GB
1216
K3

Kauffmann, John M.

Flow east

20968 -2

DATE			

Flow East

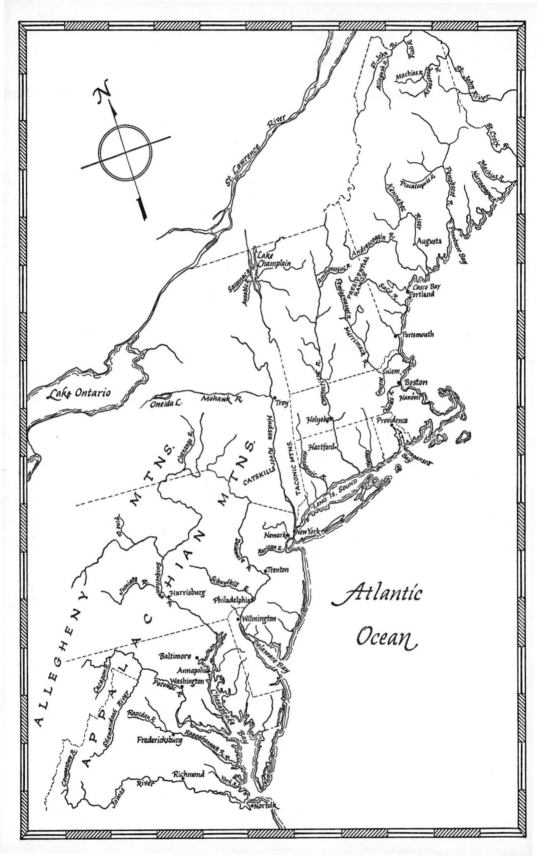

FLOW EAST

A Look at Our
North Atlantic Rivers

by
John M. Kauffmann

McGraw-Hill Book Company

New York   St. Louis   San Francisco
Düsseldorf   London   Mexico   Sydney   Toronto

Acknowledgment is made to the following for their kind permission to publish or reprint material from copyright or otherwise controlled sources:

Samuel French, Inc. (*Poems 1908–1919,* by John Drinkwater, Copyright © 1919 by Houghton Mifflin Company, renewed Copyright © 1947 by Daisy Kennedy Drinkwater); The Conservation Foundation (*Future Environments of North America,* articles by Dr. Lynton K. Caldwell, William Vogt, and Raymond F. Dasmann); Anthony Netboy (*The Atlantic Salmon*); Ben Schley (*Trout,* "Quest for Quality Fishing"); *American Forests* ("The Hemlocks of Mianus Gorge," by Alexander B. Adams).

Library of Congress Cataloging in Publication Data

Kauffmann, John M
  Flow east.
  (American wilderness series, v. 3)
  Bibliography: p.
  1. Rivers—Northeastern states. I. Title.
II. Series.
GB1216.K3   333.7'8   72-8747
ISBN 0-07-033375-0

A river forms life. It provides peace.
It's life running along.

—*Michael Peters, aged thirteen*

446133

Preface

THAT prefatory flourish of humility known as an Author's Apology is long out of fashion, but a sincere one is in order here. I wish this book could be a thorough guide to all the rivers I have mentioned. By canoe or trail I would like to take you down these rivers, mile by mile, pointing out all the interesting features, and imparting useful information on times, distances, water conditions, special pleasures and hazards and other lore to help you to plan and enjoy successful future river outings.

I wish I could help you better to know all the trees, and plants, birds, mammals, reptiles, invertebrates, even microorganisms in and along these rivers. I wish I could tell you all about their geology and hydrology as well. And there is history and prehistory to tell about, too—enough to stir the heart and fire the imagination for a lifetime.

I wish I could give you case histories of the many problems that beset our rivers, discussing them and the issues behind them in depth. And I wish I were a poet who could sing of the rivers as they deserve to be extolled and interpreted, for are they not water in loveliest form and setting?

I have been able to do none of these things for our North Atlantic waterways, alas, but only to introduce them. I can only bid you behold them; study, and understand them, to appreciate and to protect. For is it not time, in this Age of Aquarius, that we give our rivers the care and love they deserve as resources to grace our land and gladden our lives?

THANKS to my companions and mentors of paddle and pen, particularly John Berry, Carter and John Bowles, Jack Burchenal, Randy Carter, Kip Dalley, Bob Dennis, Fred Eubanks, Don Fletcher, Bart Hague, Sam Hamill, Doreen and George Hamilton and George IV, Bob Harrigan, George Harter, Bart Hauthaway, Gordy Johnson, Rudy and Chris Kauffmann, Warren King, Sam, Alan, Matthew and Andrew Marsh, John McPhee, Dick Saltonstall, Paul Schaefer, Jeffrey Smith, Dick Stanton, Maurice Sullivan, Bill Verner and John Wilson.

And to Minor Barringer, Art Hendrick, Al Kellar and Ben Schley, who are among those appreciatively remembered when fishing so often comes to mind.

Thanks also to all those able, thoughtful, dedicated conservators of rivers, serving with federal, state, county and city government and private organizations and enterprises, who shared with me their time, their knowledge, their interest and effective concern.

They agree with Henry Van Dyke that "every river that flows is good, and has something worthy to be loved" and that "it is the part of wisdom to know and love as many as you can."

So did R.M.K., the source, to whom this book is dedicated.

Table of Contents

Flow East

The Joy
of Running Water

THE walk through the hayfield seemed interminable, and excitement made it even longer. He had begged for the honor of carrying the tackle box, that jewel casket of sparkling fish lures; now it was heavy, and banged against his small bare knee. Shifting it to the other hand meant changing the grip on the equally precious coffee can of worms, however, so, resigned to his burden, he plodded on behind his father and older brother.

Past the clump of young balsams, past the big yellow birch in which a couple of cedar waxwings perched, they wound along the edge of the field, careful to trample as little hay as possible. The day was warm for northern New Hampshire, and squadrons of grasshoppers took flight before them. He resented the sweater and hat his parents had insisted were prudent outing garb. It would have been cooler to have gone up the brook.

He knew the brook. It was a close friend by now, and he liked its talk. He knew where a big trout lived under a ledge. The moss was wet-cool there, and ferns cascaded down the bank to match, in green, the white cataracts of the stream. Sometimes he tried to dam the brook, but it always escaped and trickled free, and that was all right; that was brookness. The brook made its own pools, some foamy, some quiet, where fish were shy.

But this was to be something more than pools and cascades. This was graduation to the river, the place whence his father, brother, and their friends returned with fish and stories and a look of happiness.

The two figures ahead stopped. He saw the knapsack swung off his brother's shoulders, and his father peering into the alders. He scurried to catch up, tackle jangling, and saw, resting in her leafy bower, a serene majesty. That she was a queen well past her prime could not dim his admiration, for all grace and beauty seemed inherent in the symmetry of that old canoe.

Every craft that runs and glides and darts has to man's eyes a certain special gracefulness, and in a canoe this poetry of form is manifested simply and with timeless appeal. The boy gave the old canvas-covered hull the same caress that birchbark hulls must have received from red-brown hands in times long, long before.

No water was to be seen or heard behind the wall of alders. The brook always announced its nearness, calling through the woods, but here only the wind in the maples was speaking. A path of sorts led through the underbrush, however. He investigated, tumbled down a steep sandy bank, sprawled upon a strip of beach, and beheld a silent, deep, but moving river. If it did not bind its spell with song like the brook, this too was alive with an even stronger and mysterious allure. Its shallows were pale topaz, and through them, like flashes of light through a faceted gemstone, living creatures glinted. There were minnows so small and frail that they were but eyes and tails, myriad, so as to texture the water through and through with life. Schools of larger fish darted to left or right in unison, as if following the cleavage lines of the watery jewel in which they lived. On the bottom fascinating things crawled among the sticks and sands or dove into muddy hidey-holes and pebbly grottoes. They seemed to dance a slow counterpoint to the surface ballet of water striders and dipping dragonflies. Deeper, almost beyond his sight, water weeds trailed downstream, undulating slowly in a current that betrayed itself on the surface only by an occasional dimple or the nodding of a half-submerged stick. Beyond, in the umber pool beneath the tree roots, down in the dark cool depths, there surely dwelt...

"Hey," called his father, "come help with the gear. Let's go!"

And they went, down the river in the morning—past the muskrat den and the beaver house and the bank swallows' nesting holes; round shady bends and across sunny shoals, and under gnarled trees leaning so that their branches brushed at hats and sometimes left a distraught, evicted spider clinging to the gunwale. A snag standing at water's edge turned into a heron that flapped away down river to become a snag again. Something slim and furry spied them from a high bank and vanished, and something else, which had been basking on a log, plopped hurriedly into the water, then raised a bullet head to check on the intrusion.

They paused in their journey to push into one of those backwaters called logans in the north country. All was still there, except when the breeze ruffled the leathery carpet of water-lily pads. Yet the boy sensed that the place brimmed with life. It burst into action when a pickerel swirled for the spinner his father twitched through the water. His own excitement burst out as well, requiring stern advice on canoeing conduct.

When the paddlers returned to the river, leaving the logan to regain its serenity, their small passenger was so beguiled by a long sleek trophy with chain-patterned sides and vicious jaws that he did not at first detect the quickening current. Suddenly, it seemed, the rapid was before them. It was really little more than a single white-edged wave curling between boulders, but he felt the canoe leap forward, his small hands gripped the gunwales, and, as they glided down the V of slick water between flecks of white, he heard the river speak.

Who can say which is the more impressive, a river's voice or a river's silence? Some exult in tumultuous waters. Sigurd Olson recalls it as "a sense of fierce abandonment when all the voyageurs of the past join the rapids in their shouting." To Henry David Thoreau, the river's spell was cast when "we seemed to be embarked on the placid current of our dreams." Enchanted by both the music and the silence of that river voyage, the boy entered for life into the joy of running water.

Although only a three-mile childhood journey, it was rich beyond both chronicling and appraisal. The joy of fish and fishing had much to do with it, of course, though the river fish were not firsts; *they* had come wriggling from the brook. But there was ecstasy in each bite, each catch. In the deep river bend where he was permitted to drop his worm, the perch swarmed around it and, unlike the nibbling shiners, plunged his bob under with mighty tugs.

There were collateral joys as well: visiting his brother's favorite fishing spot where strange creatures were caught at night (eels and burbots and "miller's thumbs"); the dell where his father unpacked lunch, dipped water from a spring, built a little campfire for cocoa, and waved at a passing train.

Encompassing all experiences, however, was the magic river, where ducklings vanished into shadows, and their mother, often seeming so wounded and distraught, took powerful flight; where a princely frog sat motionless until a kingfisher rattled the silence. The river was the way and the world, its surface embroidered with yellow water lilies, its edges fringed with iris and meadowsweet. When the canoe, whispering to each paddle stroke, had glided back upstream through the shadows, with supper done and day's adventures recounted to appreciative maternal ears the boy's mind swam with dream fish down a river into sleep.

For child or man, such a river adventure is a sacrament as old as humanity, for "a river went out of Eden," and mankind has loved flowing water ever since. Gratitude has had much to do with it, of course. Life-bringing rivers have meant survival and fertility. They have made Earth usable by man. Moreover, ever since roving, curious men first straddled logs and pushed off in answer to a river's irresistible beckoning, waterways have been, as Thoreau observed, "the constant lure to distant enterprise and adventure."

But there is more to this age-old love affair than thanks. Man has empathy toward rivers because of all the inanimate elements of nature they are the most personal. Rivers have a birth, a strengthening youth, a majestic maturity. They move. They speak. They have moods, laughing or angry, brooding or serene. They can be beneficent or destroying, generously open, yet filled with mysterious secrets. Man, who yearns for immortality, observes the eternal life of rivers with admiring awe.

Rivers have what man most respects and longs for in his own life and thought—a capacity for renewal and replenishment, continual energy, creativity, cleansing. "A man's life should be constantly as fresh as this river," mused Thoreau. "It should be the same channel, but a new water every instant."

Beyond even such characteristics symbolic of our aspirations and ideals, rivers have that most admired of all qualities—beauty. They are the most expressive components of landscape, and the human mind, rapt by the esthetic qualities of rivers, or soothed by their music, can glide with the current into reflection and revery.

Rivers, which have been major designers of scenery, remain the central elements of most pleasant landscapes. Look at a river and the landscape it has created and you will discern, moreover, a graceful, reasonable design for living. The broad bottom lands provide fertile space for farming that keeps the valley attractive to behold yet open and capacious enough for the occasional flood that will come. The bogs and swamps are great natural sponges to store excess water that will steady the river's flow. They and the wooded marges provide wild lands offering not only a beautiful and intriguing contrast to man-built environments nearby but also a home for the animals, birds, and plants of Earth's life community. The terraces and uplands above the valley bottom offer logical sites for residence and industry, now largely free from the necessity of seeking the riverside for power or transport. These good building areas can enjoy the river itself for landscape and can count upon its natural openness for recreation. Above them, mountain slopes provide forests and a conserving watershed, and an invitation for roaming.

The river's course and banks themselves offer a unique dimension of recreational experience. Although it may now have become but a byway for our transportation and commerce, a river can still be a boulevard of quiet beauty; an avenue of awareness and understanding of our common cause with nature. Jostled and hustled and cajoled away from our earth parentage; often driven like dry windblown leaves down the concrete channels of modernity, hoping a next invention will assuage our strange yearning, we need routes inviting us into the natural world. Along riverways we may gain serendipity, and perhaps quietly perceive who we are, how we fit in, and where we are going.

That this is not romantic fancy has become clearer as scientists watch the impact of modern life upon the human psyche. "As a support for his own immortality strivings, man needs the sense and the security of the timeless duration of nature," wrote psychiatrist Edward Stainbrook. "As contemporary society accelerates and multiplies the demands for constant change ... the need for a relatively permanent frame of reference which can allow change to occur without the sense of being lost in the process becomes increasingly important. Just to be in frequent perceptual contact with the reassuring, enduring earth is a psychological security factor of considerable importance."

Sigurd Olson, doctor of the wilderness, has put it more specifically: "Joys come from simple and natural things, mists over meadows, sunlight on leaves, the path of the moon over water. Even rain and wind and stormy clouds bring joy, just as knowing animals and flowers and where they live. Such things are where you find them, and belong to the aware and alive. They require little scientific knowledge, but bring in their train an ecological perspective, and a way of looking at the world."

Of all the natural elements of the landscape, rivers can most easily provide that reassurance, those joys, whether one voyages on them, walks beside them, or just knows they are there and available. And they are, almost everywhere, coursing through the mountains, winding across the farms, gliding past towns, offering, as Thoreau put it, "wild and noble sights . . . such as they who sit in parlors never dream of." His friend Ralph Waldo Emerson noted, even in that quieter era of our history, "With one stroke of the paddle I leave the village politics and personalities, yes, and the world of villages and personalities behind, and pass into a delicate realm of sunset and moonlight."

If you have had childhood adventures like those touched upon at the outset of this writing, you know the delights into which a river's way can lead, and you can recall a time when water magic cast its spell. Was it at a swimming hole in the creek behind town; along a fishing stream? Are you the grandfather, ensconced in your riparian rocking chair, remembering how sons and grandsons "learnt to swim and to row" on the river you have heard for fifty years? Or are you the mother explaining her lateness after a woods excursion with her children: "Our walk was along a brook, so it took twice as long." If you are young, the city world may have walled you away from such pleasures, so easily come by in yesteryear's small town or farming community. But perhaps a teacher or counselor once introduced you, a wide-eyed city child, to the happy fascination of a riverside adventure.

One of our greatest blessings is memory, for even if circumstances cut us off forever from continuing contact with the out-of-doors, memory can resurrect a once-enjoyed experience again and again to our heart's delight. Anglers know particularly well the delights and comforts of recollection. W. C. Prime, writing a century ago, remarked that "It is delicious to remember the last year's enjoyment, to recall the music of waters which have long ago run to the seas; of trees shaken by winds that have died to rest." In our own time, the eloquent Western angler, Roderick L. Haig-Brown, confesses "sheer happiness in remembering a bend or a run or the spread below a bridge as I saw them best, perhaps open in sunlight with the green weeds trailing and a good fish rising steadily, or perhaps pitted by rain under a grey sky, or white and black and golden, opaque in the long slant of the twilight. . . . I carry them with me wherever I go."

Fluviography

---

*The rivers are the veins and arteries of a country.
... He has seen the land truly, with its wealth and
strength, who has followed the rivers from their
sources in the hills down to the tide-pulsating ocean-
heart.*

*—John Boyle O'Reilly, from "Canoeing
Sketches" in "Ethics of Boxing
and Manly Sport"*

IN the seventeenth century a Dutch cartographer compiled an intriguing map. Diagonally across its atlas page he stretched the East Coast of North America, from North Carolina to Nova Scotia, in an alluring rhythm of capes and bays. Out in the Atlantic, amid a sea serpent or two, he set brave little ships sailing westward toward that coastline of promise. And from the opposite direction, out of a challenging blankness spiced with pictures of wild beasts and savage villages, flowed the rivers of Eastern America, opening to the oncoming vessels their capacious and inviting estuaries.

Across those sea lanes, into those estuaries, and up those rivers came the ancestors of most of us, and in the chronicles of explorers and colonists we can still share in the beauty that they saw, the hopes they entertained and the destiny they had pledged themselves to meet and fulfill. Wistfully, today, beside our sick and filthy streams, we sense their excited appreciation as fragrant land breezes and pure rivers greeted them.

"This is the sweetest and greatest river I have seen, so that the Thames is but a little finger to it," wrote a missionary, Father Andrew White, as he sailed up the Potomac in 1634. "All is high woods except where the Indians have cleared for corne. It abounds with delicate springs which are our best drinke. Birds, diversely feathered here are infinite ... by which will appear, the place abounds not alone with profit, but also with pleasure."

Rivers, Robert P. Tristram Coffin has reminded us in his story of the Kennebec of Maine, "once were important parts of the earth. They were bright wedges driven into the New World forests. And the first Americans cut their teeth on their rocks and were sung to sleep by their white music. They cradled the first towns. The rhythm of their flow was built into their children's hearts. They were the first highways. But today railroads and motor roads have cut across them and sucked their life away. The people now move against the grain of rivers. But rivers did their work for our country and did it well."

The rivers of the East have been main arteries of America's destiny. Their fertile bottomlands beckoned and fed the pioneers. As routes of commerce and communication they bound East and West together with bonds of everlasting water. Their water power founded America's industrial might. In all, the skills they demanded and taught went west to help complete the building of the nation.

What of these rivers now, these old friends that reared and trained and tested us and sent us on our way to greatness, giving us much pleasure in the process? Is their life indeed done? Do we need their music and their bright courses any more? Of course we demand their water more than ever before to fill our taps and flush our toilets and cool our giant engines, to make our paper napkins and our steel. But can they, as Father White so long ago suggested, abound not alone with profit but also with pleasure? Henry Van Dyke maintained that "there is no country so civilized, no existence so humdrum, that there is not room enough in it somewhere for a lazy, idle brook, an encourager of indolence, with hope of happy surprises."

Here in our civilized, humdrum East there is probably a greater wealth and variety of streams than in any other part of our country.

Large and small, they crash wildly through mountain forests, wind serenely through valley farms, well silently from swamps or ebb and flow with tides. Few cities and towns have not their river or creek nearby, and few back forties are without their spring or brook. How fortunate that waterways are abundant where so many people live and where our close-packed urban environment needs a fluvial element to insinuate openness and greenness and the joy of running water into the stolidity of our well-paved North Atlantic seaboard.

Or do we care?

Well, let us see. There will be some happy surprises, but for the looking you may need a strong stomach and an even temper and perhaps a handkerchief for weeping.

If ever you should have to go to jail, particularly if the sentence is to solitary confinement, try to take a good set of maps with you for entertainment. I don't mean maps like the old Dutch one, full of blank spaces, but as comprehensive and detailed as possible— maps which show hills and valleys, small streams as well as big rivers, forests and swamps as well as towns. Once a farmer surprised a field hand goldbricking under a tree while perusing an aged issue of *National Geographic*. Unabashed, the fellow grinned and said dreamily. "You know, I've just been to Australia!" So it is with maps. Learn to read them and you can journey for months and years, ambling through towns, climbing mountains and voyaging down rivers "at liberty [as Thoreau put it] to imagine the most wonderful meanderings and descents."

Even the old Dutch map, however, depicted Chesapeake Bay, probably the world's greatest estuary, gathering the waters of three major rivers and many smaller ones. Let us begin there with the southernmost of those rivers, the James, as the first English colonists did, not lingering at tidewater and its sea story, however, but probing those blank spaces of beautiful hinterland.

One tidewater stop must be made—at Berkeley Plantation, where Americans first knelt and gave thanks for the unblighted, untrammeled blessings of the New World's bounty. Even today, visiting Berkeley's riverside at sundown, you will not find it hard to kneel beside the little arbor where the lawn stretches down to meet the river, and give your own silent thanks. Look upriver to the right and you will see, to be sure, the costs of progress: the smokestacks and the smog. But across and down the James the islands are still green and quiet, and the ducks wheeling above them or floating in squadrons on the silver tide bespeak the beauty and fecundity that has ever nourished the American dream.

Beyond those smokestacks, the James pitches down the fall line, that rocky drop out of the Piedmont onto the coastal plain so typical of streams of the Middle and South Atlantic Coast, where water power and harbors come conveniently together. There stands Richmond, Virginia's capital (and once the Confederacy's), below 254 miles of majestic freshwater flow.

The James begins in the waters of the Jackson and Cowpasture rivers, flowing out of Highland County, Virginia, through valleys pink-white with springtime dogwood and redbud; bronze-gold with fall foliage as beautiful as any in the East. The Maury River augments the James in time to crash through the Blue Ridge west of Lynchburg, where the river shows its age—older than the mountains folding upward as it cut. It took a big tough river to fight its way eastward through those rising billows of rock. The James made it. So did the Potomac; the Susquehanna; the Delaware and its tributaries the Schuylkill and the Lehigh; the Hudson. Smaller streams, diverted by the rising crests, had to flow northeast or southeast along the troughs to join the larger streams.

East of the Blue Ridge the James winds and riffles through Virginia's rural Piedmont where you can enjoy a Huck Finn existence camping or fishing for bass in a big beautiful river almost no one has yet remembered to hurt.

If you pass the James by and sail on up Chesapeake Bay, past the York River, where Cornwallis surrendered his sword; past the Rappahannock, where boys in blue and gray sang together in the evening and fought each other when the bugles blew at dawn, you will come into the Potomac (no royal name for it, just that of an Indian village). Great homes of thought and deed overlook the broad Potomac estuary: Stratford of the Lees, George Mason's Gunston Hall, George Washington's Mount Vernon. And Washington's namesake city is set as he had wished, midway between New England and the deep South, where tidewater met a river that could link West to East, keeping the states united.

However, pass by for now your alabaster capital, shining beside its cesspool, and follow up along the old Chesapeake & Ohio Canal, a monument to America's canal-building era.

Once canals laced the East together, following rivers or linking them, and their remains show masonry that would have done credit to pyramid builders. The effort expended on American canals, some in use only for a few years, seems preposterous until one remembers that before railroads there was no other good way of moving heavy or bulky cargoes. On land, there were only wagons and rutty roads. The Erie, from Albany to Buffalo (succeeded by the New York State Barge Canal, still in use), was the most famous canal. Others followed the Susquehanna, Delaware, and James river systems.

Most canals are gone now or are mere traces, their rights-of-way often taken up by roads and railways. A few, like the Delaware and Chesapeake & Ohio, have been made into delightful linear parks. The C & O, following the Potomac for 184 miles, though mostly dry and derelict as a canal, remains a splendid relic, and its towpath is now an historic trail. Its secluded, near-wilderness qualities beside the upper Potomac offer a welcome change of pace from nearby superhighways, railroads and urban living.

Follow it through the Potomac Gorge, where wilderness reaches down to Washington City, past Great Falls' grandeur only ten miles from the Capitol, and proceed on to Harpers Ferry, West Virginia, target of John Brown's raid and Civil War fighting and now the site of a national historical park. There at the water gap, the beautiful Shenandoah swirls over washboard ledges to join the Potomac in a scene that, Jefferson declared, is "worth a voyage across the Atlantic."

Above the water gap, the Potomac loops around valley farms, and is baffled by mountain ridges. Near the old frontier trading post and Indian settlement of Old Town, the South Branch flows in through fertile bottomlands and out of craggy canyons from sources, close to those of the James, in the Virginia–West Virginia highlands.

Marylanders like to call the Potomac "Maryland's River" and so it is, entirely within the state (save for the South Branch) and forming Maryland's southern boundary. The North or Main Branch comes down past Westernport and Cumberland in the Appalachians, through the only major industrialized area on the entire Potomac. The river's official source at the southwestern tip of Maryland, ringed now with strip mines, flows out from under the vandalized replica of a vandalized earlier monument, the Fairfax stone, set there by that colonial landlord at the corner of his vast domain.

If, instead of turning westward into the Potomac Estuary, you sail straight north up Chesapeake Bay, past the Nanticoke and Choptank that well out of Maryland's eastern shore; past Maryland's capital, Annapolis, and the great port city of Baltimore, you will come to Havre de Grace and the mother river of the Chesapeake, the Susquehanna. The bay itself was probably once the lower Susquehanna, and the Potomac and James mere tributaries to it before the whole was drowned in a sea rising with the melting ice age. Even now, this "Long Crooked River" drains the largest basin in the East: 27,500 square miles, including half of Pennsylvania and much of New York. Once it was mightier far, when a wall of ice stretched across the midsection of the East and the Susquehanna carried much of its meltwater.

In a sense the Susquehanna is a "backwards" river. Its lowest reach is steepest, while its headwaters course blandly through cultivated fields and gentle hills. Hydroelectric power plants have dammed and harnessed its wild lower section in Maryland and southern Pennsylvania. Farther upstream, however, it swirls down on Pennsylvania's capital, Harrisburg, with a broad though rocky magnificence that is unequaled in the East.

The Susquehanna has three great branches. A few miles above Harrisburg one can turn west, up the Juniata River, as the canallers did, to reach the Ohio watershed. Its well-farmed valley has bucolic charm, and is not without rugged beauty as well—in the gorge near Lewistown, up the Raystown and Frankstown branches that flow in from the south, and in its Allegheny head-waters near Tyrone. The Raystown Branch valley soon will be filled with reservoir waters which, if their levels can be kept stable, should provide a spectacular lake. The canallers went up the Frankstown Branch past Hollidaysburg to Allegheny Mountain, where, for a time, a cable-drawn railway hauled canal boats in sections over the ridge to the Ohio watershed.

The other two principal branches of the Susquehanna join at Northumberland near Sunbury. The West Branch valley leads north; then west past Williamsport, once a lumbering capital that processed millions of logs rafted down the river or down tributaries like Pine Creek. Above Lock Haven, where the valley route heads northwest, it offers one of the most spectacular drives in the region, especially when the autumn foliage is bright. Above Keating the river is incised in a deep, forested canyon traversed only by a railroad and crossed by few roads. Near Clearfield it is more open again. Then the mountains close in once more, one valley now filled with the Curwensville Reservoir, and the river's sources are in the Alleghenies, even farther west than the Juniata's.

The beauty of the North (or Main) Branch is of a different sort from the West's—generally quieter, more subtle and feminine in its charm as it courses past fields and hills that seem to rearrange themselves constantly around it. Through the Wyoming Valley, where settlers died under Indian tomahawk blows, the Susquehanna has also suffered, from man's attack on coal. Yet much beauty remains, and above the Lackawanna, the Susquehanna Valley seems an agrarian Eden, much as it was when French aristocrats waited in vain for Queen Marie Antoinette to escape to the rustic Asylum they had prepared for her there.

The entrance of the Chemung forms Tioga Point, at Athens, Indian portage and base of General John Sullivan's Revolutionary War campaign against the Iroquois. Then the Susquehanna Valley route enters New York, where the pastoral Chenango enters at Binghamton. The Susquehanna's Great Bend loops back into Pennsylvania, however, before its broad valley receives the Unadilla's drainage, and, flanked by ice gentled hills, leads on to Otsego Lake, the "Glimmerglass" of James Fenimore Cooper's *Leatherstocking Tales.*

Just above Chesapeake Bay another big estuary opens to the Atlantic and the shipping which sought and seeks the New World: Delaware Bay—named for a colonial governor, Baron De la Warr of Virginia, who never saw it. Sailing up the bay past Wilmington you would go by Brandywine Creek, where a fall of 125 feet in 24 miles was, by the late eighteenth century, turning the wheels of half a dozen different industries, and which attracted a young French gunpowder maker named DuPont. At Philadelphia you would pass the Schuylkill, home of the oldest sporting club in the world, the Schuylkill Fishing Company, and repository of billions of tons of anthracite dust washed into the stream from the Pennsylvania mines. The Delaware River's fall line is at Trenton, New Jersey ("Trenton Makes, The World Takes," the big sign reads), where the running river ends a graceful journey.

Upriver, where George Washington crossed to victory at Trenton on Christmas Eve, 1776, the Delaware glides and riffles down through a landscape of gentle hills and fields. Canals flank the river on both sides: a feeder for the Delaware and Raritan Canal follows the New Jersey shore to Bulls Island above Lambertville, while the Delaware Division of the old Pennsylvania Canal System runs up the Pennsylvania side to Easton and the Lehigh River, coming down from coal country.

The Delaware Water Gap, where the river has cleft the great arching rocks that structure Kittatinny Mountain, has long been a famous scenic area and is a feature of the recently authorized national recreation area that bears its name. Above it, the terrain is gentler, though the mountain edge of the valley follows close in New Jersey and an escarpment in Pennsylvania creates the handsome waterfalls for which the region is noted. Here a dam at Tocks Island may impound the Delaware for 45 miles.

At Port Jervis, New York, where the Neversink comes in from the Catskills, the Delaware becomes the Pennsylvania–New York boundary. The valley bends sharply westward, and, coming down from the forks at Hancock, New York, the river flows clear and lively between steep mountainsides. There is an air of wildness here. It is not hard to imagine Tories stealing through the timber to ambush patriot countrymen near Minisink Ford, or raftsmen riding their lashed logs through the river rips.

Above Hancock, the two branches once were famous trout streams. They have been dammed now to assuage New York, but the tributary Willowemoc and its Beaverkill, rising cold and clean from Catskill springs like the Delaware's own headwaters, are still magic names to fly-fishermen.

Exploring the little rivers of New Jersey, about which James and Margaret Cawley have written so engagingly, requires a close look at your sheaf of maps, for the waterways *are* little. However, they are also very important in that most highly urbanized state in the Union. Perhaps the most surprising are the pure waters of the Mullica and its tributaries that well out of New Jersey's Pine Barrens, a forest surrounded by megalopolis. Better-known rivers are the Raritan and Passaic, rising in New Jersey's highlands and ending in the urban morass of Raritan and Newark bays. They have seen much history and endured much abuse, and they can offer much delight if protected and restored to decency.

When Henry Hudson sailed his little *Half Moon* past Manhattan Island and up the river which now bears his name, he was disappointed. He had been searching not for a river but for a Northwest Passage to China. Yet the fabulous waterway he explored became one of the great avenues of American destiny and remains today one of America's most noble scenes. Many a writer and painter of renown has extolled it, anticipating the recent "See America First" exhortations by ranking Hudson scenery above Europe's finest. Few rivers in the United States have mountains so near their mouths—mountains rising steeply from the water's edge—and in the Hudson Highlands, between Peekskill and Newburgh, the river makes the deepest cut through the Appalachian backbone of any northeastern waterway. That magnificent reach is of national park caliber, and might have been so designated had the river not been an historic artery for commerce and industry. As it is, much of the Highlands are protected, though epic conservation battles are being fought to preserve the mountain scenery further and protect the river's fishlife as well.

But the fiordlike Hudson of fame is in reality a tidal river, its valley drowned by the sea when it rose following the glacial age. Although salinity extends only part way—about sixty miles, to the vicinity of Newburgh—tides are felt as far as the dam at Troy, 154 miles from Manhattan.

At Troy the Hudson is joined by its largest tributary, the Mohawk, westward route of the old Erie Canal and its successor the New York State Barge Canal, and now heavily industrialized and hugged by motor and railroads.

Above Troy, past Saratoga where Americans stopped England's Hudson campaign to split the colonies, the river is at last fresh-running (if you discount the dams and locks that turn its reach from Troy to Fort Edward into navigation lakes for barges leading to and from the canal to Lake Champlain). Tributaries like the Hoosic and the Battenkill come in from the Berkshires and Green Mountains, and above Glens Falls the upper Hudson beckons toward the Adirondacks.

From its beautiful falls at Luzerne, just above the mouth of the Sacandaga, to its source in tiny Lake Tear of the Clouds on the slopes of Mount Marcy, the Hudson is largely a wild river, the only one of its size left in the East outside of Maine. Its clean water holds trout, and its rapids shout as great a springtime challenge to whitewater canoeists as can be heard in the East.

When you come to New England, old charts will not do. Save for the Connecticut, the Penobscot, perhaps, and a few others put on at random, the New England waterways were too numerous and often too small to command the attention of the early cartographers. Spread out your modern maps, however, and you can see what a marvelous lacework of streams adorns the New England landscape.

The rivers are not normally grouped at large estuaries such as Chesapeake Bay, Delaware Bay, and the Newark–Hudson area, but empty into the Atlantic at numerous small harbors that seem to multiply as one goes northeast until they become a maze of havens that have made Maine a famous cruising area. Only at Narragansett Bay, Boston Harbor, and Casco and Penobscot bays in Maine do New England rivers meet extraordinarily large embayments.

Numerous falls are characteristic of nearly all New England streams, and most of these pitches or sharp rapids were dammed during the era of water-powered industry. Still more dams have since been built for hydroelectric power, water supply, or flood control. As a result, free-flowing rivers in New England usually consist of fairly short stretches. They are interesting and often beautiful, nevertheless, and offer much to the canoeist, fisherman, naturalist, or rambling scenery viewer.

The Housatonic, the "Place Beyond the Mountains," is the first major valley that slices down just east of New York State's Taconic Range, to empty into Long Island Sound at Stratford. It is also one of the most beautiful in New England. As one drives along it heading north from New Milford, Connecticut, to its sources in the Berkshires of western Massachusetts, the Housatonic Valley seems a fitting gateway to New England's world of white church steeples, covered bridges, and stone-walled fields spreading below hills clad in pine and birch.

It is the Connecticut, however, that is the main riverway through New England. Extending from Old Lyme, east of New Haven, all the way to the Canadian border at the tip of New Hampshire, it is the longest river in New England—410 miles. Its name, derived from an Indian word meaning "Long Tidal River," is apt, for the Connecticut's tidal reach extends nearly 50 miles to the state capital, Hartford. Except for Middletown, which it passes midway, it is surprisingly secluded even today, a favorite for scenic boat and railroad tours. Just below Hartford, the river loops through huge flat meadows, an astonishing area of attractive still-farmed open space (and natural flood protection) to exist near such a large metropolis.

These bends, the huge river loops beneath Mount Holyoke, and the Connecticut's winding through White Mountain meadows undoubtedly prompted Timothy Dwight, traveling in 1837, to comment on the "elegance of its meanders." Yet, overall, the Connecticut is a straight river, cutting along an old earth fault reamed out by south-moving glacial ice.

The valley was an ideal avenue for advancing settlement of its rich agricultural lands and for the commerce resulting from harnessing the falls along its lower half. Later, log drives thundered down from the northern forests: eight million board feet of spruce and pine as late as 1911. The Connecticut has no great branches or tributaries to match a Mohawk, a Lehigh, or a Juniata. However, its numerous smaller tributaries have a steadiness of flow characteristic of New England streams, and "water privileges" along them brought settlement and economic importance. The Farmington comes in at Windsor; the Westfield at Springfield; and the Chicopee, whose tributaries drain giant Quabbin Reservoir, also enters nearby. The Deerfield and Millers join the Connecticut at Greenfield. Along the 236-mile course where the Connecticut River forms the boundary between New Hampshire and Vermont, it gathers the flow of the Ashuelot and the West, the Ottauquechee, the White, the Ammonoosuc, the Passumpsic, the Upper Ammonoosuc, and the Nulhegan to name a few.

No Eastern river save Maine's Kennebec-Androscoggin system has a handsomer ultimate source than the Connecticut. The three big Connecticut lakes and their satellite streams and ponds jewel what was long a wilderness corner of New Hampshire. Roads have scotched it now, but it still has a wild atmosphere. Following up that last slope above tiny Fourth Connecticut Lake seems like a journey to the ends of the North Woods, until you reach the top and gaze far down across the gentle well-tilled farmlands of Quebec. New Hampshire's north border is one of the few state boundaries that follow a hydrographic divide. How much more simple would our water management problems be today if all state lines were thus so sensibly located!

The White Mountains of New Hampshire, which provide half of the upper Connecticut's watershed, also give rise to two other important New England river systems—those of the Merrimack and the Saco—and contribute to the Androscoggin as well. Between the Connecticut and Merrimack basins are scores of smaller rivers draining eastern Connecticut, Rhode Island, and eastern Massachusetts. Among the larger are the tidal Thames, debouching at New London, Connecticut; the Blackstone at Providence, Rhode Island; the Taunton at nearby Fall River, Massachusetts, and, of course, Boston's famous Charles. But the Merrimack (or Sturgeon) River, some 110 miles long, is the next that taps far water sources.

It begins as the Pemigewasset, coming out of a New Hampshire wilderness south of Mount Lafayette and picking up water from Profile Lake beneath the stone face of the Old Man of the Mountain. It becomes the Merrimack when joined by the Winnipesaukee, draining New Hampshire's largest lake, plus Squam, Winnisquam, Newfound, and other water bodies that give it assured flow. This natural storage and the numerous sharp drops in the river's course made the Merrimack New England's premier water power river. Below falls where Indians once speared salmon now stand the long mills of cities like Manchester, New Hampshire, and Lowell and Lawrence, Massachusetts.

Only one third as long as the Connecticut and with far less

drop, the Merrimack water nevertheless produced almost as much horsepower or more than half again as much per square mile of drainage area. As early as 1809 in the thirteen mills then at Manchester, the Merrimack's flow was dammed and then channeled through canals to operate more than 12,000 looms and nearly 400,000 spindles. In his water power report that was part of the census of 1880, George F. Swain, Assistant Professor of Civil Engineering at the Massachusetts Institute of Technology, called the Merrimack "the most noted water power stream in the world." Although industrial methods have changed, the cities remain, and the Merrimack now is noted for something else. When it reaches the sea at Newburyport, it is one of the filthiest rivers in America.

The Saco River flows off the slopes of Mount Washington itself, and its intervales provide a river foreground for that highest peak of New England. The Reverend Thomas Starr King, writing in *The White Hills* in 1859, said of the scene, "I did not suppose that there was on earth a landscape so exquisite as this."

But for most of its 124-mile length the Saco is Maine's river, from Fryeburg to tidewater at Biddeford. It is closer than any other to the bulk of the state's population, and consequently much loved for outings and for the pleasant scenery it affords. It is a favorite for boys' and girls' camp outings, and an old channel, which cuts across the bed of an ancient glacial lake and connects with the river below Fryeburg, permits a twenty-mile circular canoe tour.

So rich is Maine in rivers and streams, not to mention lakes, that imaginative map reading may fairly intoxicate you with vicarious adventures. There are at least 4,000 miles of canoeable streams in Maine, and thousands upon thousands more of smaller brooks.

Many of Maine's rivers are coastal. As you sail up the Maine Coast, you can turn into the mouths of a score of these, whose estuaries help to make the region such a favorite cruising area for sail and power boats. The Machias and the St. Croix, both "down east" and the latter forming the border with Canada, are the largest. They and the Sheepscot, Narraguagus, Pleasant, and Dennys are well known to anglers who cherish the vestiges of our once-great salmon runs.

Maine has large rivers as well as numerous ones. Like the Connecticut, the Androscoggin and Kennebec rivers, which mingle in the tides of Merrymeeting Bay, flow out of beautiful lakes. The Androscoggin's source is Umbagog on the Maine–New Hampshire border, and it in turn is fed by the water of Maine's big Rangeley Lakes chain. The Kennebec has its source in Moosehead Lake, thirty miles long, a veritable inland sea by Eastern standards. Its storms often give ocean-size yachts a rough time. But its beauty—and that of the more mountainous Rangeleys—is such that, had they been discovered in a later time, they might have been established as national or state parks. The same is true of New Hampshire's Winnipesaukee.

The Androscoggin's uppermost (and only clean) reach is in New Hampshire. Beyond Gorham, where the Presidential Range towers above it, the river crosses into Maine. Below Rumford, where the falls must have been stupendous before industry took them over, the valley is flatter, but still redolent (between industrial centers) with New England's brand of rural charm.

This is even truer of the Kennebec, serene and full. Along it one realizes how much a river forms the very keel of the countryside through which is flows. This is the route up which Benedict Arnold's men set out to attack Quebec in 1775, cursing their leaky bateaux up the Kennebec and its tributary Dead River toward the height of land in that bitter fall.

The Penobscot, too, is a great steady sweeping river, though in its lower reaches the flatter terrain makes it less noticeable than the Kennebec as a central feature of the landscape. Its lowest reach is a long estuary, and at the head of navigation is Bangor, Maine's largest seaport after Portland. The Penobscot has two big tributaries, the Piscataquis and the Mattawamkeag, and its own two branches as well, East and West, which wrap around the

Mount Katahdin massif. North and South branches form the West. They rise along the Quebec border northwest of Moosehead Lake (drainages are crazy-mixed-up in this glaciated country) and flow east into Seboomook Lake. Its outlet is the West Branch, flowing northeast to Chesuncook Lake; then southwest through a gorge and many heavy rapids beneath Mount Katahdin to Lake Pemadumcook and the town of Millinocket. At East Millinocket the East Branch comes in from above Grand Lake Matagamon, in places a swift river of many falls and sheer pitches, thundering through wilds dominated by Traveler Mountain.

One can journey down the St. John River for 423 miles with but one carry around Grand Falls. One of the East's largest watersheds, it is the Province of New Brunswick's river for the lowest 204 miles. From above Grand Falls to the town of St. Francis it is the United States–Canadian boundary, and, above the settlement of Dickey, it is Maine's biggest wild river. From the five little St. John Ponds to Dickey, 148 miles downriver, it brawls its way through low hills and a spruce-fir backwoods that are crossed by only one logging road. With all its tributaries, the St. John has no equal in the East for the number and diversity of the wilderness canoe trips it offers.

Three big tributaries are better known to Maine people than the St. John itself: the Aroostook, with headwaters near those of the Penobscot's East Branch, flows through Ashland and Caribou to join the St. John in New Brunswick; the Fish River, draining a big chain of lakes, comes in at Fort Kent (scene of much sword rattling during the United States–Canada boundary dispute of 1842); and the Allagash. The Allagash, a hundred-mile-long system of streams, lakes, and rivers, has become a symbol of wilderness tripping in the East, and now has been preserved as a wilderness waterway by the State of Maine.

It is endlessly entertaining to study fluviography, whether you are in your cell or your study, or "passing by" to some civilized destination. "But the real way to know a little [or any] river," Henry Van Dyke reminded us years ago, "is not to glance at it here or there in the course of a hasty journey, nor to become acquainted with it after it has been partly civilized and spoiled by too close contact with the works of man. You must go to its native haunts; you must see it in youth and freedom; you must accommodate yourself to its pace, and give yourself to its influence, and follow its meaderings whithersoever they may lead you."

Then you will turn acquaintance into friendship, knowledge and experience into understanding and love.

Zombies

When you defile the pleasant streams
And the wild birds' abiding-place,
You massacre a million dreams
And cast your spittle in God's face.
                —John Drinkwater, "To the Defilers"

THERE used to be a brook at the bottom of our street. It rose behind the Garden Theater and flowed through the whole neighborhood. It had all the magic things streams have for kids; you know, crawdads and frogs and minnows, but it's paved over now." So a friend of mine, not yet forty, recalled recently." His was a small town, with plenty of green space around it and larger streams nearby, but the loss was a poignant one nevertheless. I thought of it when, flying over the Passaic River near Paterson, New Jersey, I looked down to see Willowbrook Shopping Center, said to be one of the largest in the world. Its immense apron of cement sealed the land on every side. I wondered where Willow Brook was, and if the people of that endless urb did not need a Willow Brook even more than they needed a shopping center.

In a recent report on the troubles besetting that "beautiful sewer," Rock Creek in Washington, D.C., author John Graves noted that "most of our cities conceal beneath their paved and structured surfaces living waters that once were called brooks or springs or creeks, as do most European cities. Streams are natural sewerways, and during the cities' growth in the years before waste treatment, covering them over was the easy way to get a nuisance out of sight and smell. So through masonry tubes underneath the topless towers and gray sidewalks of Manhattan and Chicago and Philadelphia flow streams, or what is left of them, that once sustained willows and mayflies and small boys' dreamings." It is said that at least a hundred such streams still flow beneath New York City, which once, a seventeenth-century journal records, had "many brooks of fresh water flowing through it, pleasant and proper for man and beast to drink, as well as agreeable to behold, affording cool and pleasant resting places."

Of course, strolls down Manhattan will never again overpower us with the fragrance of wildflowers as they did Jasper Danckaerts three centuries ago, nor shall we enjoy the luscious, foot-long oysters that once came from what is now Brooklyn's Gowanus Canal. Yet, folly though it may be to wish now for an Arcadian America again, it is nevertheless intriguing to imagine what our cities—and their inhabitants—might have been like if such amenities could have been preserved. It may not, however, be a waste of thought to consider whether or not we are wise in concreting up that next small stream—the one on the edge of town where land values are high and extra lots can be sold if the brook is buried.

Entombed streams may still babble "for no one's ear's delight" (as John Graves remarked), but for us they are dead and gone. Perhaps we should place tombstones above the vivisepultures to remind us of the murderous losses. However, it is to the still "living" waterways that we must turn our thoughts and consciences. I say "living" because many of them have become zombie streams. They move, they feebly flow (or gush as open drains), but as far as mayflies or fish or man's pleasure are concerned their grey, blank-eyed water—poisoned, bacteria-ridden, oxygenless—is dead. What life remains can be measured in sludge worms and rat-tailed maggots, and the few other creatures that can survive in their excremental ooze.

One such zombie stream flows through Salem, Massachusetts (once noted for witches). They call it North River, though it's a small thing that creeps through tanneries and industrial yards. Its grey-brown current is full of grease and hair and acid and raw sewage when the sewer pumps get overloaded. The good citizens of Salem, who established a park atop the hill overlooking this miserable valley, have deposited many valuable adornments to the river's bed: bedsprings, sets of tires, an astonishing number of grocery carts, and, symbolically, even a broken toilet bowl. Atop the river's mouth, where an underground pumping station helps North River into its fetid estuary, a purveyor of tombstones has appropriately set up shop. Across a road from the river, fenced off from dingy streets where children play, a cemetery blooms with flowers. Stately pines give shade. In Salem, as in many other places, the dead have flowered beauty, while the living have only a sewer.

There is another North River in Massachusetts which water pollution monitors call one of the cleaner streams of the Commonwealth. Rising in the Hanover area and flowing into the sea below Scituate, it has little industry nearby, and urban growth has still dealt with it lightly. It is therefore a pleasant community resource, its long tidal estuary renowned for fish, wildlife, and fall foliage.

But according to a fishing tackle dealer who lives beside it, nobody cares about that North River either. "It's the only unpolluted river in the area, but they're ruining it," he lamented. "The river used to be loaded with muskrat, mink, and otter. But where I used to fish and hunt are now sewer beds. Go up and look at the laundries dumping their suds three feet deep and their cesspools overflowing. I used to fight like hell for it, but I've given up. Now the factions just fight among themselves. Why, they'd fill in the marshes and build houses on them if the state would let them. The towns don't care. They're just after more taxes. I wish they'd save the North, it's the only one we have. But nobody cares."

An Environmental Protection Agency official remarked: "I don't know of a river in New England that is clean because it was cared for. The clean ones are so because no one has hurt them yet." It's human nature, I guess, to kick somebody or something when they're down. Once a river is sufficiently degraded, so it no longer is an object of affection and respect, its course becomes a gantlet of abuse. Indeed, one part of a river can be beloved while another part, potentially as fine, is despised. Nobody cares what it *could* be; it *is* a dump. In Waltham the banks of Boston's famed Charles, long prized as a park in Cambridge, are thought fit only to park oil trucks, or for dumping. Tributaries with evocative names like Beaver Brook are choked with junk and jetsam, and one "rapid" in the main river is caused largely by accumulated debris. Well, that's industrial Waltham. Up in more residential Newton Lower Falls the banks of the pretty little river have earned designation as a parking lot and a lumber yard, and farther up still, near Charles River Village, a small riverside preserve maintained for public enjoyment by the Trustees of Reservations became the place to plant a transmission line tower.

One does not have to journey down a river very far to see what manner of offerings men now sacrifice to the river gods. At North Stratford, New Hampshire, auto parts cascade into one of the most beautiful of Eastern rivers, the Connecticut, which ought to be the town's most cherished asset. Easiest access to Virginia's James near Iron Gate and Glen Wilton is via riverside dumps. Lawrence, Massachusetts, adds insult to the Merrimack River's pollution injuries with a city landfill dump on the river's edge—very edifying, no doubt, to the training school next door. "There's a small stream in my town but you can't get any pleasure from it," a schoolboy remarked to me. "You name it and they've got it in that stream."

Paul Brooks was right when he wrote: "America has turned her back upon her rivers. Once her life blood, they are now too often her drains; the path to the front door has become the back yard dump." I remembered that when I saw the shabby backyards of Renovo, Pennsylvania, stretching down to the West Branch of the Susquehanna. It's a picturesque town, though it has seen better days, and house owners keep their street fronts as neat and spruce as they can. But to the stately Susquehanna, the town's principal scenic asset (and one of some recreational merit judging from the kids swimming off the bridge), Renovo offers its old, dirty, unbuttoned backside.

A group of Becket Academy boys who canoed the Connecticut River from source to mouth recently learned quickly enough how careless and callous we have become toward even our handsomest rivers. After toasting the trip with pure water of the river's source lakes, they appointed committees to observe animal, plant, and insect life, wind and temperature, geology, and pollution, and started down. The sewer counter quit after two days and one hundred sewers. One was fifteen feet from a Vermont sign prohibiting dumping. Below the "infamous" Upper Ammonoosuc River, grossly polluted by paper mill and municipal wastes, they found toilet paper clinging to their paddles. Near Lancaster, New Hampshire, they paddled through mile after mile of meanders where banks were lined with wrecked cars used as rip-rapping. "There was no river bank this morning," they recorded. "There was only a continuous junk yard."

Going down that river, once called the "Fresh," they found that the Connecticut flushes itself out just in time to be ready for the next load of pollution. Twice they had to halt their journey temporarily because power companies had shut down the entire river flow. "They should reevaluate their ecological responsibilities," the boys noted in their journal.

At Sunderland, Massachusetts, pickle factories were mingling their solutions in the sewage outfalls, and many of the boys spent the night vomiting. Two days farther on they recorded that "We can only say that Holyoke has done some horrible, wicked thing to the river. The river and its banks are strewn with litter and spewing pipes abound . . . we did not get out of sight of sewer pipes for the entire afternoon. When we got to the I-91 bridge we

came onto an oil slick. In the oil slick and on the banks were
uncounted dead fish. In our preparations for the trip we had
found that surveys of the shad on the river have been having
great difficulty finding the shad fry. We found them. They were
dead!"

The boys, who were taught that every individual on earth is
responsible for his own wastes, called the Holyoke–West Springfield stretch their worst day. "This stretch of water has been so
utterly abused that it can no longer be called a river," they later
chronicled. "The banks, the water, and the river bottom have
been so completely inundated by refuse that the area is no more
than a slimy liquid dump." And there were oil and scum, dyes
and refuse, hot water outlets, transmission lines overhead, rats
feeding on dead fish and "ooze that you would sink into up to
your knees." "Unbelievable," they said.

Well, let's not believe them. (Do we want to?) After all, they're
just sharp-eyed kids; so can we not pooh-pooh their superficial
alarm? Let's go down a comparable river, the Merrimack, this
time with scientists, by reading (in condensation) a biologist's
tour:

As part of the study of water quality, a detailed biological
survey of the Merrimack River, extending from Franklin, New
Hampshire, to the mouth at Newburyport, Massachusetts, was
conducted to evaluate the effects of municipal and industrial
wastes on the benthic fauna.

An assemblage of bottom organisms commonly found in clean
water stream beds (mayflies, stoneflies, caddisflies, beetles, and
certain midgeflies) was difficult to find in the Merrimack River
Basin. No such area was found in the Merrimack River itself.

The principal streams and smaller tributaries were found to be
polluted not only in the general vicinity of the confluence with
the Merrimack River but also for many miles upstream.

The Merrimack River is formed by the confluence of the
Pemigewasset River, draining the northern mountainous region

of New Hampshire, and the Winnipesaukee River, which drains a large lake system in the central portion of the state.

Raw and partially treated sewage was discharged to the stream by most of the towns bordering the banks of the Pemigewasset. These wastes supported a lush growth of algae found covering the rocks and rubble in the stream bed.

In the Winnipesaukee River the water was gray-green, very turbid and sluggish. The bottom sediments contained brown fibrous matter in abundance and smelled like decomposing sewage sludge. Insect predator species, such as stoneflies, which cannot tolerate poisonous gases resulting from the breakdown of sewage, were not found. Mayflies, stoneflies, caddisflies, and certain beetles cannot withstand the low oxygen levels that occur here. Other more tolerant species, including the snails, leeches, and certain midgefly larvae, were found in large numbers. A total of 2,033 individuals and seven kinds of bottom fauna, mostly leeches, were found per square meter of stream bed. This large number of a few tolerant species of bottom fauna, gases of anaerobic decomposition rising from the bottom sediments, and the abundance of raw sewage discharged to the stream indicate that these headwaters were grossly polluted.

Downstream of the confluence, the stream was rapid, shallow, and passed over a stream bed primarily composed of sand with some rock. This same stream bed under unpolluted conditions would be suitable for the development of many different kinds of bottom fauna, especially certain mayflies, caddisflies, and waterpennies. However, only certain midgeflies, a few leeches, and sludgeworms could tolerate the grossly polluted environment. Further evidence of gross pollution of this area was the huge numbers of rotifers found clinging to the body surfaces of the midgefly larvae and leeches. These rotifers feed on the bacteria and microcrustacea in waters where active bacterial decomposition of organic sludge is occurring.

Dense growths of aquatic plants covered the stream bed downstream of the Winnipesaukee and Pemigewasset rivers. In relatively unpolluted streams, prolific numbers of herbivores such as certain midgeflies and mayflies may be found feeding on the tissues of these plants. Innumerable snails browse on the debris near the roots, and predatory carnivores such as dragonflies and leeches search for sludgeworms and insects burrowing into the substrate for food or shelter.

However, such a community of bottom life did not exist at this site. The assemblage of bottom life found was impoverished both in kind and number.

Benthic fauna found in sediments farther downstream were chiefly sludgeworms. Except for a few midgefly larvae and these sludgeworms, no other form of benthic fauna was found in these sediments. Other forms of benthic fauna such as clams, mussels, and snails may have been smothered by large quantities of grease and oil found in the bottom sediments.

No benthic fauna were found in sediments from the Merrimack River 0.55 miles downstream of the confluence with the Nashua. During dredging of the stream bed, nauseous gases of anaerobic decomposition bubbled to the surface. This portion of the Merrimack River was in a state of active decomposition. Benthic fauna dispersed to this area from upstream locations would face death by exposure to this septic environment or be smothered by fibrous matter found in abundance in these sediments.

In the backwater of the Essex Dam, downstream of the confluence of the Concord and Merrimack rivers, gas-lifted fecal matter and putrid sludges floated about the water surface.

This, a river with only two treatment plants on its entire main stream, is the Merrimack immortalized by Thoreau, who wrote, in *A Week on the Concord and Merrimack Rivers,* "Man tames Nature only that he may at last make her more free than he found her, though he may never yet have succeeded." He seems to have flattered man, who has certainly not yet succeeded on the Merrimack!

The tradition of riverine sewage and trash disposal goes back to the roots of humanity, of course, and when we today throw something into a river, to be swept away out of our ken, it is an instinct that dates from the ages when it didn't much matter. Certainly, the Nile at Memphis and Thebes, the Tigris at Babylon, the Tiber at Rome, the Seine at Paris, the Thames at London must have been vile indeed, but the people of those times had no technology to cope with the problem. Moreover, cities were small and compact by our standards. In most places, rivers could assimilate the sewage that men deposited in them; material things like metal, cloth, or glass were too valuable to throw away; industries used water mainly to turn wheels and flung few poisons in the face of nature.

And so the tradition came down that the use of rivers to carry away wastes was not only customary, it was free, and American communities and industries grew up on this economical assumption. The only investment needed for waste disposal was a pipe. Otherwise it was not a part of the cost of doing business. Water-using industries that otherwise might have had to clean things up to operate spaced themselves far enough apart so that special treatment was not necessary.

So effective pollution control has not been in the municipal and corporate budgets. Other things, from schools to dividends, came first, and, anyway, a little more pollution was not readily detectable except by organisms that neither vote nor buy. "With the school growth and other necessary growths and departments," an official whose town had doubled told a pollution conference recently, "now to contemplate the expenditure of funds for a sewage disposal system would be completely out of the question."

But the free ride on the environment is over, or at least we are beginning to understand that it is not, cannot, be free. As President Nixon said, "Through our years of past carelessness we incurred a debt to nature, and now that debt is being called." An aroused nation is at least becoming aware that its environment—indeed, survival itself—is threatened by our poisonous assault upon water, air, and the delicate mechanisms of nature which support us. My, such a squealing and scurrying and slithering around by the polluters; such excuses and foot-dragging and weeping and muttering about having to go out of business and leave towns unemployed! Then come sly smiles when Congress declines to provide sufficient federal money to help, and state and federal pollution cops go to pointing fingers at each other.

The failure of Congress to ante up enough does aggravate the situation terribly. Pollution abatement costs rise some ten percent per year, and backlog demands by states for matching funds since the enactment of the clean water laws have grown to beyond six billion dollars. Meanwhile, federal enforcement officials brandish the law, pointing out that in it there are no "ifs" or "buts" or financial contingency clauses.

Industry, which causes much more pollution than do human wastes, wrestles with enormous pollution problems. Those that want and try to do a conscientious job—and there are many of them—often find that their plants are such old conglomerations that they scarcely know where the pollutants come out. Others find themselves "out of the sewer and into the dump" with a solid waste disposal problem on their hands once they stop using the river.

But many are not yet about to be brought to heel. "We still have six recalcitrants and they are among the biggest corporations in the country," an official of the Delaware River Basin Commission admitted sadly. He was talking about the lower Delaware. "If you put your boat in below Trenton, the acid would eat it up." A State planning official told me that conditions there have forced New Jersey to write off the lower Delaware as a recreation area, even though that is where recreational opportunities are most needed.

I did not realize what a few industries could do to even a large river until Bart Hague and I took a two-day canoe trip on the Androscoggin in New Hampshire and Maine. Three paper companies have been responsible for more than 90 percent of the pollution in the Androscoggin, and the near-destruction of a recreation resource the Indians used to call the Fish River. Above Berlin,

New Hampshire, the Androscoggin is a great pride to that state, its fishing and boating renowned. When we launched our canoe below Gorham, however, we found ourselves not on the crystal waters of the Great White Hills, but on a torrent of foul and sulfurous soup. Instinctively we tried to dodge the foam that formed a thick scum upon the water and the sludge that floated by like dinosaur stools. Instinctively, too, we raised our nostrils to try to catch what breeze of sweet air might blow down from the mountains to dispel the river's fetid breath that rose from its mires in nauseating bubbles.

Since the river was disgraced, men abused it further with offerings of refuse, two cascades of which graced our campsite; another relieved a Bethel sawmill (love that river!). Near Newry dead cars nosed into the water like drowned ducks. At Rumford, forty miles below our start, the river's pollution remained noticeable, and there it received its next massive dose.

Insofar as its setting is concerned, however, the Androscoggin is probably the most scenic river in the Eastern United States. The majesty of the Presidential Range towers above it to the west The Carter Range looms to the south, while to the north stand the stately peaks of the Mahoosucs. The nearby scene is as impressive, with its cliffs and birch-clad hills, its broad meadows and glimpses of the steeples and white houses of New England hamlets. The Androscoggin Valley is New England in all its glory, surrounding a big strong lively river that sweeps magnificently through its heart. What a treasure to this land of recreational opportunity! And what a sewer, with more heavy industry proposed along its banks!

Up in northeastern Maine citizens are outraged over what a potato-processing complex has done to little Prestile Stream. "Once it was a fabulous trout stream; now it's completely ruined," growled a local newspaper editor. When the plant is in operation, the stream is so clogged with rotting residue that local residents have had to use bulldozers to scrape up the piles of dead fish. It is the equivalent of the waste of a city of 270,000 people going into a small brook. "We couldn't sleep at night for the stench," one woman said. New Brunswick residents on the Canadian side of the border, which the stream crosses, were so angry they dammed up the mess in protest and erected a concrete monument to the fight. Maine had downgraded the Prestile's water standard to "D" —the lowest rating—to encourage the industry, and some legislators said it would be discriminatory to up the rating again too quickly. Said one state representative: "It's simply a matter of keeping industry here; besides all the fish are gone anyway." And a state senator added, "Two wrongs don't make a right, and there's no reason to be vindictive." The company said it's trying to cope with the problem, but the Maine State Biologists Association called for a boycott of the products produced at the Prestile's expense.

Apparently it is not yet clear to industry that complete cleanup of wastes must henceforth be an essential part of the cost of doing business. Some corporate minds may not get the message that environment is more important than dividends until, in the midst of an annual stockholders' meeting, the chairman of the board is led away in handcuffs to the pokey. Perhaps the pillory will be revived so that the populace can pelt him with choice specimens of his company's pollution. Better yet might be to bring back the ducking stool!

Much of our rivers' misery is so old, so massive, and from such myriad sources as to defy cure, however. We have induced a river leukemia in our land. Eighteenth-century Potomac seaports like Port Tobacco, Maryland, and Dumfries, Virginia, which once rivaled New York, are now nearly half a mile from tidewater, silted in by the erosive agricultural practices of the past. A soil conservation expert informed a Potomac study conference recently that the best and most thorough erosion control practices could now only hold the line in keeping the river from becoming muddier. A Washington *Star* headline after a local storm read "Potomac Dirtier *Than Usual*" (my italics).

The rate as well as the massiveness of river pollution is appalling, for it has taken us less than a century to ruin the purity of our streams and their beauty built up over eons. Americans not yet middle-aged remember swimming as kids in rivers now so filthy that, as one put it, "You splash yourself and you feel like taking a bath." Former Secretary of the Interior Stewart Udall has pointed out that, as our requirements for water were doubling, pollution more than doubled. For the Potomac, pollution warnings were sounded as early as 1913. By 1932 the problem was termed "critical." Now, with the area population doubled and $150 million invested in antipollution measures, it is at least a third more serious than before. "We have repaid its beauty and importance with . . . excrement," an Izaak Walton League spokesman exploded at a pollution enforcement conference in 1969, calling the situation "little short of treason to the heritage of a nation."

"George Washington goofed," a conservationist commented sarcastically. "He should have located the capital above Great Falls and let the estuary turn into a vast morass."

More disquieting than the anger, however, is the tone of hopelessness which many concerned people have expressed over the years. Chard Smith, for one, writing about the pollution problems of the Housatonic and its tributaries concluded, "Since the Naugatuck is entirely controlled by industry, all hope of curing this condition must be abandoned."

A Water Resources Survey of the Schuylkill River called it "a classic example of man's eternal propensity for sacrificing natural resources in order to meet his increasing appetite for a better life," and noted that "by the end of the first third of the twentieth century, the Schuylkill was but a shell of its former self." "Water quality in practically the entire main stem of the Schuylkill River is now severely degraded for significant periods of time," the survey report concluded, and continued:

Some portions of the river are persistently of poor quality, the headwaters mostly from a chemical standpoint, the middle portion from chemical and bacteriological standpoints, and the lower reaches are contaminated from almost all standpoints. The future outlook is extremely bleak at all points if immediate water quality control measures are not instituted. Unquestionably, immediate *total* relief is impractical from almost any point of view, but many measures can now be instituted which will afford significant alleviation. An expenditure, by all affected sectors of the economy, of probably hundreds of millions of dollars will be necessary to provide any lasting solution to water quality problems in the Schuylkill River.

Coal mining, which has probably ruined more Eastern streams than any other cause, very nearly destroyed the value and usefulness of the entire Schuylkill River. The hydraulic washing and sorting of anthracite coal along the Schuylkill's headwaters choked the river with coal silt, raising flood heights, ruining navigation, reducing the river's capacity to assimilate wastes, and destroying its beauty. Pleas to remedy the problems went unheeded for fifty years, and by the 1940s three million cubic yards of silt were being dumped into the Schuylkill annually. Finally, a state–federal desilting project was undertaken, and in the nineteen-year period from 1948 to 1967 some thirty-four million cubic yards of silt were removed from the river at a cost of more than $43 million. As a result, river conditions have been improved and stabilized, but the problem goes on. More than thirty million cubic yards remain accumulated in the Schuylkill, even though anthracite mining is mostly past, and controls are in effect. Huge "culm banks" of waste materials piled up in mining days erode into the streams, and the annual siltation rate is still half a million cubic yards per year.

Of all the chronic diseases which industry has bequeathed to our Eastern rivers, the most insidious is acid mine drainage. Sulfuric acid, formed when air oxidizes the sulfur that occurs in coal deposits, leaks out with water drainage. This acid mine drainage is Pennsylvania's worst single pollution problem, infecting sixty percent of the State's streams, and it is an affliction shared by twenty-five other states as well. Pennsylvania is gamely trying to cope with it. Mines are sealed when possible. Neutralizing installations that treat the acid water with lime have been placed in many streams, operating like artificial kidneys and frequently overtaxed. Now the commonwealth has teamed up with the federal government and Pennsylvania State University on a pilot treatment plant to chart the way for more massive control.

I never fully realized just how awful, how spooky, is this curse of the coal mining region until Kip Dalley and I went canoeing down the West Branch of the Susquehanna from Shawville to Renovo. This spectacular and secluded stretch offers one of the most satisfactory canoe camping trips in the Mideast, despite its beginning.

That was discouraging and depressing, I must admit, though it was what we Eastern canoeists must expect to encounter often. We put in below a power dam, where the water was as hot as your bathtub. Summer cottages clung to one bank beside the dusty road, while on the other a power shovel grubbed gravel from a river bar. A power line sliced across the valley, and a work train ground along slowly while crews squirted massive doses of yellow herbicide on the surrounding trees and shrubs. A mile or so downstream we began to see strip mines atop the escarpment, looking like the earthworks of giants engaged in trench warfare across the gorge.

But the soothing, exhilarating river at length took us quietly away from this offensiveness. Its bouldery course and gentle rapids (which must have vexed the old-time lumber raftsmen) kept us pleasantly exercised and alert, and Moshannon Falls, a mile above that beautiful wild tributary, gave us an especially exhilarating ride. The grassy riverbanks were brightened by summer flowers— leopard lilies and pinks and early asters. Above, hemlocks and rhododendron forested steep mountainsides that rose to nearly a thousand feet above us. They folded about the river as we threaded the tortuous canyon, misty in the shaded morning, or back-lit with gold in the hazy afternoon, and we seemed to be traveling a far wilderness. Only the railroad, an occasional bridge, and a house or two reminded us we were still close to civilization. Our campsite amid the ferns beside Sterling Run could have been a thousand miles in the wilds.

And the river, which had cooled, seemed like trout water. I peered down to look for fish, but not even a minnow could be seen. I looked also for the birdlife one expects along a river—herons, kingfishers, ospreys. All were gone, for the West Branch was a sterilized stream.

We saw positive evidence of the acid in the brooks feeding the river. Their rocks were stained bright yellow-orange from "yellow-boy," the ferric hydroxide often associated with acid-mine drainage. The whole watershed seemed thus to bleed. It is reported that more than 1,500 tons of acid per day go into it. On a sportsman's map of the mountain wilds of northcentral Pennsylvania—a map marked "GOD'S COUNTRY"—skull and crossbones symbols mark the beautiful West Branch of the Susquehanna River.

Such are the river diseases from the past that linger and fester on. What of the present and future? As our population burgeons, each individual demands his more than 50 gallons of water per day to keep clean and cool and contented (once three or four sufficed, so that shows progress). He also demands more goods from industry, which require 200 gallons of water to make a dollar's worth of paper, 500 for a yard of woolen cloth, and 1,400 for a dollar's worth of steel. It is not only the backlog of neglect and the reluctance to meet a costly challenge, but also the sheer volume of sewage that caused one anguished city official to ask not long ago, "Is there anybody in this room who actually believes that the sewage treatment plants are doing what they are supposed to do?"

A wit once remarked of the Housatonic River that its water was so pure it should be used "only for baptism." Now, apparently, we must accept Chard Smith's directions for canoeing the river: "Paddle on down with the soap suds through the meadows where the Indians used to live."

The environmental doom which a population increase threatens is beginning to show up in other new forms of pollution. One is pesticide poisoning, which has now tainted every part of the world, including Antarctica. In the 1930s a Swiss chemist discovered that an astounding man-made substance, dichlor-diphenyl-trichloroethane or DDT, could effectively deal with insects which carried disease or attacked crops. What a boon to humanity! In 1947 he received a Nobel Prize for the discovery.

Other pesticides were developed also. Many have proved relatively safe when used properly, but one group, the chlorinated hydrocarbons (DDT, dieldrin, endrin, aldrin, toxaphene, heptachlor, lindane, and chlordane, for instance), are persistent, lasting as long as ten years or more, and are passed along the food chain to fish; then to birds and animals; and at length to man. A few scientists were nervous from the start, knowing they were dealing with mysterious poisons, but their concern went largely unheeded in the welcome for pesticide magic. Rachel Carson's galvanic warning in *Silent Spring* was attacked as an overstatement.

Then the toll on wildlife began to tell. Some chemicals kill animals almost immediately. A two-ounce-per-acre application of aldrin for grasshopper control, for example, killed nearly a third of the young waterfowl present in the area. DDT accumulations in the yolk sacs of embryo fish have killed them soon after they hatched. Larger doses attacked the nervous systems of fish, small animals, and birds, and killed them. The poison also broke down sex hormones in birds, inhibiting calcium metabolism and producing thin-shelled eggs. As a result of orchard spraying around Lake George, New York, lake trout reproduction was almost totally destroyed. Spraying for black flies and mosquitoes around Sebago Lake in Maine caused landlocked salmon fishing there to decline sharply. DDT accumulations in the fatty tissues of fish in such Eastern streams as the Delaware and Hudson increased alarmingly, for the food chain of aquatic life, from plankton and insect larvae to fish, concentrate the chemicals as much as 100,000 times in twenty-four hours. As for birds, the peregrine, the world's most valued falcon, is now gone from the East, and the American Bald

Eagle has been decimated. Osprey colonies in Connecticut and on Gardners Island in Long Island Sound have been reduced ninety percent in two decades.

It is ironic to read a description of this graceful "fish hawk" written a century ago (almost before our "conservation era" began): "The sportsman delights to gaze upon this bird of solitude, as she returns from her excursions up the lake in quest of food, bearing the struggling trout in her talons. . . . None disturb her domicile or question her right of protection."

Sure, sure, but we're loath to ban the persistent poisons that will do her, and perhaps ourselves, in. Analyses are finding DDT residues in every animal species. However, there is not positive proof yet that the chlorinated hydrocarbons will kill man. We're still guinea pigs in this profitable experiment though most of us have much more of them in us than we permit in food we buy, and we know they are transmitted to unborn children. We are at last getting scared enough to phase them out—not stop, just phase out—after the whole chain of life has been polluted. After all, dollars are at stake.

More sickening than those pesticides could be the ingestion of mercury, another substance millions of tons of which we have been adding to our waters in the name of progress. The discomforts of chronic mercury poisoning, caused by exposure to small amounts over a long time, can include inflamed gums, tongue, or colon, loosening teeth, loss of appetite, nutritional disturbances, diarrhea, anemia, kidney damage, and hypertension. It can affect the central nervous system, killing brain cells and impairing coordination, vision, speech, and hearing. It can cause behavior changes, irritability, insomnia, shakiness, fatigue, and occasional hallucinations. It can also cause brain damage in an unborn child even though the mother has no poisoning symptoms. Chronic mercury poisoning is very resistant to therapy, and victims may remain out of health for years.

Death from mercury poisoning has been rare in the United States so far, and the extent of low-level poisoning is unknown.

What has been discovered is the scary fact that mercury, long believed to sink harmlessly as an inorganic substance into stream and lake sediments, can be transformed in the environment into an organic form. It then enters the food chain ending up in fish and birds in thousandfold concentrations. Some fish caught have contained fifty times what the Food and Drug Administration has tentatively established as a safety limit. Lake Champlain and a number of Eastern rivers have been contaminated. The discovery of mercury pollution has brought about the complete closure of some fishing waters, the seizure of commercial fish hauls, and warnings to anglers not to eat their catches. Dollar damages to commercial and sport fisheries are in the millions.

Fortunately, drastic action has also reduced industrial mercury discharges by some eighty percent and has banned most mercury-treated materials. However, even if all mercury pollution were halted immediately, existing deposits, which break down slowly, could continue to contaminate the environment for many decades to come.

Heat, as well as chemicals, threatens the web of life. Rivers are heated in the process of cooling electric power generators. The demand for electricity is doubling every six to ten years, the Environmental Protection Agency reports, and, by 1980, 200 billion gallons of fresh water—one fifth of all that is available in the country—will be needed to cool electric power generation. If one subtracts spring runoffs, the portion needed amounts to half the flow in other seasons. In the Connecticut Basin alone the demand for power is predicted to increase some twenty-eight times by the year 2020.

The effect of heat on aquatic life is marked but as yet imperfectly known, hence the many arguments on the subject. But thermal pollution can affect the entire ecological balance of a stream. Power plants often discharge water ten to twenty degrees warmer than the natural river water, and an increase of only three or four degrees can, under certain conditions, seriously affect aquatic life. It can stop spawning, and make fish eggs hatch too early or not at all. The hotter the water the less oxygen it can hold, yet fish double their consumption of oxygen for each ten-degree temperature rise. Hot water has less capacity also for assimilating wastes than do cooler flows. Heat can harm the usefulness of water for recreation, industrial use, and irrigation, and encourages the spread of noxious aquatic growths and rough fish.

Some results of thermal increases seem good: increased oyster production, improved winter fishing, warm swimming areas. Yet to emphasize these and go on with thermal meddling when the ecological consequences are not fully known is folly and scientifically indefensible. We bash on, nevertheless, for we the public must be served—now. Industry tempts us with more power-consuming devices, then cites resultant demands as needs and mandates.

Some power projects seem arrogant indeed, oblivious to environmental impact, cooking rivers until the very bottom mud is hot. New plants mushroom. Local officials and citizens at Saratoga on the Hudson were unaware of one such start until the foundations were already dug for a nuclear power plant (there being no local laws to preclude it). It not only would have affected the river but also was right across from an historic area—Saratoga National Historic Park. The Hudson River Commission's incisive questions faulted the engineering premises for the project, and that plus enraged local opposition finally shooed the plant away.

The power industry is, fortunately, beginning to use closed cooling systems—cooling towers and ponds. These, however, are more expensive than using natural water bodies, and he who gets between business and a buck can get into trouble even when he is elected government. Realizing that public concern has now made ecological considerations unavoidable, the power people are also now making their own studies of thermal pollution effects on waterways, though conservationists often charge that they are either inadequate or rigged. Be that as it may, even if a company can demonstrate little harmfulness in its new power plant proposal, it is the cumulative effects, up and down a river or around a vital fish nursery, like Chesapeake Bay, that could be disastrous. This possibility caused one conservation leader recently to make the astonishing suggestion that Americans might soon have to make a choice between environment and, say, air conditioning. What—limit ourselves, our use of resources in high-wide-and-handsome America? Stay our hands? How naïve! How preposterous! Down with fish; up with air conditioning! It's an American birthright.

Flexing our technology to meet population demands is causing yet another kind of pollution along our rivers: visual pollution. Power lines, needed to transmit all that electricity, and bigger than ever before, have caused particularly grievous offenses against the scenic beauty of rivers, and have brought on some major controversies. A proposal to run a transmission line near Antietam National Battlefield brought out the Secretary of the Interior in full battle array. The outrage caused when the huge steel skeletons begin to march across a beautiful or historic part of America has prompted increased efforts toward underground transmission, which is very expensive and difficult, and also toward better siting and design of overhead lines. But bad siting is everywhere. Along the Connecticut River the hill behind Guildhall, Vermont, so typical of New England's village charm, is scalped by a power line cut. The spectacular water gap of the James River at Balcony Falls is whipped with power lines. A huge one has been rammed up the pretty little Brandywine Valley—in fact, right between the stream and artist Andrew Wyeth's charming home. One of West Virginia's loveliest views of the Shenandoah River has a power line right between the eyes. Nobody cared. Power goes from here to there the cheapest way. That helps the electricity rate payers a bit, it is said, so score them seven, the environment zero.

Power plants and other water-using industries have, of course, been located as close to rivers as possible, without any regard for what the huge complexes of buildings, smokestacks, transformers, piles of coal, do to the beauty of what is often otherwise rural riverscape. Two squat on the banks of the Delaware below the water gap like giant toads. Similar monsters affront the Susque-hanna and the James. A plant on the edge of the Potomac has not so much as a tree left to screen it. Even for the new nuclear plant on the Connecticut below Middletown, interesting though it is architecturally, no effort was made to screen it or blend it har-moniously with its natural surroundings.

Moving the plants back a bit, blending them in, meant bigger pumps, more pipe, costlier siting. It was cheaper to rape the river-scape. An example of the fact that it need not happen is the Charmin paper plant on the Susquehanna, low in profile and set a thousand feet back from the river, it is almost entirely hidden from view except for its stack. The railroad and the summer cottages along the river's edge are more intrusive than the forty-acre factory.

Industry makes a convenient whipping boy for much abuse of our landscape, particularly our rivers. We ourselves, with our frantic urge to get from here to there faster and faster, have de-stroyed much river beauty. Valleys are natural avenues, of course, and our routes of transport sought and followed them. The old roads and canals usually followed the river meanders and were well-married into the landscape. Railroads cut and filled, but were usually narrow and generally empty. Our superhighway builders, however, have become geologic forces almost as powerful as the glaciers. Neither mountain nor canyon turns them very much as they thrust arrogantly through the American ideal of rocks and rills and woods and templed hills. Wherever they follow a river, they usually dominate it. The lower reaches of the Willowemoc and Beaverkill, those beloved New York trout streams, are now scenically enslaved by a dual-laned Route 17.

The valley of the Winooski River from Vermont's capital, Montpelier, to Burlington on Lake Champlain epitomizes the scenic beauty of the Green Mountain State. Farm fields flank the little river's bouldery edges, pools, and riffles while behind stands Camelback in green majesty. All that is now subordinate to mighty

Interstate 89. Admired for its design and the views it offers, it is lord and master, now, of the valley the Winooski made.

Good design can mitigate the scenic impact of highways, of course; could even attain the simple objective of allowing glimpses of a pretty river through or over the bridge railings now usually designed to block the view completely. And highway construction often gives opportunity for protection of rivers and of making them enjoyable. If rights-of-way are expanded sufficiently in places to include a nearby riverside, its beauty can be preserved and perhaps made accessible as a rest area. Highway departments generally are interested in transportation only, however. The conservation of nearby scenery, being nonessential to that purpose, and being also an added expense, is ignored. One citizens' group interested in the Still River near Brookfield, Connecticut, has helped to correct this failing. The local residents have urged that when Route 7 is improved through the little Housatonic tributary's green flood plains and across its meanders, an additional width of right-of-way be provided to accommodate trails, river access, and scenic protection. Though the project as now planned still will have a serious impact on the riverway in places, it will provide some of the green space and river access that have been suggested.

Fortunately the intrusion of big highways is often screened by vegetation and topography when one is actually on a river or perhaps wading it a-fishing. The Winooski can hide you from I-89. The Schroon in New York can make you forget the Northway though it is practically on top of the river. Others, like the Pennsylvania's Juniata near Amity Hall, are open victims of highway hegemony, and few are free of the noise. When a highway and a river converge, as they must through the Delaware Water Gap, the roar is constant and dreadful. Even the Susquehanna, so broad above Harrisburg that it dwarfs the paralleling highways, is bathed perpetually in the roar of truck traffic.

The impact of road construction along rivers is most tragic

in the cities, for it has cut people—millions of them—off from one of their few sources of scenic beauty and recreational pleasure. It all started out quite reasonably and appealingly, of course. Back in the days of buggies, even the horseless variety, not only were urban banks important travel routes for commerce, but also a Sunday drive along the river was a pleasant and harmless outing. Park roads along the lower Charles River in Boston must have once been delightful for this purpose. So must also have been the esplanade along Harrisburg, Pennsylvania's, Susquehanna waterfront, and Hartford's Connecticut Shore. When Potomac Park was constructed in Washington, its riverside road, though it was referred to as "the Speedway," was really just a pleasant Sunday driving way. The roads enhanced rather than detracted from park use. Now that we are enslaved to automotive travel, swaths of concrete have usurped much of the green riverbanks in all these places. In Boston (where the road builders and park protectors are in bed together in the same agency, the Metropolitan District Commission), the parkland has been steadily gnawed away to make more room for cars and less room for pedestrians. People without cars, just trying to enjoy the riverside on their feet, can get out of the way as best they can.

Washington's George Washington Memorial Parkway, designed especially for scenic enjoyment and one of the most beautiful riverside parks in the world, was built for autos only, and trail and bikeways are now being added in some stretches only as an afterthought. Its most beautiful part, along the Potomac Palisades, is still only for those who drive.

In downtown Washington, more than 60,000 cars a day sluice through Potomac Park, turning Independence Avenue into a river of steel. Plans now call for cleaving the park with a freeway chasm in order to get the river of steel underground and allow people to cross to the river of water. I-295 paralleling the Anacostia River blocks off from riverside parklands residents of the southeast part of the capital who need parks desperately. At the other end of town, Georgetown's historic waterfront cannot be restored and developed as the cultural treasure it could be until the elevated freeway now dominating it is redesigned below ground.

Along Harrisburg's waterfront is such a whirring wall of traffic that the comfortable old riverfront homes are being abandoned to business offices. Interstate 81 threatens to gut Wildwood Park that surrounds a Susquehanna River channel. The city itself gave the right-of-way, but court action has stopped the project pending ecological studies.

Philadelphia's Fairmount Park, largest urban park in the world, was sliced through by the Schuylkill Expressway which, depressed along the riverside in the central city, has destroyed the usefulness and beauty of one side of the river there. Philadelphia managed to prevent the rape of the Delaware riverside in the heart of town: the Delaware Expressway was depressed and covered to allow free access across parkland between the famed Society Hill historic restoration area and the Penn's Landing development of marinas, parks, museums, and promenades along the river. The Schuylkill shore in downtown Philadelphia across from the Schuylkill Expressway is also scheduled for park development. Other cities are fighting also to keep or make their riversides meaningful to people once again. Binghamton and neighboring cities of Broome County, New York, are trying to do so.

Richmond, Virginia, has undertaken one of the most dramatic rescues of riverfront. Where the falls of the James provide potential for one of the most beautiful riverscapes any major city ever enjoyed, the waterfront had been preempted by industry and cut off by railroads. Instead there will be a 2,000-acre preserve of tree-arched, flowered riverbank and islands, with trails and bridges and landings, giving Richmond its first legal access to the river within memory. As this project progressed, however, the Richmond Metropolitan Authority was preparing, farther upriver, to run a four-lane toll expressway along the James, ripping up trees, paving over riverbank, even filling part of the river itself, and shadowing the rapids with pylons.

But private citizens organized a Richmond Scenic James

Council, which organized tours of the river, had its status as a navigable waterway reestablished to bring Federal controls to bear, and invited City Council members to meetings to hear the citizens' views. As financial feasibility of the toll expressway was shaky and in view of the widespread concern with its environmental impact, plans for a bond issue commitment to build the highway were dropped. Now the Scenic James Council is proposing a special "Historic Falls of the James" scenic designation to protect the river, and the city has cleared the proposal for the Virginia legislature to consider.

If all of us who live in the North Atlantic Region of the United States would only stay our hands as Richmond did, we could keep a significant heritage of rivers and riverscapes that are still attractive and enjoyable. Much is being said these days about massive programs to undo the ravages our waterways have suffered. We talk of billions to exorcise our zombie streams in ways that range from building huge water treatment plants to the moving of highways. It is well that we admit and are prepared so to atone for the hideous sins we have committed against our most beautiful and delightful of all natural resources. Yet we tend to think of cures for our lack of conservation in the same terms which caused the ills. Money and technology, we believe, can cure what they caused. No doubt that they will do a lot, and they should. How much more we could do by simply protecting what is still fair and wholesome! The adage that an ounce of prevention is worth a pound of cure applies well to pollution. Although our Eastern waterways are nearly all sick to some degree, our heritage of still-beautiful, enjoyable streams remains a significant one. Much as our go-go national personality hates the terms, it is time we said "Don't" and "Stop" as well as "Go and fix it." We shall have become affectionate, respectful stewards of our environment rather than wizardly masters when we protect the living with the same enthusiasm with which we would revive the dead.

Dammation

But when his fair course is not hindered,
He makes sweet music with the enamell'd stones,
Giving a gentle kiss to every sedge
He overtaketh in his pilgrimage.

—*William Shakespeare from*
"Two Gentlemen of Verona"

IF you drive through Vermont's Green Mountains along Route 100, threading Granville Notch and following the White River southward, you will pass through a countryside you will swear you saw on a Vermont Christmas card or calendar. It is the quintessence of Vermont scenery, that blend of birch and pine, farmhouse and stone wall, green meadow and sparkling river which has made Vermont landscapes preeminently admired. Enraptured, you will say to yourself, "*This* is Vermont!"

Now guess what was going to happen to that perfect Vermont valley; what may still happen. That's it—you've got it! They were going to dam it up. They still may, for dam builders do not give up. Rebuffed, they roll up their plans and await a more propitious occasion for offering again their engineered solutions to problems of flood control, water supply, dilution of pollutants, electric power needs, and "demands" for lake recreation. Of course, you may have gotten a hint of the plans from a sign, nailed to a tree, that reads "DAMN THE DAM." That was just the work of the few people who live in the valley or have come to love it, and to quote the despairing comment of a state planner who also loved the valley, "They don't have any political muscle."

A past governor had once said that to dam the White was acceptable, and the United States Army Corps of Engineers marched. The Corps had been beaten back on a proposal to build a reservoir long authorized for the Moose River in the town of Victory, Vermont. People began talking about ecology and wildlife wintering areas, however, and the State Game Commission stepped in to buy a key part of the site as a game refuge. The White River damsite at Gaysville apparently seemed a good fallback position.

And the plan was not frivolous. The White can be a terror. In flood its three branches hit like a one-two-three punch. A 1,000-acre reservoir could lower flood levels as much as five feet at White River Junction, where the White enters the Connecticut, and half a foot at Hartford, Connecticut, 200 miles away. Thus, there would be substantial downstream benefits to people who perhaps should not have settled and built where they did. For towns and cities were placed according to the necessities of an earlier era on the banks of a river then of steadier flow out of untouched upper watersheds. The damsite was not only efficient, it also affected a sparsely settled valley. Only one hundred homes would be flooded out, and relocation could be arranged. Drawdown of the reservoir, exposing unattractive mud flats, would be made in winter, after the recreation season, when snow covers the ground for much of the time. When attacked as would-be scenery murderers, the Corps politely pointed out that while Vermont is very conscious of its beauty, there have been few controls to protect it. The Gaysville reservoir area has been wide open to any kind of commercialization that whim or profit motive may dream up.

But something irreplaceable, precious beyond price, would be lost if that reservoir were constructed. Part of the smile of Vermont would be wiped away forever. "Ours is a 'little land,' " the Stockbridge Planning Commission wrote to Governor Deane C.

Davis, "small mountains and hills, little valleys and streams, villages and hamlets with country houses strung out through the valleys over the hillsides. This is rural Vermont, and it is what attracts the visitors to our state. . . . They like the tranquil setting, the unpretentious way of life. There is much being said today about 'keeping Vermont natural, conserving our natural assets.' This is what *we* are saying. We want to keep our natural environment."

If muscle cannot twist the arm, sometimes eloquence can touch the conscience and the heart. Governor Davis, evidently concerned about Vermont's deteriorating environment, decided there would be no Gaysville dam, at least for a while. The legislature now is considering a bill to designate and keep the White a scenic, free-flowing river.

Our past sins and blunders plus our prolificness and our demand for engineered solutions to the needs we generate may well cost us some of the most melodious rivers and beautiful river valleys America has left. Scared that places we should not have built upon may be flooded, that our fifty-gallon-a-day-per-person water-sopping gadgets may go thirsty, or our electrical comforts powerless, we send out the engineers to find new water supplies. And true to their credo that "Nothing should interfere with good engineering" and that they must do things in the most efficient and least costly way, they find a handy damsite.

Now dams can be fun, much more so than digging wells, building desalting plants, surcharging gruff voters for using excess water, or forbidding profitable flood plain construction—and certainly more so than finding new power sources. First of all, dams take a lot of machinery and cement and manhours and other such prosperities which give a community an economic shot in the arm. Dam building is construction, and "America Progresses Through Construction"—at least that's what is emblazoned on a Washington office building. When it's done, the dam is a magnificent monument. It soars above the valley like the wall of some noble castle. You can fly a flag from its crest and put a bronze plaque on it and everything.

Moreover (and this is the real frosting on the cake), you can water ski on the reservoir the dam creates, angle there for big easy fish, and swim too if the water level is up over the mud flats. (If it's down in winter, who cares, except perhaps some life that doesn't matter.) Really, you just about have to admit that dams are the most, unless you're an old fowf who can't stand change, one of the bug-and-bunny set who babbles about free-flowing streams and how pretty they are, or else one of the hicks who lives in the valley to be flooded out. Some say that reservoirs, unlike streams that go on giving pleasure, fill up and lose their usefulness after a generation or two. Well, we won't be around in a generation or two. Let them worry about it.

I do not believe, as do some conservationists, that all damming is wrong, a wicked dereliction of moral duty to harmonize better with our environment. They may be justified in saying that engineering surgery on the landscape is no substitute for a basic cure. In many cases, however, we cannot cure the ills, often past ones, which now cause our rivers to flood, or fail to fulfill our demands. We cannot expect our fellows to relish the thought either of going thirsty or of floating down some flood crest astride their own rooftrees, when a well-placed dam could prevent such possibilities. Nor would we abandon a standard of living which is causing society's increasing demands for harnessed rivers. Sometimes dams seem the lesser of two evils. For example, it may be more acceptable to produce hydroelectric power than to pollute the atmosphere by other means of power production. Where there are no natural lakes, a reservoir, if properly managed, can be a scenic asset, providing a dimension of outdoor recreation otherwise unavailable in the area. Feasible solutions to our problems of managing our water resources, in short, involve social, economic, and political as well as scientific and technological considerations.

Yet each one of us should be fully aware of what endless population increase, endless construction in our valleys, endless demand for more water and more power will cost in terms of the beauty and integrity of the American landscape, and its intangible values that enrich our spirits. The money we gladly pay for a dam today may constitute a check drawn on the birthright of the future. In fifty or a hundred years, the dam may be "spent." The valley could have smiled, the river could have laughed for us forever.

If pollution, like interest or a debt, is a continuing (and often increasing) drain on the American treasury of beauty and wholesomeness, the sacrificing of beautiful valleys for reservoir construction constitutes lump-sum disbursements of capital. Whereas the pollution mess is chronic and we at least partly adjust to it, the sudden loss of a chunk of beloved scenery to dam construction can be traumatic. Of course, those who have not been fortunate enough to see it (and they are far too many) may not relate to the problem. Others can coolly measure "benefits" against "losses," and, if the former are mightier, order the execution of a river valley. But those who know the valley and love it fight and weep, for they know how great will be that debit to the dwindling account called "America the Beautiful."

If you like scenic valley wanderings, move down to New York State's Susquehanna River watershed. There Charlotte Creek winds for twenty-five miles among wooded hills that glaciers smoothed, and joins the river at Oneonta. The bottomlands along the creek provide some of New York's finest dairy farms. In all, those who love it call the Charlotte Valley "an enchanting piece of rural America," yet they have been fighting off a multipurpose dam there for thirty years!

Thrice they have been able to get the proposal knocked out of congressional public works programs, but it never goes away. Now it is back again as a double dam in the latest Susquehanna Basin plan. More than half its "benefits" are counted as recreational space and, according to one opponent, "for the paraphernalia of Americans at play." Flood control for downriver urban centers like Binghamton is also a major purpose, though the last flood was in 1933, protective works are now in place there, and the steady Charlotte contributes little to floods. However, New York's Water Resources Commission, calls the Charlotte Creek damming "a necessary part of the total development for the Susquehanna River."

The engineers have infinite patience. Like starfish opening an oyster, they apply never-ending pressure to pry apart the resistant shells and insert their project. Yet a dedicated band of Charlotte Valley people fight doggedly on. "We're sick and tired of being harassed," said dairy farmer Ray Christensen, who heads the Charlotte Creek Watershed Association and leads the fight, taking fifty speaking engagements a year to plead for the valley. "People cannot continue to live under these conditions; farmers must be able to plan ahead. It's a terrible strain."

The tactics of the battle are to challenge and, with hired experts, refute the justifications for the damming, and to enlist broad public and political support to dismiss it. But as one Charlotte Creek writer, Henry Kernan, has explained, "the larger issue is how Americans view their land and their lives . . . all the engineering efforts could not design a valley more suitable for pleasant living than the Charlotte." Other Susquehanna Valleys are also under the shadow of dammation, so do not delay too long in taking your valley tours. For example, the Unadilla, of which farm organizations are particularly proud, is mentioned for three damming possibilities in the future.

And hurry down to Virginia, where the Jackson, Cowpasture, Calfpasture, and Maury rivers and Craig Creek form the upper James. With all due respect to New England scenery, which is supreme in the East in summer and winter and where architecture seems so cleanly fitted to the land, montane Virginia in spring and fall is unsurpassed. In the spring it is a world of redbud and white dogwood, its pastures greening and its streams gushing amid the wildflowers. In autumn it is bronze-gold, not as brilliant perhaps as New England's renowned autumn glory, but with a subtler and wider range of foliage colors. Corn still is often shocked in the fields and blue smoke rises from a farm chimney to match the soft haze upon the hills.

Well, a number of Virginia's valleys are accused of being useless scenery, and at least one is already convicted of the crime. The sentence? Dammation. What else? Where else? These young rivers in their narrow valleys are easy to plug. Few people live there to object, and there is much old grundginess that has to be protected downstream—where the votes are. After all, youth must often be sacrificed to preserve the investments of old age.

Condemned to die, with gallows under construction, is a delightful portion of the Jackson in what is known as the Gathright Preserve. The valley was once owned, mountain to mountain, by a gruff-kind giant known as Uncle Tom Gathright, who operated it as a sportsman's vacation club. Later the state bought it for a wildlife management area. In public ownership, how cheap and convenient a site it was for a dam—no land to buy, no residents to fuss with. Floods could be checked a bit, downriver pollution could be flushed out, and gas-driven recreation could be provided. Quality-minded sportsmen were mollified by promises of a trout fishery downriver, maintained by cold water releases from the reservoir, although landowners are reportedly opposing the access that implies. The Gathright "Preserve" was regarded not as a beautiful Virginia vale to be held in trust, but merely as a land-bank deposit.

One October, when sycamore leaves floated down the little river like wrinkled coracles and walnuts plopped in the pools, we went camping down the Jackson, John Bowles and I, so that he might bid farewell to the river. As a boy he had chored in the summers for Uncle Tom and had come to know the charm of a river. He learned its trout riffles and bass holes; experienced the ecstasy of an exploding covey of quail and the majestic approach of a wild turkey gobbler. We caught few fish but many memories floating down the Jackson that day. John caught his limit of them of course, but my own mental creel was well filled too. Turkey Ridge was ablaze, and fog wisped down the river. Its water was chilly-clean on our legs as we waded to fish the tourmaline pools, deep under rooty banks. Bars of water-smoothed stones that seemed infinitely varied nudged the canoe into swift channels, and ribs of rock, criss-crossing the river bed with ledges, made the water crinkle. Moss and ferns chinked the slatey cliffs that often formed the riverbank and pines clung to one high escarpment soaring above the water. Every bend brought a new scene and a new expectation. The last one was a huge gash in the cliff face, with raw stone rubble spewed down beside the water, and we knew this was the end. "Why can't kids in the future know the Jackson as I knew it?" muttered John. "Good-bye, Gathright."

We may soon have to bid good-bye to other valleys of the upper James Basin, valleys as beautiful as any in the Land. Ever since the flood ravages of Hurricane Camille in 1969, many Virginians have called for regulation of the "capricious" James, not only for flood control but also for industry. "The realities of modern life make industrialization a necessity," the Richmond *Times-Dispatch* editorialized, adding that the Old Dominion cannot provide prosperity with an economy "geared to an agrarian past." The little agrarian valleys that lend Virginia so much charm and delightfulness do not contribute to such a dream in their present state. To the urban, industrial mind, the penalty for such uselessness is death by drowning. "If the basin's promise is to become reality, men must pick up where nature left off," the newspaper opined. "They must not allow the James to remain a capricious stream, victimizing the basin with floods today and with droughts tomorrow."

Thus the same round of despoliations which have stilled so many singing waters and drowned so many lovely valleys comes again in the name of Progress. Sportsmen who love to float and fish Craig Creek, another beautiful James tributary flowing in near Eagle Rock, soon may mourn its loss, for it is next on the death list. The Appalachia program proposed a dam there, and Army engineers are consequently beaver-busy, having the backing of most local governmental bodies. Though Craig Creek has many admirers, landowners along it have kept away most of its would-be friends and defenders. Some who have been run off by the property owners say flood-out would serve them right. Conscience whispers wrong, however. Craig Creek, recommended as a state scenic river, is too beautiful to drown. Perhaps with a Virginia Scenic Rivers System now authorized, something can be worked out to make the stream accessible, keep it beautiful, yet still leave the landowners undisturbed. Hipes Dam, as the reservoir project is called, cannot really do much to control floods, for Craig Creek is not subject to dangerous flooding. And to use a dam to dilute pollution instead of treating it at the source certainly seems an immoral flushing away of sin against environment. As for recreation, if the area is to be publicly enjoyed, should it not be on a beautiful natural waterway instead of a reservoir?

A Roanoke businessman who manages to float the stream nearly every weekend with his family believes that if enough people could experience the stream just once it would be beyond dammation— its value measured not in tourist dollars or acre-feet of storage but rather in melody of moving water. "Every state should have a place like this so our kids can get at least a little taste of wilderness," he said. "Once in a while you need to get off in a corner by yourself and enjoy nature."

It was another aspect of progress—power—that for a time threatened another death-row river in Virginia, however. The river bears the name Calfpasture because, some say, the buffalo calves liked its grazing long ago. The little waterway of deep pools and bright riffles caresses lush, stone-fenced fields that lie between Mill and Great North mountains, under the far suzerainty of Elliott Knob. The stream struggles in summertime. Folks are few and struggle also, though some families have been there since the eighteenth century. The only bumper crop is quietude. "Listen," said one farmer walking out at sundown. "All you can hear in this valley is birdsong. How many like it remain?"

What matters a peaceful valley, however, when customers need more electricity? Indeed, so dependent on power are we that if a major failure were to occur, power companies might well get almost any valley they wanted. Although hydroelectric power was dropped from the Gathright Dam project as not economically feasible, the Calfpasture Valley seemed ideal for a new kind of hydropower generation—from pumped storage. To vary the power output of the big steam power plants run by nuclear or fossil fuel is considered neither efficient nor economical. Instead, the surplus power they generate during periods of low consumption is utilized to pump water to high storage atop some mountain. When power demands soar, the water is released down penstocks to produce hydroelectric peaking power for meeting the increased market. There are less than twenty pumped storage facilities completed or under construction in the country as yet, but power companies are avidly searching for sites.

Called the Marble Valley Pumped Storage Project because of a local geographic feature, the plan was to construct a seven-mile-long reservoir in the heart of the valley plus a high reservoir on Mill Mountain in George Washington National Forest, where a Federal Power Commission license could be granted regardless of the Forest Service's views. Such is the power of power. Virginia acquiesced to the scheme on the agreed-upon condition that it would provide some flood storage, flow augmentation, and recreation. Many Virginians wondered, though, how good would be recreation on a lake drawn down ten feet every night and weekend when water was pumped out of it up to the upper reservoir. They wondered, too, how the little river's low flow out of the reservoir could be increased in summer without drawing down the lake even more.

These serious questions about benefits do not supplant the biggest question and deepest principle involved: Whither the quality of the American environment? And why should that quality be destroyed, not to save lives or quench thirst but to make power company stockholders a profit? One stockholder wrote, "I am pleased with the operations of the company. My investment has increased in value and the dividends from it have increased, but there are some things that we cannot buy with money and once destroyed they are gone forever." Another critic of the proposal added: "We are now called upon to prevent pollution of the air, but the pollution of the Virginia landscape is just as serious a matter. I just cannot bring myself to imagine that valley, filled as it is with beauty and history, filled with water. There is something more to be held in value above the mere financial considerations of the moment—such beauty as that which the valley possesses can never be restored after the age of electricity has been replaced."

Luckily nature saved Marble Valley from dammation. Late in studies of the project a geological flaw was found that made the upper reservoir site unsuitable. The license application was withdrawn. But residents in other pretty valleys in the region rest uneasy, for the project builders are looking for a new place to dam. Some fear it will be the scenic gorge of the Moorefield River in West Virginia. Or it could be Back Creek, another Potomac tributary. At this writing, the Russian roulette of pumped storage dam building is still at play.

Although sparsely settled rural valleys like Vermont's White, Virginia's Calfpasture and Craig Creek are its special victims, dammation stalks urban open spaces, too. Massive efforts were required, for example, to beat off a huge dam at an efficient site twenty miles up the Potomac River from Washington, where open space in that fast-urbanizing area will be desperately needed in another thirty years. On the little Passaic River in urban New Jersey, I sensed the full tragedy inherent in dam proposals, however urgent, for the shreds of green space still remaining in asphalt America. Although the Great Swamp surrounding the Passaic's upper reaches has been saved from jetport pavements, other meadows that sponge up water and nourish wild creatures and breathe oxygen into choking megalopolis have steadily been encroached upon. Piece Meadows in Caldwell and Montville remain largely intact, though they have been drained, and I put a kayak into the Passaic one day to see them from the water. That water was as foul and slimy as any I have seen, and the muck it had carried down covered all the banks. At one place the river was dammed completely by a pile of 150 old auto tires. That is how we Americans revere a pretty little river in New Jersey. But the world of the river was beautiful still! Huge trees—maples, sycamores, oaks—soar above a lowland kept open by the frequent wet. Ducks flared up as I rounded each bend, and squadrons of turtles fled their sunning logs to seek safe depths. A muskrat's wake creased the water. Around me the freeways roared in the distance, and for miles and miles on every side was concrete and urban clangor. But here, despite the defilement of the stream and surviving it bravely, were natural beauty and the life it supports. Into the vortex of megalopolis, only seventeen miles from Times Square, I had escaped into a micro-wilderness. And they say they need to drown it out. The natural meadow sponges are not enough, according to the engineers. More land, more water is in demand. Recreation is urgent. Private conservation organizations and the state have made a feeble effort to protect Piece Meadows, but dollars speak louder than trees and birds.

I saw not a soul on my half-day's journey on the primitive Passaic save one man. I don't know why he was there, idle. Perhaps he just enjoyed the scene. But he was astride a bulldozer. He seemed to be waiting.

Much of the damming and industrialization of riverine beauty in the East is already an accomplished fact. A number of Catskill and Adirondack mountain streams and other Hudson River tributaries have long been impounded for New York's water supply. Most of the larger waterfalls and rapids which so beautified Eastern riverways, particularly in New England, have been harnessed for industry. The Connecticut River's famed Fifteen Mile Falls were dammed as late as 1958 to create the largest hydroelectric power generation complex in New England. Falls like those of the Passaic at Paterson, N.J., have been industrialized since the early days of the Republic. Many were once scenic resources of renown. Of Berlin Falls on the Androscoggin River in

New Hampshire, the Reverend Thomas Starr King wrote more than a century ago: "We do not think that in New England there is any passage of river passion that will compare with the Berlin Falls. But if we stay long on the borders of the gorge, as we ought to, we shall find that the form and the rage of the current are subordinate in interest to its beauty and to the general surrounding charm." The general surrounding charm today is made up of one of the grubbiest paper mill complexes in New England, surrounded by one of its dreariest industrial towns. So went *that* little gem of American river beauty, grossed out by the indubitable importance of paper towels.

Not all the attempts to still the flowing waters of Eastern America have been successful, however. There have been those who cared enough to fight valiantly and, so far, victoriously to save certain beloved river reaches from dammation. The Androscoggin above Berlin Falls is an example. Unlike the mess below the mills, the upper river gushes clear and clean out of Umbagog Lake and down through the Thirteen-Mile Woods. To countless travelers heading for Dixville Notch, these are the North Woods, an almost unbroken stretch of spruce and fir, and this a North Woods River. Fishermen try for its big brown and rainbow trout and landlocked salmon. Canoeists test themselves in its churning rapids. A road follows much of it rather too closely sometimes, but it is a small road, and the view and picnicking spots along it are charming. Near Berlin one can see (through the smog and fumes of the paper mills) the massive Presidential Range.

Well, sure enough, the Corps of Engineers suggested a high dam that would turn most of the upper Androscoggin into a reservoir. Principally for hydroelectric peaking power, but with flood control and recreation also, the multipurpose dam project would have been a $60 million expenditure, a real shot-in-the-arm for that none-too-rich section of New England. The upper Androscoggin had quality, however: quality scenery, quality fishing, quality canoeing. It was a rare treasure in a State where many streams have been degraded and lakes ringed with vacation slums.

Flood out the Thirteen-Mile Woods? Never! The Society for the Protection of New Hampshire Forests, the Federated Sportsmen's Clubs of New Hampshire, and other conservation organizations rallied to the river's defense. So did journalists and radio commentators who cared, spreading the news that quality was at stake. Perhaps New Hampshire people remembered the words of John Dodge, one writer who decried the dam, pointing out that "the quality of the recreational experience will determine the quality and behavior of the participants. . . . Such land is too precious to be prostituted to anything less than its highest potential use." Did the people of New Hampshire "want to see their last big wild river watered down to become just another man-made lake so they will have to travel many miles outside the state to find another?" Dodge asked. "No," said New Hampshirites, rejecting recreational "benefits" of perch fishing and water sports on a fluctuating reservoir set amid the State's own beautiful natural lakes. The Brown Paper Company, which already regulated the river flow by means of its own small headwaters dams and which saw its timberlands threatened with inundation, put its considerable muscle into the fight. But it was the local power company, which owned the damsite, that pulled out the rug and became the hero of the fray, announcing suddenly that its own report showed the power benefits to be less desirable than other generation methods elsewhere. The company gave its land for a state park, the governor called for the Engineers' sword of surrender, and the Corps retreated across the mountains to other dam campaigns in the Connecticut Valley. Now the upper Androscoggin is being talked about in terms of a New Hampshire scenic monument.

With many of their dams and their pollution problems facts of long standing, this battle for quality and free-flowing scenic river was a new, exhilarating experience to the conservation minute men of New Hampshire. Over in New York, however, it is an old familiar fight to the veterans of the Adirondacks who have been fending off dams for years.

If you want to know how it feels to propose a dam in the Adirondack Park, strip down stark naked and knock down a hornets' nest. "The anti-dam feeling is so strong in the Adirondacks it is almost unbelievable," declared an Adirondack conservation leader. "People don't want this country monkeyed with. It is unique and deserves a better fate than being drowned out with fluctuating reservoirs." A State official agreed. "There is an Adirondack sanctity that pervades the State," he explained. "People in New York City who have never seen the Adirondacks are among its strongest supporters. They don't want their Adirondacks dammed. They want to know there is a wilderness to which they and their children can go."

To understand this better requires a word about the Adirondack Forest Preserve. This comprises the state-owned lands within a "Blue Line" drawn around the Adirondack Mountains designating an "Adirondack Park." It is not a park in the usual sense, not being managed as a unity, and with more than half of the nearly six million acres within it privately owned. The lands which are owned by New York State—some 2.35 million acres—are required to be kept "forever wild" under the New York State Constitution. This constitutional cure for the kind of forest butchery that shocked and outraged New Yorkers a century ago is more comforting to the public mind than it is effective in keeping the Adirondacks forever wild. Except for thirteen large chunks, the Forest Preserve holdings are scattered in bits and pieces throughout the Adirondacks, heavily used in places, and sometimes misused, and riddled with resorts on the private lands that surround or checker the Preserve.

But the Adirondack region with its 2,300 lakes and ponds and 20,000 miles of streams, has, since 1849, been regarded as New York's wilderness playground, and the Forest Preserve lands, in principle if not always in actuality, are sacrosanct. That means no dams.

Many of the major waterways leading out of the Adirondacks were dammed, of course, long before the conservationists of the

Adirondacks mustered. George Washington Sears, who canoed the Fulton Chain of Lakes in the 1860s and, under the penname Nessmuk, wrote widely read magazine articles about them, complained bitterly about their damming. The lower Saranac and Raquette rivers have long been dammed, and the Sacandaga is penned in what is now popularly cited as *the* horrible example of a fluctuating reservoir. Many favorite streams in the Catskill Park area have also been sacrificed for water supply.

So when a state water control agency proposed to dam the Moose River at Higley Mountain, and flood out the best deer yarding area in the Adirondacks, all hell broke loose. The fight, using such modern weapons as TV and billboard advertising, lasted eleven years—from 1945 to 1956—and was carried to the Supreme Court of the United States.

New York voters finally gave the dam project the coup de grace by plugging a hole in the constitution that permitted river regulation in the Adirondack Forest Preserve. The dam builders tried again on the Moose with the Panther Dam proposal, this time asking for a specific exception to the constitutional prohibition. New Yorkers beat the proposal down by one and one-half million votes.

A more recent Adirondack battle was fought over the proposed damming of the upper Hudson River. Eighty miles long from its source in Lake Tear of the Clouds to the town of Luzerne, the upper Hudson is New York's premier wild river and the only one spotlighted for special study and designation by both federal and state agencies. Its tributary Cedar, Indian, and Boreas rivers add to this wildwater resource. No, it is not wilderness in the purest sense of that term. A road and a railway run along parts of its lower section, and an occasional camp stands on its banks. Civilization visits it briefly at the hamlets of Newcomb, North River, North Creek, Riparius, and The Glen. But in secluded, brawling, rugged beauty it is wild, offering probably the most exhilarating river adventure in the Empire State and one of the finest in the East.

Once the Hudson's beguiling current takes you downriver from
the bridge at Newcomb, the wilderness spirit of the Adirondacks
claims your entire consciousness. It is as if you stepped into one of
Winslow Homer's watercolors, or had been magically transported
into some Canadian north woods fastness. The white throated
sparrow pipes his clear call for "Old Sam Peabody, Peabody, Peabody," and the bordering conifers roll out their clean fragrance
with the clean calm current of water. Only old traces of log driving days remind you of man, and the not-so-far away Northway
is leagues out of mind. If you look behind, Santanoni Mountain
and its neighbors lend a far blue backdrop to the river scene. Rumbling ahead promises action. It comes first at Long Falls; then Ord
Falls. If the water is high, the ride is a wild one. But relaxation
comes again along Blackwell Stillwater. The wilderness mood is
broken where a timber company has permitted a scattering of
cabins to be built along the stillwater, and has bulldozed a spiky
dam and former road crossing necessitating a portage. Wilderness
soon reasserts itself in atmosphere and current, however, and the
Cedar River adds its own wild flow to the Hudson's. A beautiful
campsite invites you to stop at the junction, but the day is early
yet and the Hudson rushes on. Below the Gooley Club, perched
on its bluff, the river turns abruptly left, the Indian River brawls
in, and the Hudson drops ominously deeper between its dark
forested shores. The gorge begins to yawn, and the cold, damp
breeze, like the breath from a cave, sends a tingle along your spine.

May's high water roars and spumes through this canyon in
drop after drop, tumultuous in giant waves and gushing chutes,
dazzling, awesome in the somber cleft. Only decked boats and
rubber rafts can then navigate this grandest of all whitewater runs
in the East. Highwater time is not the occasion to enjoy the details of natural beauty in the Hudson Gorge; attention is totally
preoccupied with surviving the monstrous rapids. In June, however, when the water has subsided and an open canoe can, with
care, run down, the camping is delightful. Then you can examine

the water worn rocks, undercut into weird grottoes. Each niche at river's edge seems a Japanese garden of gnarled trees, shrubs, creeping vines and winking flowers. Blue Ledge, its beetling precipice long as an eagle's eyrie, overlooks a favorite fishing place, where a father may bring his boy, backpacking in to taste wilderness and catch a fat rainbow in the misty morning. Mink Pond Brook, draining one of the score of ponds set in the plateaus that flank the gorge, flashes white through the trees, tempting you to stop and explore. O.K. Slip leads to a gossamer cataract higher than Niagara.

Typical of many glacier-gouged rivers of the north, the Hudson drops in steps, each pitch spewing into a welcome pool or stretch of quieter water. Below its confluence with another beautiful wild tributary, the Boreas, the Hudson seems to brawl along continuously, however. After passing the settlements of North River and North Creek, its rush of white rapids disappears into rock-studded, forest-flanked seclusion. Civilization touches it again at the hamlet and cottage colony of Riparius eight miles downstream, and once more at The Glen. Then roads tag along, and by the time it nears Warrensburg and its confluence with the Schroon River, the Hudson's character begins to change. It becomes placid at last, though still moving steadily. Mountains—the Three Sisters, Number Seven, Deer Leap, and others—guard a channel now divided by islands and edged by occasional pasturelands. This last fourteen miles to the waterfall at Luzerne marking the end of the upper river is in many ways the most beautiful reach of all. It is one still surprisingly little used, but offering an idyllic journey, a hope for bass and a campout or lunch hour long and pleasant to remember.

It makes no difference to New Yorkers that the Hudson's white water is too tough for any but experts in spring, and often too low to be navigable in summer, or that its trout fishing, while fairly good, is not widely enjoyed because access is difficult. The Hudson is the shining, roaring gateway to Adirondack wilderness. "It's

unique," explained a state forest ranger. "There's nothing else
like it. It's part of the soul of the Adirondacks. To dam it up and
destroy it would be like bulldozing off the high peaks."

But New York City needs more and more and more water and,
as a newspaper columnist pointed out, the upper Hudson is "a
dam builder's dream." So the state's Water Resources Commission, which has to find water somewhere, suggested the dam as
the cheapest and most efficient source now available. Patiently, as
if used to the pain of hornet stings, a state water resources official
explained the rationale:

New York City will need another 500 million gallons of water
per day by the 1980s; in fact, use is already close to supply, and
lead time is necessary to develop additional resources. Although
other sources of water, such as desalinized sea water, may some
day be economical, they are more expensive now. So are alternative
reservoir sites, such as a twenty-dam system suggested for eastern
tributaries of the Hudson. Included is that famed and beloved
trout river the Battenkill. It might cost $100 million to control
water use by metering New York's largely unmetered water, a
situation much criticized by conservationists who cite the pro-
digious waste encouraged by free water (and tell about a "spring"
in Central Park which turned out to be a broken water main).

The Adirondack Hudson River Association, a leader in the
fight against the proposal for a dam below the Gooley Club or
farther down the gorge at Kettle Mountain, called it a last resort,
however, one that could waste through evaporation enough water
to supply a city of 80,000. Control water use instead, the Association argued; use subsurface water; reuse waste water; consider
desalinization, the cost of which is approaching standard water
supply costs. In short the Association agreed with that terse New
England advertisement: "Costs more—worth it!"

For the essential conviction was the same one which helped
to save the upper Androscoggin: To dam the Hudson would re-
duce the quality of American life. As one leader in the fight
asked, "Are we willing to lose the best trout water remaining in

our state, excellent big game hunting country? Shall we replace the challenging five-hour white-water canoe adventure, through country federal officials described as the 'most spectacular river scenery in the East,' with boating on a fluctuating narrow pond? Shall we drown out miles of fine hiking trails and wilderness campsites, replacing them with a cemetery of stumps and dreary mud flats?"

Or as another put it, "Why destroy something unique for just a temporary solution to New York's water problem?"

The Hudson fight was nip and tuck, for the water users too were pressing the governor. But he finally signed a preventative bill, passed in the New York Legislature unanimously, to ban all dams on the upper Hudson. This decision was confirmed in recommendations of the Temporary Study Commission on the Future of the Adirondacks, appointed by the governor to see how threats to the wild recreative beauty of the Adirondack Park might best be met. "The preservation of free-flowing streams and the unique wild forest environment of the Park is at least as important to society as the construction of reservoirs, particularly where other solutions appear to exist to the water supply problems of southeastern New York," the Commission stated, and declared that "No further large-scale impoundments should be constructed within the Park for municipal water supply except as a last resort."

As for the Upper Hudson, the Commission emphasized that "the Upper Hudson and its principal tributaries rank among the finest natural resources of the Adirondack Park and their preservation in a wild free-flowing state is vital to the integrity of the whole Park. The construction of the proposed Gooley Dam would not only be a devastating blow to that integrity, but would, also, destroy one of the last remaining unprotected wild river systems in the eastern United States. . . . No impoundment should be constructed at Gooley site under any circumstances."

Even so, it is an uneasy victory, an uneasy truce, for the defenders of free-flowing rivers know that they must win over and over again. The dam builders only have to win once. The conservationists know also that, bob and weave, faint and dodge as we may in America, calling upon science and technology to perform feats of magic to offset our waste, we must in the last analysis face the fact that, like mice in a grain bin, we are breeding and squandering ourselves out of the right to any quality at all.

If the Androscoggin was saved by New Hampshire minute men, and if the Hudson was reprieved by well-generaled conservation veterans, the little Rappahannock in Virginia may well be rescued from reservoiritis by the love of one man.

From its source at Chester Gap in the Blue Ridge to the town Remington, the Rappahannock is typical of the attractive little rivers and creeks that wind through the rural countryside of piedmont Virginia. For the thirty-six miles between Remington and tidewater at historic Fredericksburg, however, the Rappahannock is unique in being virtually a wilderness river at the doorstep of megalopolis. Only one small road crosses it and scarcely a house is visible from it, though the river is but an hour's drive from Washington, D.C., and Richmond. Its rapids at Kelly's Ford are challenging enough for whitewater races and so beautiful are their small cascades and chutes and beachrimmed pools that local landowners have promised to dedicate their land for a county park if the dam is not built. The river is relatively clean, its bass fishing is excellent, and though it has no scenic grandeur, it possesses an intimacy and charm that quickly captures an outdoorsman's heart. To find anything even resembling it you have to go beyond the Blue Ridge.

So of course there has been a dam proposal for years at Salem Church right above Fredericksburg. It would flood out the entire wild section of the Rappahannock. Authorized by Congress, the dam would give Fredericksburg a water supply, for which there are other sources, dilute pollution, relieving city and industry of cleanup responsibilities, and by regulating salt water dilution in the Rappahannock estuary it might improve 16,000 acres of oyster beds to compensate for the 21,000 acres of land, including much farmland, it would inundate. The factor which made Salem Church dam ring the feasibility bell, however, was recreation. Recreation made up 41 percent of the dam benefits. What a glorious impoundment for fishing and watersports right at Fredericksburg's doorstep. Bonanza! Of course it was right next to the Rappahannock Estuary, the Potomac Estuary, too—nearly half a million acres of flat water for boating, sailing and fishing. But that is salt and there are jellyfish, so a $109 million dam and the destruction of a unique river was justifiable. If a third or more of the reservoir area was exposed as mud flats during periods of drawdown, wild grain could be planted to cover that up.

Everybody thought it was great. Even Secretary of the Interior Stewart Udall, leading advocate of wild and scenic river protection, was constrained to say something nice about Salem Church to support a Virginia candidate for Congress, for had not his Department's Bureau of Outdoor Recreation touted the reservoir's fun benefits? Udall later had second thoughts about the matter and suggested that it be reopened, but time ran out for his administration. Salem Church Dam was authorized, and, when the Nixon Administration budgeted money for further design studies of the dam, all hope to keep the Rappahannock natural seemed lost.

Randy Carter, however, never gave up. A county building inspector who is more widely known as author of a labor-of-love guidebook on Northern Virginia and West Virginia streams, Randy began canoeing the Rappahannock in a home-made craft in 1933. And if rivers are close to Randy's heart, the Rappahannock is the great aorta of his river love. Patiently, with quiet eloquence, he testified at hearings, countering and refuting pro-dam sentiments. Indefatigably he wrote letters, recruited support for his beloved river's defense, and begged high officials to let him show them the stream. Finally one of them accepted—the then-Deputy Under Secretary of the Interior, Boyd Gibbons. Seeing the river, he understood. He also understood that the Nixon Administration, criticized by conservationists for tightening pursestrings on conservation projects, here might save a scenic river and a good many million dollars too. Interior outraged the Department of the Army with notification that the Bureau of Outdoor Recreation would take a new look at the Rappahannock. It did.

Meanwhile, much had happened to support the change of mind. Virginia's own scenic rivers study had come up with the Rappahannock as first priority. Power company impoundment projects on other streams of lesser stature near the Rappahannock promised to take care of the reservoir recreation demand. Conservation organization chapters in Virginia switched their thinking to support a natural river. When B.O.R. reported back, it was to champion the free flowing river as worthy of National Wild and Scenic River status. No dam should be considered until non-recreational benefits from impoundments had become paramount needs.

The dam proponents did not take this lying down. A revised, slightly smaller proposal emphasizing (without previous discussion) water supply for all of northern Virginia received the governor's formal approval, to the consternation of his own Council on the Environment, the Commission of Outdoor Recreation, and the Water Control Board. With a cost-benefit ratio of 1 to 1.7, the revised proposal still relied heavily on recreation and on water quality control by dilution. By merely flushing out the pollution, mixing in cleaner reservoir water until quality standards were met, the effect of local waste treatment could be put off —at national expense and the river's. The Federal agencies had already pointed out a better recreational alternative on the nearby Potomac, while the Water Control Board denied flushing as a solution to water quality problems. It pointed out also that up-river communities would have to bear heavy costs of further cleansing of water that flowed not down a river but into a water supply lake. Above and beyond that was the unnecessary loss of a unique and beautiful recreation resource, and the battle to save it goes on.

When Randy showed me the Rappahannock, springtime's green was still pale upon the trees, making the pines stand out darkly amidst the deciduous branches. Along the shores the hornbeams were tassled with long conical masses of flowers; box elders were fringed with pink. Ferns were uncurling from crannies in the rocks, and spring beauty and dogtooth violets brightened the dun carpet of old leaves. Enroute to our launching place we passed lush green fields where cattle grazed. If the dam goes in, all will be under water, to be exposed again as thousands of acres of mud whenever the reservoir's water level is drawn down.

We had decided not to challenge Kelly's Ford Rapids this day and instead put in below the long peaceful deadwater that stretches below the rapids. Harold Comer had allowed us to launch from his farm pasture, and calves pranced after us as we reclosed the pasture gates.

Below Kelly's Ford and the deadwater, the Rappahannock varies delightfully between smooth stretches and short pitches of rapids. Though not difficult, they are exciting, each different, requiring navigational tactics to be carried out smartly. Each also offers promise of a big bass lying behind one of the granite boulders that break the current. We ran our first rapid where a tall rock is crowned by a sentinel pine. Once it was the site of a mill and a small settlement, but all has gone to wilderness now. So has the old canal that once followed the river. In use only for five years before the Civil War, it nevertheless was built for the ages, and we marveled at the huge stones of the locks still securely in place.

It has always surprised me how the old-time works of man, no matter how mighty, are so completely recaptured by time and nature. How fortunate that civilization retreated here, when not needed, and wilderness has come back when we need its opportunities as never before! Will our current developments ever melt away thus? I fear men are now too numerous to retreat from anything, and their earth moving and refuse dumping is too tremendous. We no longer work simply with wood and stone that blend soon again into the landscape. Our machines now have geologic power and our detritus is of awesome substance.

Despite spring's promise and the exhilaration of the lively water, the gloom of death hung over the river, for, like a corpse stripped for burial, the riverscape for miles had been logged of every salable tree. If the river is spared, the forest will grow back in time, of course, and the feeling of freedom still survived along the Rappahannock. A high cliff where hemlocks grew sheltered our island campsight. That evening as I stood amid the rushing water, a stout bass bent my flyrod. Randy's campfire scented the evening air, and I imagined myself as far from nearby Washington as one could possibly hope to be in the American outdoors.

I felt the freedom strangely again at our nooning next day. Violets and bluets embroidered the greening bank where the Rapidan and Rappahannock rush together. A wan spring sun glinted on the water. Martins swooped low for the new hatches of insects, and an osprey circled high. It must have looked just that way when Indians dwelt at the confluence. Here was living, talking water sweeping around a thousand rocks and islets with enough pools and eddies to keep a fisherman excited for days. Down through the giant boulders and foaming rifts we swept to our landing, where the dragon head of a transmission line tower, rearing above the forested hill, reminded us that our wilderness voyage was over.

Then occurred a meeting which brought home to me a saddening though correctable reason why rivers are often so little understood today. Modern conveniences and city living have not only cut us off from contact with the natural world but have also dulled our sensitivity toward it, aborted our knowledge of its lore and atrophied our outdoor skills. I feel this poignantly when I grope in my mind for the names of plants and birds I should know as familiar acquaintances, or when, fumbling with a paddle, I try to meet the physical challenge of fast water.

But industry surfeits us with marvelous toys which speed over the surface of life without ever giving us the chance to peer in or test ourselves. In the name of speed, of power, of ease, convenience, even safety, we are insulated from the outdoor matrix of our lives, and outdoor recreation has come largely to mean the use of gadgetry in the country. Reservoirs, giant gadgets in their own right, are ideal gadget grounds, and, muttering the old adage "Gimme something I'm used to," we head for them with our motors and trailers, eschewing the age old disciplines of hand and eye that rivers require to unlock their treasury of delights and satisfactions.

So it seemed with the party packing up as we landed. For two days they had dragged and cursed a big aluminum boat and outboard motor down that little river, missing water song and bird song too. They were still struggling and muttering when we found them lashing the battered hulk down atop their truck and stowing their array of gas cans, tool boxes, and countless other outing accessories.

"Goddam river!"

Attraction

So I the Fields and Meadows green may view
And daily by fresh Rivers walk at will.

—John Davors, as quoted in
Izaak Walton's "Compleat Angler"

THE world seemed fenced with lofty peaks of snow. Distant, but dominating all, rose the immaculate immensity of Mount McKinley, backlit by the ebbing light. Downward from its flanks Muldrow Glacier wound like a striped and frozen river, and the roar of its meltwaters filled the frosty air. Caribou browsed a tundra brilliant with the hues of approaching autumn. Beneath the highest mountain in North America, I could drink in the incomparable Alaskan scenery of Mount McKinley National Park. But slumbering snug in my tent that night, with the glory of that glittering wilderness round about me, I dreamed I was on the Shenandoah River once again.

Count on the perversity of dreams to bring, amid all that splendor, the vision of a small, polluted rural waterway. But it *is* a beautiful river, infinitely varied and inviting, with a touch of wilderness and liveliness about it in places, never awesome and aloof; a very winsome waterway. No wonder the chanteyman sang wistfully of it long ago, "Oh Shenandoah, I long to see you, and hear your rolling river." I missed it, even in Alaska, for it has captured my own heart as well. I like it best of all the scenic rivers of the East.

For fifty miles, the Massanutten Range splits the Shenandoah Valley into two parts, each with its own fork of the river. The smaller North Fork flows out of Brocks Gap to the west, crosses the broader part of that famed agricultural area which once was the Confederacy's breadbasket and then winds north along the Massanuttens' base. Writhes is a better word, for few if any Eastern streams are more tortuous. In the twenty miles between Edinburg and Strasburg, the river covers fifty miles in twenty-nine bends. It is an intimate little river, flanked by both farm and forest land, with the Massanutten ridge rising above it like a great green rampart.

The South Fork, formed by tributaries near Port Republic, also winds deeply when confined within its narrow Page Valley. Each reach of the South Fork offers a new and charming mountain prospect, first of the high Blue Ridge in Shenandoah National Park, and then of the Massanuttens in George Washington National Forest. Broad bottomlands alternate with steep, forested bluffs and an occasional beetling cliff. The river never lets you lose interest in the flow. At the end of each short lazy stretch is a shallow ledge or two to awaken a dreaming boatman to the necessary art of quick-water navigation.

The Massanutten ridges end at Signal Knob near Front Royal, and the two forks flow together there. The confluence could have been a regional beauty spot but instead has been ignored, crisscrossed by roads and railroads and scarred by quarries. Front Royal further honors its river with pollution and occasional fish poisoning. Despite this, the main Shenandoah is still delightful, winding northward between lush fields, with the mountains following at a respectful distance.

The river regains its mountain aspect as it enters West Virginia, for the Blue Ridge comes close again, and near Harpers Ferry and confluence with the Potomac, the Shenandoah partakes of the drama and grandeur of that historic water gap. Escarpments rise on both sides, and the river takes its only real canoe-breaking plunge over the five-foot ledge of Bull Falls. Below, whitewater canoeists know the river as the Staircase, for it flows over a washboard of rock serrations that make navigation a test of boating skills.

There is something special about getting on the Shenandoah in May. The whitewater buffs are out much earlier, of course, often when sleet is still flying, on little rivers abrim with wild challenge. But the Shenandoah is for that time when the camping gear and fishing tackle cry to get out of their closet, when the sun first feels warm on a bare back and your favorite campsite has not yet replaced spring's violets with summer's rank and riotous tangle of vegetation.

Summer, too, is fun, of course, especially with kids along who flop over the side like otters (no, they probably shouldn't; the water *is* polluted); and even gray-haired kids are tempted to climb that rope dangling from the old ferry cable and plummet into the cool depths.

Fall is a golden time for fishing the Shenandoah. It has been called by experts the finest small-mouth black bass stream in the Nation. Many will challenge that, of course, but it is among the best nevertheless. Not being especially skilled at taking Mr. Micropterus, I accepted this dictum only on faith until one enchanted afternoon when all the mayflies on the Shenandoah seemed to hatch, and the river went wild. Every bass and bluegill was rising, revealing the incredible fecundity of the Shenandoah. More and more heavily fished, the river yields fewer big ones now, but the poundage of pleasure brings city folks in canoes and country folk in boats or flat bottom skiffs to try for bass or bullheads, and the prettiest girl I ever saw was a solitary fisherwoman on Shenandoah shores.

Fall trips send the wood ducks crying off in flocks and suggest that a jump shooting expedition might be profitable. The woodies depart early, but leave the black mallards to listen for the telltale sound of canoe touching rock. A grouse thundering off in frosty woods atop the bluffs suggests that Shenandoah rambling is now best done afoot, until the dogwood blooms again, and a full channel and the rush of whitewater down Compton's rip asks how your paddling muscles are this spring.

There is always a certain special elation when you first push off from shore on a river trip. You feel freedom yet commitment to a new life and exacting adventure. It tightens your belly and whets your eye, especially if around the first bend the river wants to wrestle. You worry, feeling rusty. The Shenandoah tussles with you a bit, just to wake you up and let you know this isn't a beer-float, and soon you're with it again. There are the sights you remember. They always have a freshness about them: Kennedy Peak and the high meadow that reminds you of Vermont; the rocky bluff and the dark inlet of Jeremy's Run. Here comes the V-shaped fish weir of rocks, probably Indian, with the hole you must duck through down a tongue of slick water just before the point of the "V." You glide down the quiet deadwater with the mossy cliff beside just before you tense for the Compton Rapids sleigh-ride. You never cease to marvel at the high limestone cliff just below; wonder how deep it goes beneath the surface, and vow to bring a diving mask next time and try to see.

You wish the state hadn't run the new road so close, knocking trees down the bank, but you forget that along Burner's Bottom, where the shallowness fools you into thinking there are no bass about. Then the intricate quick-water maze before the pool at Overall, and the beautiful run below, under the bluffs, where there's a steep ledge with but one opening that sneaks up on you and you almost hang up the canoe.

All along the way are fishermen on the bank or in the stream, and you pass the usual "Any luck?" time of day, and they ask about the journey. You're tired when you pull out, and probably a bit sunburned, but you feel as if you've visited an old friend once more and wonder how long it all will last. Each year you expect to find a house at your favorite lunch spot, with a radio blaring out of the woods where the birds used to sing. It's not there yet, but others are, elsewhere.

From the lookout tower atop Massanutten Mountain near Woodstock, you can see seven bends of the North Fork. Long fingers of land stretching out from the mountain ridge, some wooded, some farmed, seem to push the thin silver ribbon far out into the valley, while other farmland fingers push the river deeply in again toward the mountainside. The Seven Bends compose one of the valley's most beautiful scenes, so recognized and advertised by promotional literature and postcards offered in the area. It is one of Virginia's great scenic assets.

If you look more closely, however, you will see the beginnings of a rash that is blemishing the fair complexion of many a riverscape in Eastern America. One of the bends is being subdivided into vacation cottage lots. Others are bound soon to be infected by the disease also, for there is nothing in Shenandoah County, Virginia, to stop it.

There is little anywhere to stop it, for it is a disease of love, and the only cures are drastic ones. Loren Eiseley was right when he said that "if there is magic on this planet, it is contained in water." Enchanted by that magic, we seek it wherever we can—at seashores, lakeshores, and along those most ubiquitous water resources, our rivers. Anywhere and everywhere there is water we, loving and longingly, rush out to embrace it. There is betrayal in that attraction, however, for we are destroying the beauty that we seek. Other manifestations of river love—our desire to clean up pollution, or to keep a stream free-flowing—restore or preserve riverine beauty, but our urge to live on riverbanks is hugging it to death. We do not realize that river beauty is a trinity of water and banks, and that ugly, crowding preemption of the riverside destroys that beauty as surely as does fouling or impounding the water.

Along some rivers, like the main stem of the Shenandoah, this disease is well advanced. The east bank of the river from

Front Royal, Virginia, to Harpers Ferry, West Virginia, is already one almost continuous platted subdivision, some fifty miles in length. The Potomac, both main stem and South Branch, is also becoming a mecca for second homes. Indeed, there is scarcely a river in the East, even in the wilds of Maine, where the symptoms of suburbanization cannot be found in a cluster of cottages or trailers, or the telltale fluttering of surveyor's ribbons and bulldozed roadways across old farm fields. Only the most obnoxious of the polluted rivers or those whose banks are held in large and secure ownerships are still free from the creeping—and often galloping—plague which seems destined eventually to urbanize every attractive river course in America not immunized by special legal protection.

The origins behind this problem are so natural, the motivation often so deserving of sympathetic approbation, that it is difficult to think of this as an environmental problem. A group of amiable local fellows up in the country, lacking means and time for far-away vacations, ask a farmer neighbor to let them erect three or four shacks down along the river at the foot of his pasture, where they can go on weekends, fish, drink a little beer, and loaf pleasantly down by the riverside. Why not? They are friends, and it means a few bucks of rent money in the farmer's overalls at a time, perhaps, when crops are poor. Not having much money and knowing, too, that old man river may come along and sweep them away some spring, the boys invest in their vacation homes as lightly as possible. Perhaps one is an old bus body propped up on cinder blocks, or another is a tarpaper shack chained to a couple of big sycamore trees. A privvy takes care of the plumbing problem. Simple; cheap; fun. What harm in that? Why criticize a poor man for trying to have a little pleasure along the local river?

Or it might start back in the city where a couple with growing children yearns to acquaint them with the out-of-doors—have a weekend place they can escape to, wear old clothes, barbecue a steak, swim, boat, catch fish. There's a river lot advertised for sale with easy payments and a man who will build them a modest cottage. Maybe several friends band together and buy an old farm and put up cottages. Perhaps a club is formed. Can you think of a more wholesome instinct than the simple desire to get your wife and kids out of the hot city on a weekend and let them fall asleep in a cozy cabin where one is lulled by a river's murmuring?

Such are the individually worthy instincts and purposes that are destroying the natural beauty of our rivers, for the shacks and cottages, like us, are proliferating. The isolated cluster of shanties becomes sizable, like one blighting the Shenandoah that, with some candor, was named "Hobo Flat." The small cottage community becomes a city of second homes like another Shenandoah subdivision which envisions a population of 30,000. As four become eight, and eight, sixteen, and sixteen, thirty-two, the forests give way to lawns, river banks to boathouses, wildlife retreats, bird song is drowned by the whine of outboards, NO TRESPASSING signs ward off river pilgrims. The valley has become a linear suburb, the river itself a city street, with water paving, and those who once came seeking rural beauty and quietude have helped to destroy what they sought.

Many did not seek that, of course. Gregarious, city bred with city ways, they simply have transplanted the urban life to another locality, destroying something refreshingly different for more of what they had before, and effacing forever, with irreversible land-use patterns, the central beauty of the valley: its riverscape.

Few who have participated in this erosive process seem concerned. If they were among the early comers, they accept the deteriorating environment as inevitable. Often it changes slowly enough for them to get used to it. If they are late on the scene, they feel lucky to have gotten their quarter-acre piece of paradise before the next guy grabbed it.* They probably never knew the river as an unblighted solitude of forest shore and wheeling osprey. The time is past when they could, like Thoreau, exclaim,

"How fortunate were we who did not own an acre of these shores, who had not renounced our title to the whole." So long as we get the site we like, and proximity to pleasant places we enjoy, we care not how we look to the world or who else may be deprived. The presence of a river beside our house is a good prospect. The view of us from the man in the boat is beside the point; he owns no land, so too bad about him. Yet if we remain oblivious of how poorly we fit in with the world around us, or harmonize with the elements of topography, vegetation, and wildlife from which we derive our pleasure and well-being, we shall destroy all natural beauty, particularly along major design elements in the landscape, like rivers. Moreover, we shall be caught in our own carelessness when we become the boatman, when our own river recreation is blocked, or when the opposite shore is, like ours, built up and the good scenery destroyed.

Large rivers will provide much recreational use from boats on the water, but recreation on streams and small rivers, which generally takes place from the bank, requires movement along the bank to seek the holes, flats, or riffles where the fish, wildlife, or swimming, perhaps, is located or to enjoy the diverse attractions of the waterside. Each little portion of stream or small river makes a contribution to the whole. Small parcels of frontage will seldom contain all values, and owners and users of these will also be dependent upon other frontage and locations for their package of recreation activity.

As edges of streams and small rivers become splintered into small holdings, the ability to enjoy free movement up and down the banks diminishes, and improvements by private frontage owners in the form of lawns, gardens, buildings, and sewage disposal change the environment substantially.

In a few places we have foregone individual possession; have stood back and now can count upon the natural design of rivers which so enhance the American landscape. Through the foresight of influential men and by dint of great effort, Congress bade Washingtonians stay back from Rock Creek, and the whole city now enjoys a woodland park winding through its heart. Philadelphia has its Wissahickon, Boston its lower Charles, and there are other examples, a few.

The vulnerability of attractive stream valleys near cities—valleys that will soon be engulfed by them and which could, like the old city parks, offer beautiful open spaces—is usually ignored. Boston's Charles River has, since the nineteenth century, been a shining example of foresight even though the parklands there are being steadily whittled away. But out in the Boston suburbs the Metropolitan District Commission has never extended this riverbank protection concept to make the upper Charles a permanent park resource.

The Monocacy River, winding through the rolling farmlands of Frederick County, Maryland, is now on Washington's urban frontier. Yet county officials have said that conservation zoning, though overturnable, protects the Monocacy "reasonably well," and a state scenic river study of it is lagging.

Naturalness is not the only category of beauty, of course, and you can very logically defend human habitations as also having aesthetic appeal, arguing further that to insist upon wild open spaces without structures is ultraconservative in both senses of that word. Look, you may say, at the landscape paintings of the Chinese, few of which are without structures tucked into the landscape. Yes, tucked—in harmony. It is true that a cozy cottage or even a romantic castle is often a welcome contrast when glimpsed amid extensive natural shores. Again we come to the matter of the saturation point. How many dwellings can a river accommodate pleasantly without becoming cluttered, its other elements of beauty displaced? Where do we stop? Can we tell Bill and John and Peter that they may build and say to Ed and George that they may not? When is enough? It took less than half a dozen buildings recently to requisition for suburbia the spectacular and long-unspoiled Potomac riverscape above Washington, a river reach unique in the world for its wild beauty so close to a major capital.

And what of the structures themselves—which are attractive and which ugly? Somebody cut half an acre of forest off the banks of the upper Hudson to give a trailer a view. I know of one solitary house on the Shenandoah so commanding that it busts the whole mellow Shenandoah scene. A slightly different siting and design might have made it a pleasurable sight, but the occupant looks out, not in. There is a lone cottage of contemporary design, well built and well kept and no doubt the pride and joy of its owners, which, overhanging the wild Penobscot below the majesty of Mount Katahdin, does to the aspect of that superb wild river about what a gold tooth does to a pretty girl's face.

Why should river-loving riparian landowners not fulfill their dreams—yet what is to save the pristine beauty of our streams if they do? Too often are developments planned without thought of a reciprocity of view and the ultimate total effect upon riverscapes that should be enduring amenities of America. Ralph Waldo Emerson once observed that "The charming landscape which I saw this morning is indubitably made up of some twenty or thirty farms. Miller owns this field, Locke that, and Manning the woodland beyond. But none of them owns the landscape. There is a property in the horizon which no man has but he whose eye can integrate all the parts, that is the poet. This is the best part of these men's farms, yet to this their warranty-deeds give no title."

We are not American Indians, who could enjoy in common their patrimony of land. We must dice it up and buy and sell it, for scenery to us is not a heritage to be protected and handed on but rather is merchandise, a commodity to be exploited. To leave a landscape alone, be it in forest or farmland, is not progress in our minds. To develop it is, and devil take the hindmost. I asked a riverside developer once what would happen to the scenic view he was extolling in his ads, once all the riverside lots were sold. "Oh it will be gone, of course," he replied. Scenery was something to be consumed. His responsibility to the American environment ended, apparently, with a satisfied customer.

With much of our national history one of necessary exploitation to open the country for settlement and wrest a living from the land, small wonder that we go on in the momentum of that tradition even though our huge numbers and awesome technology works havoc with the landscape. Major design elements in the landscape, like rivers, are first to show the consequences.

Much of the real estate along our river banks is, of course, the work of professional developers. It's their business, and they take the position that if they don't sell the riverbanks off for a profit the next guy will. Big industry, whose ethical attitudes toward environment are evident in polluted water and air and blighted scenery, are getting into the act after seeing that massive real estate development can represent profitable business diversification. Much also is the result of personal need, however, like that of the farmer renting cottage sites to friends. I sensed the poignancy this kind of situation can have at the Seven Bends of the Shenandoah. The development was not a big professional operation but rather a family affair, and the eager and affable young salesman was the owner's son, newly married and excited about his own start at dairy farming on another family farm not far away. It was the old story of pioneer America. This farm could go; there was more elsewhere; always more somewhere else. But for his dad, he said, it was hard to see this fertile bottomland sold off. Hard? Why the subdividing in acre lots, then? And I got the outline of the tragedy: three years of drought and failing crops, age coming on, then the crushing blow—the death of an older son, killed in a farm accident. What else but subdivide and sell and get the maximum income from land now yielding little but care and sadness?

Many rural citizens are still convinced of what former Secretary of the Interior Stewart Udall has called the Myth of Superabundance. When opportunity comes their way to make a killing on real estate, they, like most of us, grab at the pie, reassuring themselves that the sell-off really won't hurt anything; after all, progress and exploitation go hand in hand. A county agent up along the Connecticut almost smacked his lips when, after describing the scenic beauties of the valley, he said of two big river farms, "Now if you could subdivide them, you'd really have something—four or five hundred acres of lots with a view of Mount Washington!" And: "We must save the Adirondack Park wilderness!" a New Yorker asserted; then mused, "I wonder how I can best subdivide my land there."

New York State, where more houses, roads, industrial plants, airports, and other urban structures will be built during the next fifty years than have been built since the state was first settled, has recognized the vulnerability of its agricultural open space. A special state commission on the preservation of agricultural land has reported:

Farming means open space—peaceful countrysides, inspiring vistas, pleasant settings for homes, places to hike, fish, and hunt. A beautiful countryside is important to all the people in this state. Farming is part of what we all know and cherish in rural New York.

Since farm incomes are not high and ready cash is short, the industry is vulnerable to urban penetration. Land sold near cities by retiring farmers often goes for prices beyond what beginning farmers can pay; even operating farmers are often tempted to sell building lots. Farm land near urban fringes in this way becomes split into small holdings and nonfarm uses are increasingly intermingled among farms. Land tends to pass into the hands of investors who can afford to hold it for later development. Farmers increasingly depend on rented land.

The prospect of a large investment can place a farmer near a city in a genuine dilemma.... When even a *possibility* of an advantageous sale for urban uses presents itself, there is a strong temptation to bet on that possibility rather than invest in a new barn. The temptation is strong even when it is clear that not all landowners in the area can ever be lucky enough to make such a sale.

This "roulette" effect of urban penetration—this temptation to bet on a nonfarm sale rather than to invest more in the farm business—often begins with the first scattering of new homes in a rural area. It can destroy farming long before the area is fully needed for other uses, and it can destroy the character of the countryside that attracted the first new homes.

When new homes begin to appear, tax assessors tend to change their thinking on agriculture and tax farm land as though it all could be sold for homesites [the report continued, pointing out that new nonfarm residents in farming areas sometimes object to farm practices and may get ordinances passed making it more difficult for farmers to operate].

The problem of preserving agricultural land is a problem of preserving farming. Farming is a process. It is not a physical object. It can not be saved like a historical structure or a point of natural beauty. Men must be encouraged to pursue it as an occupation. A favorable social and economic climate is necessary if farm families are to make the heavy investments and take the risks necessary to keep their farm businesses viable.

Most of the scenic rivers in the East are pastoral or agricultural in setting. Therefore, the fate of their beauty is tied to how successfully agriculture can be perpetuated beside them. Along every river where there is pressure for development the rural landscape yields, for there is usually nothing to protect it, no laws or regulations or standards. Many of the old farmers hang on as long as they can, loving the land, wedded to their way of life. But one by one they retire, sell out and move away, or die and heirs let go a farmstead that to them means most in cash.

I remember two conversations with farmers whose velvet hayfields beside the upper Connecticut River help to create a New England Eden. Looking past the gnarled hands into eyes which had caressed that riverscape for seventy years, I heard each old man paraphrase in his own way the words of Madame de Pompadour: "After us the deluge."

"This is a wonderful country to get back to," said one, who owns a mile along the Connecticut River. "I'd hate to see my land cut up into a mess of goddam building lots. I've been offered fabulous prices to subdivide and I won't do it. But I don't know what my children may do."

"It takes only one poorly placed subdivision . . . to destroy the integrity of an agricultural area," William H. Whyte points out. "This is not at first apparent, but inevitably assessment and taxes go up to pay for the additional services and schools needed by the new residents. The load falls on the farms that don't require these services and this in turn puts more economic pressure on the farmer to sell his land for development. It's up to the community in its planning effort to grapple with these problems. It cannot be left to the pleasure of the individual land owner. Yet in some states, the farm groups which have been pushing for preferential assessment have recoiled at the idea of coupling it to community planning or even zoning."

Expectedly, the staunch men who own much of the East's riverscapes love something else we all cherish—liberty. To many of them, however, this means not only the personal freedoms but also the absolute right to do as one wishes with his property. They will not be fettered by legal restraints which might limit their options for land use or abridge their absolute sovereignty as property owners. They scorn the thralldom of the suburbanite, who is told what he can build and where, which animals he may or may not keep, where he can park his car or erect a fence. The countryman's freedom is the land-freedom of nineteenth century America, before crowding necessitated constraints, and he is determined to keep his remnant of paradise from that population disease called regulation. He looks proudly back at tradition and not forward at the need for conservation and land use controls suggested by what will soon be a third of a billion people who have a growing awareness of ecology. "We don't want the federal government or even the state government meddling. We don't want vague schemes. We have kept the status quo and we want the status quo," a New Englander declared fiercely. "After all, we don't come to the city and tell you what to do."

"We have been good stewards," a West Virginian protested,

nostalgically oblivious of the trailer camps, junked autos, and hog pens that have begun to defile his part of the Potomac River. Proud of his mountaineer heritage, he could not see what the trend of the times would ultimately do to the landscapes he loved.

Often the rural resident does see what is coming but, unwilling to accept regulatory and conservation programs to guide and contain the change and influx in wholesome ways, tries to minimize the problem. He agrees with like-minded neighbors, that "we will never let it happen here." He does not face the inevitable fact that the "we" are going to die; that no matter how perfect is his stewardship, it will last only a few short years. Despite the deeds in his strongbox, he is merely a life trustee of the land.

If we do love the land, we must make secure arrangements for the trust to carry on as well as we have borne it. But no, we are immortal. I know of riparian landowners past middle age and with no direct heirs who, while they themselves are keeping their land intact and beautiful, have rejected any suggestions for preserving it in perpetuity. Any hint that the resource might someday be important as a park and otherwise is doomed to eventual urbanization merely raises a red flag. The fact that such public ownership would not come in their lifetime does not register; they only fear and resent the thought of an ouster from their ownership. Like most of us, they cannot imagine themselves in a grave, with bulldozers tearing into their beloved fields. Perhaps we should all think more of what may be the downward view from Heaven.

Willfully blind to the sell-outs going on around him; convinced that, if he can hold the line, his arcadian America will be eternal, the rural resident often fights irrationally against any plans to retain the elements which make his countryside beautiful. He knows instinctively what the most sophisticated recreationists from the city have learned: that his is a high quality environment which is becoming precious. He therefore regards all "meddling" as attempts to raid his way of life. He even talks half seriously about building a fence and gate across the valley to keep back the city hordes. "We have something good and beautiful up here," an Upper Connecticut Valley man remarked bitterly, "and now you city people want to come up and take it from us. It's the 'have-nots' wanting what we poor 'haves' possess. Mass recreation will destroy the life offered here." Proudly resenting his land being made into "a museum for city people to look at," frightened that it may be overrun, and degraded, he, like Ethan Allen of old, resolves to "retire with hardy Green Mountain Boys into the desolate Caverns and Mountains and wage war with human nature at large."

Human nature at large these days means the nature of city people. Their habits, as they spew out into the countryside for a weekend of recreation, reinforce the countryman's attitude of resentful resistance. Their manners are abominable. They strew the pretty countryside with their trash, cut fences, trample crops, shoot up buildings, and roar around with their noisy gadgets. They are different today, as one New Hampshire man recalled, from those few city gentlemen of yesteryear who knew their sport, hired a guide, and settled comfortably with the local innkeeper or farmer. Often there is a racial bias lurking behind the fear of city visitors, and a private club or community, however slummy and damaging to open space and recreation, is often much preferred by the county fathers to protecting the scenery by means of a public park.

The problems of recreation impact boil down to the fact that the run-of-the-mill urbanite is simply not trained to respect the out-of-doors. Physically removed from the natural environment, he does not understand it, having had no such schooling, and generally he lacks the skills to use it gently and wisely. Too often he regards the rural American landscape as merely a playground across which he can heedlessly romp and which is conveniently maintained for his benefit by a few taxpayers who, while cranky, can be outvoted.

Ironically, the countryman, whom we sometimes idealize as a modern-day Daniel Boone or an Audubon in overalls, is almost as bad. Critical of the mote in the crass and thoughtless city man's eye, he fails to note the beam in his own. He takes for granted the natural resources he enjoys and treats them accordingly. There is scarcely a brook or gully or wooded back road in rural Virginia, for example, that is not filled or edged with rubbish, and it was not put there by city recreationists. Rivers are obvious victims of this rural thoughtlessness. They have always been conveniently available places to push something you don't want around anymore. They have become the alleys and gutters of the countryside and receive their full share of our mounting mass of jetsam.

When Hanover, New Hampshire, ballotted on sewage treatment funds not long ago to clean up its section of the Connecticut River, the town fathers were appalled to note that leading conservationists in the area voted against the measure. Their reason was simple though unhappy: The polluted water kept the green forested riverscape they loved from being exploited. Continuing the unnatural "conservation" provided by the river's stink for a while might buy them time to devise legal ways of preserving the natural beauty of the shores.

Sportsmen's federations in New Hampshire and Vermont reached the same conclusion. In discussing plans for the Connecticut River, they agreed informally that "once the river is free of pollution it will probably be too late to plan, zone and control key areas of the river corridor from the southern Vermont and New Hampshire lines north to Canada. Public access to the river banks will soon begin to disappear, except where action has been taken to acquire easements, options or title to selected points of access before the land boom begins. As of today, only the present foul water conditions in the river are holding speculation in check."

The beautiful woods and pastures along the Nashua River in Massachusetts, still exist only because the river water is so foul. A local conservation group that has pushed for a model river cleanup now feels that it should have started protecting the land first before going to work on water cleanup. It is scrambling to set up land trusts and other devices for keeping the Nashua's banks as a regional asset before river cleanup makes them valuable to development.

Maine people are similarly concerned about the Penobscot's riverscape when the stink and goo are gone:

"While much of the Penobscot Basin is relatively undeveloped, pollution abatement and restoration of fisheries for anadromous and resident fish species will put stream frontage at a premium," a state fisheries report on the river points out. "Without acquisition of title or easements by the state, the public may be barred from fishing, canoeing, or otherwise enjoying the streams and pools which have been restored with the tax dollars."

Belatedly, we are realizing that the much heralded new antipollution laws are discoordinately ahead of the legal tools necessary to take care of the other half of the problem of keeping our rivers attractive resources. Land control and pollution control must go hand in hand. If wishful thinking and laissez-faire attitudes, economic principles, and social pressures and antipathies paralyze efforts to preserve outstanding scenic environments like rivers, or even to channel changes in wholesome ways, our traditions of land ownership, law, and government hamstring them further. They make broad programs of riverscape protection difficult at best.

Riparian lands have for the most part always been desirable lands. Fertile, with access to water for farming or industry and often pleasant for residence, they are almost entirely in many private ownerships. There has never been an Emperor Justinian to decree the public status for riversides that he gave for Rome's sea strands. If any of the East's riversides are to be preserved in perpetuity as public parks, recreation, or wildlife areas or other scenic resources, they must be purchased, acre by acre, sometimes foot by foot, by governments or philanthropists with hard dollars against the competition of countless other purchasers, unless new alignments and types of planning authority are voted in.

Much is hoped these days for the use of easements to protect scenic values along rivers. Called scenic easements or conservation easements, they convey to a governmental body or trustee organization some of the rights which, in toto, make up a land ownership. Any of the rights can be sold or given away by a landowner and the others retained. For example, an owner may sell his mineral rights, or farming or timber rights, or development rights or rights to occupy the air space above his property. He may convey an easement for a road or trail, a power line or a pipeline across it. Scenic easements often take a negative form, the owner agreeing in conveying the easement, for example, *not* to build houses on the river's edge, or to cut trees of a certain size or in certain places; not to dig gravel or put up signs. Each easement can be tailor-made to fit the need for scenic protection and to leave with the owner the remaining ownership rights he requires. Thus a farmer who wishes to reside on and cultivate his land can sell an easement precluding subdivision or industrial development and go right on enjoying his land as before. A timberland owner may agree only to spare trees along the river's edge, or to cut selectively. Sometimes a right of access is included in an easement (or a separate access easement is acquired) to permit fishermen to walk along the riverbank or for public access to certain camping areas.

The value of the easement depends upon how important the rights may be to the owner or how damaging their loss may be to the overall property value. An easement precluding development of land that could very easily and profitably be subdivided will be costly, perhaps almost as expensive as the full fee title. The same easement on a piece of remote or steep or swampy land might have only token value. Some easements are given free, not only out of a landowner's desire to preserve the beauty of his land, but also to enhance its value. This enhancement has come about at Piscataway Park on the Potomac River near Washington where a group of landowners who gave scenic easements have found their land more valuable because of the collective force of their easements, which protects the immediate environment in perpetuity.

But scenic easements have their problems. For one thing they are hard to enforce, and penalties for violating easement restrictions do not put the ruined scenery back. Moreover, scenic easements have as yet been little tested in the courts. Some state laws leave their validity in doubt, particularly their perpetual life. The law abhors perpetuities, and legal tradition does not usually look favorably upon devices that may encumber and cloud real estate titles forever, permitting the dead hand of the past to control the uses of the future.

Government land buyers who rely on easements to encourage willing sales at savings to the taxpayer often find that sellers are suspicious of agreeing to something that may later cause them inconvenience, tie their hands or make their land difficult to sell. And easements can cost almost as much as fee title. It is often to the taxpayer's advantage to buy the land outright and have full use of it rather than to pay practically as much for only an easement. "We have enough trouble protecting the land we own outright against power lines, roads, and other encroachments, let alone try to defend the integrity of easements," a Pennsylvania park official explained.

Nevertheless, the easement concept does offer hope for overcoming many landowners' gut reluctance to part with their property outright, for keeping property on the tax rolls, for stretching conservation funds, and as a substitute for the lack of effective regional planning authority.*

Similar but more economical and efficient means of marrying conservation and private use are just beginning to be tried. These are sell-back agreements. A government buys the land on which conservation restrictions are needed. Then if full public use of that land is not warranted, whatever rights are not needed to do

---

* An alternative to easements is compensable regulations. This method of land use control simply spells out by law what land uses are permissable and which are not and allows the landowner to collect damages if he can prove them. In this way no money is paid out of the public treasury (to forestall destructive events which may never occur) until damage to a landowner is real and compensation is in order.

the conservation job are sold back to private ownership again. For example a farm might be purchased and then the farming and farm residency rights sold back to the former owner, or to someone else if he isn't interested. The government retains the development rights along with the basic title, thus insuring that the property will always remain farmland. It is a cleaner deal than an easement. The private occupant knows where he stands and what he can and cannot do. His rights are permanent, salable, inheritable, but if he abuses them he can be stopped immediately, whereas a broken easement can only be redressed by a lawsuit after the damage is done. By selling back private interests, government can get most of its investment back—up to 90 percent of its costs—and on the rights conveyed to private individuals local taxing bodies can levy most of the taxes that support community services. These same arrangements can be made on a lease basis if a less permanent deal is desired. The only drawbacks of the buy-and-sell-back approach to land conservation are that it requires a big slug of money initially to do the buying, and property owners must part with that often cherished fee-title deed with its license to exploit. In the end, however, the taxpayer gets most of his money back from the conservation investment and the private resident retains the privacy and most of the uses he enjoys.

If a riverscape cannot be preserved by means of buying the land, or an interest in it like an easement, or cannot be brought under long-term lease, the only other means of control is by the police power of government. Planning authority, zoning and sanitary and subdivision regulations, building codes and the like are all part of this governmental responsibility to look after the health and safety of the citizenry. These powers were not delegated to the federal government under the Constitution but remained vested in the States, and these in turn gave them over to local government. Consequently, the police powers controlling land use along a single river are fragmented into many town, city or county jurisdictions. The only hope for concerted action to plan for the wholesome growth of a river valley, or any other large geographical unit for that matter, is a regional authority or compact, a cession of authority back to the state, or some voluntary working agreement. Political jealousies being what they are, plus the economic advantages of being autonomous and making your own deal with developers, industries, and other land use changers, these methods are difficult. Each political subdivision fears the hegemony of another.

Here again, a noble and rightfully prized tradition of American democracy—local government—is finding itself unable to cope with the wide environmental problems that beset us today, whether they be cleaning up pollution or preserving river scenery for the general public good. In the words of Stewart Udall, "As long as each city, county, township and district can obstruct or curtail, planning for the future cannot be effective."

"Home rule is sacred here," a New Jersey conservationist remarked. "Whoever wants to make a fast buck is in total and complete charge." Using the old strategy of divide-and-conquer, those who prey upon the environment for gain find the weak laws, or buyable changes in the laws, and by bamboozling the county commissioners with visions of fat tax revenues from new housing development or fat payrolls and taxes from industry, they stick the area with a rural slum or an industrial blight permitted without the needed controls. As Udall has observed, "The modern land raiders, like the public land raiders of another era, are ready to justify short term gains by seeking to minimize the long term losses. 'Present the repair bill to the next generation' has always been their unspoken slogan."

If the land-loving farmer who doughtily fights off planning, zoning, or conservation proposals in the name of liberty should look up at the tree behind him, he would find it perched full of the vultures of land exploitation waiting for him to sicken and die. Soon stakes will sprout across his green fields, bulldozers will grunt in his woods, and billboards will triumphantly herald the coming of Septic Estates. Frequently he is not above whistling in the birds himself, after fighting off conservation proposals with ringing declarations on the sanctity of individual liberty and property rights. "You can seldom sell conservation to people who live near the resource," a New York conservationist warned. "They've seen it too much and will fight and connive to exploit it."

The propriety of local authority notwithstanding, there is always the heart-wrenching problem of human relations when land use controls are locally administered and economic gain for local people is at stake. If you are a town or county official charged with such matters, you are forced to regulate friends and neighbors. State, interstate, or federal government may be able to do the job dispassionately, impersonally; the local official cannot. To do his duty, he may have to tell a friend, a neighbor, a customer, or his boss that he may not make a pile of money from a real estate deal. How would you like to deny the sweet old lady who lives across the road from you and gave you cookies when you were a kid a profit of a hundred thousand dollars, enabling her to move her ailing self to sunny Florida, because the zoning regulations you set up won't permit the deal she has been offered? In such cases, the conscience of the right actions to protect environment is challenged by the conscience of personal relationships. In the old days no one worried about such problems. If one river valley got clobbered in the process of profit-taking, there was always another one over the hill.

As mentioned earlier, rural areas don't cotton to zoning because they infringe upon a landowner's liberty and right to do as he pleases with what is his. Faced with the choice of having to buy land outright or zone it to protect the quality of a community, landowners and governments alike grasp at zoning as the "lesser of two evils." It doesn't cost anything, nor does it deprive people of their property. Often it is regarded as a panacea for all the developmental ills that beset a changing community.

Too seldom realized is that zoning, the body of regulations to insure a place for everything but everything in its place, for a safer, healthier, more attractive community, exists to guide growth wholesomely and is not designed to preserve resources perpetually intact. In other words, an exercise of police power cannot be fairly substituted for the purchase of land or rights in land for public benefit. Only in clear cases of public safety, such as the prohibiting of building on flood plains, can zoning reasonably serve long-term goals of preserving such natural resources as open space, wildlife habitat, and scenery.

Sooner or later most zoning breaks down. Fifty years of zoning protection can be overturned by a single vote of a county board. When the monetary stakes are high enough to encourage such overturns, they happen with a frequency which surprises no one. It happens most often, of course, in high-value urban areas where the open space is scarcest and most precious, and the planners who try to keep some pleasant order in the endless urban expansion or redevelopment feel like frail referees in a dirty football game.

Out amid the nostalgic, determined do-nothingness of the country, the professional planner is often regarded as a strange and annoying prophet, preaching of a doom no one can imagine and talking of preventative measures that sound to their listeners like communism. When the planner is naïve about local political realities, when he patronizes the local people as too stupid to know what's good for them, his plans do indeed become lead balloons. The fact that he has the temerity to offer plans at all, without first consulting every landowner around, is a source of considerable irritation to the local citizenry. That problem is one of the chicken-egg variety: does the planner start with a for-instance plan that voters can chew on, or does he dare to organize "for scratch" planning meetings with everybody in the act and few knowing the principles and goals involved? Many a zoning proposal has been soundly voted down as too much fine print. Many a master plan has been rejected as a predetermined product concocted for ramming down local throats.

A witty playwright might well parody old-fashioned American melodrama by personifying the elements and attitudes involved in the dilemma of riverscape protection. The beautiful girl would be named Riverside. Her father would be the farmer-landowner, and her suitor, a young planner bubbling with idealism and new-fangled ideas Pa doesn't dig. Aunt Susan and Aunt Hattie—one president of the local Audubon Society; the other heading the League of Women Voters—try to back the boy, but they cannot prevail against Ma, who suspects that Young Planner is a communist and who shares her husband's old American feeling that he who pays the piper calls the tune. That's the slick town villain with the mortgage (or cash offer) on the farm, of course. And of course the villain wins out. Gleefully he runs the heroine through the buzz saw and has the governor fire the would-be hero, who goes sorrowfully off in search of another pretty girl to try to save. Aunts Susan and Hattie kindly pack him a picnic lunch to take along, while Pa and Ma go off to Florida in their new Cadillac.

City or country, planner or layman, we will hate to commit ourselves. We like to keep our options open; therefore we hesitate to freeze our environment by dedicating any elements in it to perpetual preservation. Even when we have, as in our national and state parks, there is always someone trying to nibble away at the boundaries, seek exceptions to the protective principles and regulations, or abolish the whole thing outright. Planners themselves, recognizing that planning is a continuous process, often shy away from immutability. ("My mother preserves things," a regional planning director told me sarcastically. "She uses vinegar.") Therefore, few communities can count on any permanence in their surroundings, no framework of natural beauty around which handsome development can be designed.

Yet we continue wishfully to think we can regard rivers, like mountains, as permanent scenic assets in our lives. Robert P. Tristram Coffin wrote of his beloved Maine river, "The Kennebec's wealth, which no carelessness of men could ever destroy, is beauty." Just wait, Mr. Coffin; no doubt many men will try to prove you wrong.

Red Gods' Call

Do you know the blackened timber—do you know the racing
   stream
With the raw, right-angled log-jam at the end;
And the bar of sun-warmed shingle where a man may bask
   and dream
To the click of shod canoe-poles round the bend?
It is there that we are going with our rods and reels and traces,
To a silent, smoky Indian that we know—
To a couch of new-pulled hemlock, with the starlight on our
   faces,
For the Red Gods call us out and we must go!

            —*Rudyard Kipling in "The Feet of the Young Men"*

SCHOOL was out. The commencement exercises were just over, and the seniors in their caps and gowns were mingling with parents and friends. The talk included inquiries about summer plans, of course, and I asked a father and son I knew about theirs. The man's eyes lit up, and he put a hand on his son's shoulder. "We're going down the Allagash," he replied. "For thirty-five years I've wanted to take that river trip. We're going to Maine tomorrow, my son and I."

I wonder how many men, how many boys, how many fathers and sons have responded to that magic word Allagash over the past century. There is something in the very liquid sound of that Abenaki Indian name that says wilderness, promising the cleansing adventure, the self-renewal, the reaffirmation of vigorous life that canoeing down a wilderness river can uniquely provide.

Through all the hurly-burly of modern living, Americans still can hear the Red Gods of the wilderness calling them out. It has been that way since we began on this North American continent. The allure of the wilderness was one of the magic forces that beckoned us and bore us on. Beyond missionary zeal or lust for gain and glory, there was always something more urging the pioneers, the voyageurs. John Bakeless describes it in his *Eyes of Discovery:* "It was the lure of the great woods, the wild free life, the strange new peoples, the satisfaction of going where no white man had been, the hunt, still lakes at dawn, new plants, strange animals, the silent over-arching trees, the spice of danger."

The call still comes, though America now is largely tamed, and our wilderness is but a circumscribed and often soiled and battered souvenir of freedoms past. As Sigurd Olson has pointed out, the never-ending search for the essence of the wild is the underlying motive of all trips and expeditions.

"America is still close to the frontier," he has reminded us. "In the mists of morning along our rivers and lakes, ghosts speak to us of unnamed waterways flowing clean and full to the sea. Moderns think they have forgotten and in their urban lives have no need of this past, but deep within them is a smoldering nostalgia that can burst into flames should existence become too crowded, boring and commonplace."

The call comes strong along our rivers, where wilderness lingers on, and the nostalgia of which Olson speaks is what has saved the Allagash from becoming just another resort area. The Allagash was a symbol, symbol of a woods freedom now nearly gone from Eastern America, an invitation to absent oneself from civilization a while and blend again into the wilderness. The symbol was threatened in the early 1960s, specifically by a giant reservoir proposal which would have drowned it out for hydroelectric power, and generally by encroaching civilization. Roads were coming in, and had opened all but a few Allagash watershed lakes to auto traffic. Cottages would soon follow; then resorts. The people of Maine, backed by a national interest, overcame the bitter opposition of Maine's powerful timber industry that owned most of the area to establish the Allagash Wilderness Waterway, a 23,000-acre strip of wild preserve down the hundred-mile length of the river and its seven big lakes. Although easement lands back up the waterway preserve, it is narrow, and Maine will one day wish it had provided some lateral dimension by including hinterland streams and ponds. Heavy use will plague the preserve, and regulation, unpopular though it may be, will inevitably be necessary to preserve quality. But the Allagash Wilderness Waterway is there. The symbol and the substance will remain.

Remember the time we went down the Allagash with your boy and friends? Like Henry Thoreau who traveled that country a century ago, we were "suddenly naturalized there and presented with the freedom of the lakes and the woods." Unexpectedly, perhaps, the country was not spectacular in the usual sense of that term. No mighty mountains soared above the shores. Though fraught with what Aldo Leopold called "those rewards and penalties for wise and foolish acts which every woodsman faces daily, but against which civilization has built a thousand buffers," the adventure was no severe challenge. Nor was the Allagash region a howling wilderness; thousands of people go down the waterway each year.

Yet there was a freedom, an expansiveness, a fresh, rugged cleanness to this world of huge lakes and little ponds, of placid current and brawling rapids, that captured the imagination and the heart. There in the presence of a browsing moose or an otter's playing, the Red Gods' call comes clear. We heard it beside embered campfires; heard it in soft wave-on-gravel scouring; saw it signaled in the pale aurora shimmering across a star-pricked sky. When, out on the lake, a haunted loon sobbed in the night, civilization dropped from memory. Our craft turned to birchbark and we were a thousand years ago.

We had chosen not the usual, old route via Chesuncook Lake and Mud Pond Carry, nor the new, drive-in way to Telos Lake near Baxter State Park, but rather the beautiful though tedious way via Caucomgomoc Lake and the three-mile portage to Allagash Lake. It was long, long for soft muscles unused to carrying canoes. The way was wet and stumbly and the flies bit hard. Wilderness is not necessarily a pretty or pleasant condition. But the very weight of the canoes and packs seemed to impress on us a feeling of belonging, of being home in a long forgotten place again. "Early in every wilderness trip there comes a moment of awareness," Paul Brooks has written. "It is as if somewhere along the way, a door was silently opened and you have been invited to come in." On that long portage we were initiated into the fraternity of the forest.

As muscles cried to quit, the breeze freshened at last and we glimpsed that indescribable beauty of water gleaming at portage end. Across the dark basaltic rocks that reached into the shallows, we launched our craft in Allagash Lake. It is the finest jewel of the Allagash system, I think—the most beautiful, most remote of the seven large lakes which the river links in its northward flow. Once airplanes could fly in, and beer cans then came floating by your campsite. Now a paddle is the only key.

Remember the steep half-mile climb up Allagash Mountain where the blueberries grow thick? From that vantage point we could preview the trip that lay ahead. Below, cats-paw winds played across the two-by-three mile mirror of the lake. Far as the eye could see, forest carpeted a land that had been molded by a mile-thick press of glacial ice. It had rounded the promontories and scooped the lakes that lay like sheets of silver amid the wooded undulations of the hills.

We cruised down the lake slowly next day, along rocky shores fringed with arbor vitae; past rocky islets that looked like ships masted with pines and spruces. Then we slipped into the waters of Allagash Stream. Each eddy in that riffled path of gold promised trout. Bends deepen into fishing holes to dream of, and we longed to stay a week to try them. We did try Round Pond, where the stream plunges over Little Allagash Falls to that beautiful big pool below. Evening came with a calm expectancy, I remember, and trout dimpled the surface. Your young bowman was discouraged at first. Inexperienced, he could not cast aright. Then he sensed the timing, and it happened as it must to all boys who fish: a surge, a taughtened line, a gasped "I've got one on!" Your net came up under the glistening, writhing captive, and I suspect the youngster's thrill ran like an electric impulse through the gunwales to your heart.

Past ledges and whitewater raceways next day—remember how we floated out onto the long glittering expanse of Chamberlain Lake, a mile wide and, with its eastern neighbor, Telos, twenty miles long? Indians called it Apmoojenagamook—"Lake To Be Crossed," a name doubly apt. Their travel route not only crossed its midsection but howling west winds also could make the trip a dreadful one. We saw the lake's teeth show that evening, I recall, when boys from a summer camp scudded in through mountainous waves, their canoes rafted together for safety. That was the eve of the rainy day in camp, with its good talk and camp craft. Wood smoke mingled with the scent of balsam, and the woods seemed hushed despite the swaying of the trees.

The weather was brisk but bright when we were on Chamberlain, however, and our little fleet raised ponchos to catch the breeze and sailed down the Lock Dam like miniature Viking ships.

As I recollect the trip, several motor boats shot past us, for Chamberlain is open to motor craft as a compromise recognizing existing usage before the Wilderness Waterway was established. Someday Maine will realize that with 2,400 lakes it need not compromise its few wilderness waters. People move slower with the paddle and must watch the weather, but they will go farther into the world of the Allagash that way than a motor can ever take them. Men disturbed the Allagash with more than motors, however, and long ago. In 1841 lumbermen connected the upper Allagash watershed with the Penobscot via a canal, the Telos Cut, and Lock Dam at Chamberlain's outlet diverted the water eastward to feed the Bangor mills. Now it supplies water to hydropower there, but enough water goes north to float canoes. We portaged the dam and headed on.

Remember Eagle Lake with its islands and peninsulas, the long bays with trout streams pouring in? We could have spent days there, exploring, trolling for togue. But we had to get on, bucking a stiff wind. It was dip and stroke, mile after mile, but a swing of the shoulders began to make paddling as automatic as walking. The boys had fun at the Tramway, where a cable once hauled logs across an isthmus to Chamberlain, and where Edouard "King" La Croix built a logging empire in the 1920s, leaving two old locomotives rusting in the woods.

Remember the lone camper on the island, puffing his pipe, watching his little fire? He didn't talk much and we all respected his privacy. But he did say he comes back to Allagash country every year. "So much to see," he remarked. And he mentioned that word "freedom" again. We found evidence of earlier campers on one of the gravel bars—flint chips from tool making and a little stone sinker drilled with a single hole.

A couple of hours' paddling closed the centuries as we arrived at Churchill Depot, once King La Croix' logging capital. There the Allagash Wilderness Waterway Authority had rebuilt the old log dam, which once gave, and again provides, a head of water with which to shoot famed Chase's Carry Rapids.

The kids were nervous as we lashed in the gear. So was I. Hearts quickened as we knelt and heard the roar of rapids below. Then came that moment of commitment, yielding ourselves to the force of the water. How thankful we were that the boys had been well trained, deftly to draw the bows to left and right, dodging the rocks, seeking the current's strongest deepest thrust, but edging away from the high standing waves below the chutes. With their sharp eyes, and good reflexes, what a ride!

Remember the Big Eddy?—a welcome place to rest after the Devil's Elbow and see the Allagash in beautiful fury. It was there we first saw the otter that accompanied us on downstream for a couple of miles, appearing every now and then as if playing tag with the canoes. The quick-water, too, had slowed, though there were a rock and a rip or two to keep us alert for the rest of the ten-mile journey to Umsaskis Lake.

The river below Chase's Carry Rapids was my favorite on the Allagash—so much variety of water and shore with birches hanging over the stream and spruces spiking the sky. It was a pleasant change, nevertheless, to drift out through the grassy delta channels into Umsaskis Lake, slender, smiling that bright midday. I recall Thoreau's writing that, "It is an agreeable change to cross a lake after you have been shut up in the woods. It is one of the surprises which nature has in store for travelers in the forest ... the lakes also reveal the mountains and give ample scope and range to our thoughts."

That was a long paddle down Long Lake next day, and the sunny nooning on the meadow at derelict Long Lake Dam was drowsy bliss. Below it the main Allagash began. We glided down it that delightful afternoon until the long light came slanting through island elms, and we entered another Round Pond, that holds the river in a mile-long basin under a tumble of hills. There we met the Old Guide, Willard Jalbert, last of a breed of Allagash woodsmen, who still maintains his fishing camp. He gave us all a drink of spring water, and tempted me to return some September when the squaretails rise.

I've learned since our trip that the Allagash was a working river once. Logs were driven down, and sixty-five-foot barges were dragged upriver by teams of horses to supply the lumber camps. Michaud Farm, which we passed sixteen miles below Round Pond, grew hay for the stock. The logging days stripped the great pines from the land, but when the loggers were gone, the old tote roads grew quickly up again. Despite his greed, man was easy on the land. His tools did not bite deep, and soon he left again. Today, when he comes he stays, or others come behind him. The Allagash showed few signs of its old working years, I thought.

But motor canoes, following the logging barge route, overpower the fragrance of balsams with perfume of burnt gasoline. Some "Moosetowners" from the St. John Valley bitterly resent the Wilderness Waterway and the people it brings. They thought the old days would last forever; that laissez-faire would suffice without formal protection for Allagash country. Thoughtful Aldo Leopold once said that "All conservation of wilderness is self-defeating, for to cherish we must see and fondle, and when enough have seen and fondled, there is no wilderness left to cherish." In a way that is true, I know, but it depends on how one defines "enough." Left alone the Allagash would never have survived as a wilderness. Protected, it will attract recreationists who will surely fondle it severely unless there is strict regulation of use. Already state administrators are plagued with side-doors into the Allagash via logging roads. Gates are broken as fast as they are locked by timberland owners trying to cooperate in keeping the valley remote. It will be hard indeed to turn away many who yearn for that wilderness experience. Turned away to wait their turn they must be, nevertheless, else all that the Allagash stands for will be destroyed. Loss of quality and of freedom of opportunity are the prices we pay for a burgeoning population. In another generation, will that once-in-a-lifetime trip be a once *permitted* in a lifetime trip? The freedom of the wilderness will have to be rationed out by regulation, and the coureurs des bois, the voyageurs, the Algonquian "People of the Dawn" will stir in their mossy graves. But for now let us hope and teach, and remember.

Who can forget Allagash Falls crashing down over the basalt in a mighty thirty-foot cataract? Ferns grew out of the potholes in the rock. One big hole beneath a cataract made a natural tub and shower, and the kids cavorted there and in the current below the falls. In the woods beside the falls, all the delicacy of the North Woods could be also found. Snowberry vines creweled the rocks. Twinflowers nodded with fey fragrance. Wood sorrel offered cups of striated pink. Green moss sprouted ivory Indian pipes.

Remember the last campsite at Twin Brook? We camped there after the boys made that perfect run down Twin Brook Rapids' sweeping "S" curve. I can still see the firelight flickering across the young faces that evening—youth in the wilderness, as timeless as the fire itself and the comradeship it generates. I too felt young again, but our reprieve from civilization was ending. The Allagash itself was changing, broader, sweeping between banks lined now with maples; here a house; there a road. Beyond Casey Hole Rapids we saw the bridge, the village and the St. John.

That's another trip, the St. John, the Allagash's big brother. We'll make that some day with the boys. (But they're older now with boys of their own to train to the paddle.) People are talking about a huge dam on the St. John for hydropower and happy pastimes. Maybe the wild river will still run there, though, when the grandsons' shoulders are muscled to a paddle's swing.

The St. John is a temperamental backwoods brawler, of course. Lacking the Allagash's big steadying lakes, it is unpredictable. Sometimes it is gaunt and bony; at others, like a lumberjack on a Saturday night, it surges full with fury. When you commit yourself to its course, as Matt Marsh and I did one June, you are in the bush for several days, and only an occasional chain-saw behind one of the low ridges wails a man-call.

Moody itself, the St. John invites moods. When Big Rapids shout at you and plunge your bow in foam, you exult in the physical pleasure of the run. Yet when spruces are black against the moon and mists are rising, and the campfire burns down to its last philosophic coals, your ebullient young bowman may tell you quietly he believes there is more to Universe than moons or men.

Nobody seems to care much about the St. John except for fishermen who know the trout lies, and a few venturesome canoeists. Apparently the timberland owners do not. In places they have clear-cut the banks or have scored them with logging roads, though they have offered a few safe-and-sorry campsites in fields, a gravel pit, or some ranger station's back yard. Engineers love the St. John, of course. They see a 30,000-acre hydropower reservoir, and some may hold that to be a lesser evil than polluting power generation elsewhere. No doubt it could offer happy hours to millions on its surface, but is Maine so lake-poor that it needs another, and at the cost of much of its last wilderness? I trust not, and if wilderness is not extirpated from the East, maybe our sons will one day take their boys down both the Allagash and the St. John.

Man cannot fabricate a substitute for the wild. He can only spare it, and, to paraphrase an old political slogan, as Maine goes, so will go our Eastern wilderness. That is particularly true of our opportunities for experience on wilderness waterways. There are more than 4,000 miles of canoe trails in the State of Maine: nearly 1,000 on the St. John watershed, 1,000 along the coastal rivers, more than 800 each on the Penobscot and Kennebec drainages, some 350 along the Androscoggin, and more than 150 on the Saco. Nearly half of these can be classed as more or less wild. The importance of Maine as a place to find adequate opportunities for a wilderness experience on rivers as well as the range of other outdoor recreation, can be gauged from the probability that New England's population alone will increase from eleven to nineteen million within forty years, and recreational demands for water will be three times greater than today. Nearly forty million persons live within a day's drive of its recreation.

Today there are eleven million acres in Maine's unorganized townships and plantations. Eleven companies own more than half of this acreage. The remainder is largely in undivided ownerships, with the landholders having to reach a consensus on management policies.

With so much wild land under the control of so few decision-makers, the opportunities for wise overall decisions protective of wilderness values are enormous. But so is the danger that a few wilderness-destroying decisions can wipe away that wilderness wealth forever. As John McKee has written recently in *Maine Digest,* "More and more, as Northeastern U.S. develops, the Maine woods are becoming an almost unparalleled resource, both for tree production and for recreational opportunity. But who is to come forward to say that this resource must not be squandered? Can we guarantee that the next generations will be able to set out a canoe and know that adventure is just around the bend?"

Maine's water wealth is so great that the State has the chance to have its cake and eat it too—to have an abundance of profitable centers for recreational development around and plenty of wilderness hinterland to boot. The old myth of superabundance lingers on in Maine, however. It almost killed the Allagash Wilderness Waterway proposal. The timberland owners are under increasing pressure to lease cottage sites along their shores, to open their roads to freer travel and, most of all, to make recreational profit from their vast domains. Fortunately some of them are seeking sage advice to master plan their land management for the years ahead. But if those master plans do not include the preservation of generous amounts of wilderness, the magic of Maine may evaporate like the mists on its wild waters.

If Maine wants to see the results of wilderness compromises past, of conservation action that was too late and has been too little, the Adirondack waterways of New York provide excellent examples.

In the Adirondacks Eastern America rediscovered the joys of wilderness recreation, and Adirondack waters became the highways of forest adventure to escape from what even in the mid-nineteenth century was becoming an unhealthy, confining urban environment.

"Yesterday, as it were, I was walking the crowding streets of New York," wrote J. T. Headley in 1846; "last evening, in a birch-bark canoe, with an Indian beside me, nearly a day's journey from a human habitation, sailing over a lake whose green shores have never been marred by the ax of civilization and on whose broad expanse not a boat was floating but that which guided me and my companions on. . . . How far away seem the strifes of men and the discords of life. Tonight my couch of balsam boughs shall be welcome, until the cloudless morn floods this wild scene with light."

Most famous of the Adirondack waterways was, and is, the route from Old Forge up the Fulton Chain of Lakes, across a carry to

Raquette Lake and down the Raquette River to Tupper Lake or over to the Saranac Lakes region.* Several thousand canoeists travel it each year nowadays. Headley avowed that a ride through the Fulton Chain "is an episode in man's life he can never forget. It furnishes a new experience—gives rise to a new train of thoughts and feeling, and opens to the dweller of our cities an entirely new world."

Even today, a guide booklet published by the New York Conservation Department tells you that "While man-made highways and railroads have, for some people, destroyed the wilderness of the woods where they have penetrated, the water routes are largely unchanged from the times they were traveled only by Indian canoes or by the trappers and hunters of colonial days." By kayak I traveled a portion of the Fulton Chain–Raquette River route to experience what a sign at Old Forge announces as "one of the longest and most scenic canoe routes in the eastern United States." It is long—nearly 100 miles to the several ultimate destinations one may choose—and it is scenic, too. The forested Adirondack hills around it are beautiful; the lakes fresh, islanded, and green-shored. The Raquette River meanders in sylvan solemnity, then crashes into a gorgeous tumble of rapids. I was soon made aware that the trip might not be a wilderness experience, however. A sign informed me that Old Forge is "snowmobile country," and another rustic emblazonment offered "woodsy gifts." The fish I ate came from the Pied Piper drive-in.

The Conservation Department's guide further prepared me. "From First Lake through Fourth Lake heavy motorboat traffic is likely to be encountered," it warned. Motorboats were few and kind the day I went through. I was half-afraid they might try to buzz me; try to bounce the kook in the kayak, but all were gentlemanly, often coming up to look me over like big curious porpoises.

"The passage to Fourth Lake is just beyond the hotel," the

* Nineteenth-century trips were, more often than not, made in reverse, upriver, because the best access to the Adirondacks was via Lake Champlain.

guidebook went on. "Hotels and motels are numerous along the shores of Fourth Lake."

I eschewed these, continuing past a hotel tennis court, several sunbathers, and a bar-lounge to the carry along the highway to the dock at Sixth Lake.

"There is also a hotel on Seventh Lake," the guidebook informed me. "Persons desiring to camp out will find state land available for that purpose on the shores of the northeasterly end of Seventh Lake."

It looked like a sophisticated, well-filled campground, and, as my little kayak was able to negotiate the small outlet from Eighth Lake and so avoid the carry, I paddled on. With shores entirely in Forest Preserve lands, Eighth seemed still as it had always been, and I made camp on a gravel spit where a spring trickled out under a hemlock canopy. I built a wee fire to greet the moon, cooked my supper, and fell asleep, lulled by the night roaring of the highway just behind the ridge.

Next morning at Browns Tract Inlet, a half-mile carry from Eighth Lake, the sun glinted on the water lily pads and made the several sardine tins submerged at the launching strand wink from the bottom. Soon I was lost in the 2½-mile quietude of the inlet as I rounded its bends enroute to Raquette Lake. Under the bridge and past the church steeple and docks of the village, I entered what the state described as "the heart of the Adirondack wilderness."

Raquette Lake is truly a remarkable body of water (so much so there are thoughts of damming it into a large reservoir). Though only some six miles in length, its many embayments and peninsulas give it a shoreline of more than forty miles. Much credit is due to New York for having secured a great deal of this shoreline in the Adirondack Forest Preserve. Summer homes command most of the points, however, and I heard a summer camp loudspeaker blare "It is time to report for your first morning's activity." I had mine already cut out for me, as Raquette was afroth with whitecaps and my kayak bucked and plunged as I ploughed on toward the lake's outlet. I lunched beside the summer cottage which commands the carry to Forked Lake, then crossed the half-mile to that equally beautiful, almost-wild body of water.

The dam at the end of Forked Lake required another short carry. I picked my way between the trailers on the campground there, and, again, the small fiberglas kayak was able to bump through the rapids below, avoiding the customary mile-and-a-half trek down the road. I had only to make the short haul over the ledges around Buttermilk Falls. Past the cottages and hostelries at the head of Long Lake, I paddled under the highway bridge at Long Lake Village, landed beside the airplane mooring and sought the hospitality of the Adirondack Hotel.

Such opportunities in the Adirondacks are not of recent advent. The truth of the matter is that travelers of Adirondack waterways have been able to enjoy them ever since the country became famous for "wilderness" recreation more than a century ago. When camping was inconvenient or uncomfortable or its joys wore off, the vacationists would stop by a convenient hostelry or private summer home, for a tight roof and a good dinner. W. H. H. Murray, the Boston clergyman whose *Adventures in the Wilderness,* published in 1869, started a stampede to the Adirondacks, tells of coming late one night to a log hotel at wildly beautiful Raquette Falls and ordering up a bellyful of hotcakes. His book lists a number of good lodgings, among them famed Paul Smith's. "This is the St. James of the wilderness," he wrote. "Here Saratoga trunks and Saratoga belles are known. Here they have civilized 'hops,' and that modern prolongation of the ancient war-whoop modified and improved, called 'operatic singing,' in the parlors."

J. T. Headley had admitted that "This wilderness will be encroached upon in time, though it will require years to give us so crowded a population as to force settlements into this desolate interior of the state." He underestimated the ardor of wilderness recreation seekers. Within fifteen years after *Adventures in the Wilderness* sent "Murray's Fools" pouring into it for adventure or to try to cure tuberculosis with mountain air, the Adirondack wilderness, at least along the waterways, was gone.

"But alas! For the romance of paddling through the forest alone," lamented "Nessmuk" (George Washington Sears) in 1880 in one of his popular letters to *Forest and Stream*. "Before I was half rested my ears were pained, my soul was sick with the shriek of a steam whistle." Of Blue Mountain Lake, source of the Raquette, Sears reported that its days of natural wilderness were gone forever: "All luxuries of the season are to be found at the hotels." Indeed, the 300-room Prospect House was the first hotel in the world to have electric lights.

Some people who know and love the Adirondacks say there is little or no real wilderness left; that it is just a matter of degree of degradation. Nevertheless, some 2.25 million acres—some 40 percent of the area delineated as New York's "Adirondack Park" —today are preserved "forever wild" under provisions of the New York State Constitution. The development of that remarkable, indeed unique, protection came about as the result of horrifying depredations on Adirondack timberlands. Diverse interests united in determined measures to preserve such virgin wild lands as remained and give many others a chance to recover: canal and other water resource users apprehensive lest the waterways would suffer from the ravaged watersheds; owners of vast private acreages in the mountains who feared the raging fires that often followed logging operations; outraged recreationists and sportsmen. And so came laws, a constitutional amendment and a continuing program of land acquisition to put as much of the Adirondacks as possible into public ownership and be "forever kept as wild forest lands."

It is possible still to take many a lengthy hike through wild mountain country in the range, but as far as Adirondack waterways are concerned, the state's action was locking the barn after the horse had bolted. Unlike logging in Maine, undertaken long before recreational development became feasible, the logging which prompted New York's conservation action and the resort development that preempted much of the best land were roughly concurrent. Except for a few big tracts, the forest lands which New York has been able to buy up over the past ninety years are scattered, interlarded with private holdings, much of it waterfront, whereon the developments have been ensconced.

Not that New York has failed to do a creditable job of buying up waterfront property. In view of the demand for it for private use, the state has managed to acquire a surprising amount for public recreation. But wilderness canoeing and boating opportunities have been practically gone for a century. Without a vast roll-back to wild status, most of the famed Adirondack waterways which captured the heart and imagination of eastern America in the last century are destined to be forever only partly wild. People who seek a truly wilderness experience in the Adirondacks now look rather to the mountains than to the rivers and the lakes.

Canoeists develop a certain ambivalence toward the semiwild-ness of Adirondack waterways. I know I did. They are beautiful and woodsy still, and, as with a child's pretended wilderness tenting in the back yard, a little imagination can piece out the illusion of primality. Sears, who paddled his 9-foot, 10½-pound *Sairy Gamp* more than 250 miles through the Adirondacks, extolled the "delicious air, the free, open-air life, the lakes, the scenery, the balsam-laden breezes," and recalled at one bivouac that "There was not a soul within miles of me, and the shriek of the steam whistle was afar off, beyond the keenest earshot." Yet when the frail "Pennymite" woodsman found a convenient streamer, he "Went on board of her and became resigned to steam and a teeming civilization that increased nearly every hour."

The early lovers of the Adirondack wilderness were not jealous of it as many are today, though they knew that civilization was fast encroaching. Not only was there wilderness a-plenty, but they charitably hoped that its benefits could be as widely shared as possible. Murray wrote that "Hotels will multiply, cottages will be built along the shores of its lakes, white tents will gleam amid the pines which cover its islands, and hundreds of weary and overworked men will penetrate the Wilderness to its innermost reaches, and find amid its solitude health and repose."

State Surveyor Verplanck Colvin, who, having tramped the fastnesses of the Adirondacks knew them best and wrote of them eloquently, was startled by the rapidity of their civilization, and he recognized that to many who loved wilderness its thronging was deeply regrettable. "The old romance is gone forever," he recorded just ten years after the "Murray rush," noting resignedly that, "The genius of change has possession of the land; we cannot control it." But then he added, "When we study the necessities of our people, we would not control it if we could." Inherent in his thinking was the old myth of superabundance. The Adirondacks could be a pleasuring ground for the poor cooped-up city dweller. Somewhere else the old romance would linger still.

And as wilderness faded to woodsiness, Adirondack buffs adjusted. The essence of the Adirondacks remains, they assured themselves—the rippling waters, the cool woods—they are eternal, so all is well.

"The encroachment of the modernizing process left no salient disfigurement in its train such as all too frequently results from human enterprise set foot free in virgin fields," Joseph F. Grady asserted in a 1933 book on the region. "It is the same continuity of shade and cool rippling water that it was generations ago: and being now the cherished ward of a nature-minded commonwealth, it is not improbable that its deeply satisfying, natural, intimate beauty will remain forever unaltered."

Yes, it is forever wild; the New York Constitution says so. I kept reminding myself of that while kayaking down the solitudes of the winding Raquette. Soon I was rocking in the wake of a motorboat that plowed the narrow channel. Slowly the water quietened. Silence returned. Another boat; another change of pace—out of the wilderness, into modernity; then back to forever wild. I kept telling myself that the blue smoke hanging above the water was not really engine exhaust but the mists of early evening, or perhaps an Indian wraith.

Yes, one of the prime elements of Adirondack woodcraft is a good imagination. It takes a deal of it in that collection of once-wild little ponds which lies just west of Upper Saranac Lake. What a place to take a little boy on a canoe trip! Carries of a few hundred feet lead you from pond to tiny pond, each one Hiawatha's own. Not Fish Creek and Rollins Ponds, anymore, however. There the constitution has been circumvented in the name of fire protection and concentration of use to preserve other areas. More than 600 campsites along some 2½ miles of waterfront now banish the wild forever. And there I confess, I lost my ambivalence and my cool toward what New York has done over the years to this tiny jewel box of wilderness waterways. The could-have-been wilderness was being lounged upon with beach chairs, for the Empire State was saying welcome, city man, to the wild Adirondacks on *your* terms. And the little boys who camped there in the elaborate tents and trailers would never, in old age, dream back to a first adventure in the wilds. Above the portable radios, they would not hear the Red Gods' call.

I cite this to indicate how management can fatefully affect the wilderness values still remaining in the Adirondacks. At present two Adirondack worlds coexist along the waterways. While the beautiful people of the resorts lounge on their motel and cottage lawns and race back and forth in their spray-flinging speedboats, the woods people, like elves or peasant folk of long ago, pad silently by, canoes and knapsacks on shoulders, or paddle steadfastly past the proud prows of launches. At dusk, firelight before a lean-to answers the floodlights and neon glitter across the lake. How long this will go on, in view of developments and pressure on campsites and shelters, I do not know. Perhaps forever, though New York's fragmented holdings of Forest Preserve land would seem to make management of increasing use difficult indeed. If, however, the state can set aside a few major areas for canoeing, it can at least perpetuate a remnant of what water trekking in the Adirondacks once was like. This will mean extensive purchasing of private lands or easements in a few places, but perhaps this can be done at the end of a life estate or timed in such a way so as not to discomfit present ownership. A million acres of private land in the core of the Adirondack Park are held by fewer than forty owners. When the clubs and the private landlords and the paper companies realize they are in some places growing trees on $1,000 an acre land, change may come fast. And as one state conservation official observed, "Government had better be ready to pick up the pieces; otherwise there will be a hot dog stand at the foot of each rapid." The state already has a good basis for a semiwilderness boating area, comprising Raquette and Forked Lakes, which offer long, various and beautiful shorelines. Another area, different and equally beautiful, is Long Lake and the main Raquette River to Tupper Lake.

Long Lake, really a glacial widening of the river valley, fairly demands a boating voyage down the 9½ miles north of Long Lake Village. The Seward Range towers in the distance, and the narrow lake is flanked by the ice-smoothed masses of Buck, Blueberry, and Kempshall mountains. Tall pines fringe the rocky shores and islands loom ahead, beckoning the canoeist onward to explore them. Past pine-backed beaches, patches of water lilies, and brushy glacial bars, one slips quietly into the Raquette's strong silent flow. It is a contrast to the noble lake, this intimate, mysterious channel, lined first with maples, then arbor vitae, winding through lowlands until, after six miles, low hills and the thunder of water herald Raquette Falls. The Falls actually consist of a mile and a quarter of heavy rapids dropping eighty feet in their course, and punctuated by two pitches twelve feet or more in height.

The carry, an old tote road, remains aloof from the stream, but a scramble path carpeted with conifer needles as it winds between venerable hemlocks, arbor vitae, and yellow birches, follows atop the steep bank along the rapids. That walk must surely be one of the most beautiful in the East, though the hard work of portaging has not been conducive to appreciative descriptions of it.

Below the falls, the Raquette resumes a stately, tortuous course, with many backwaters to tempt a canoeing naturalist. One may work up the outlet to Stony Creek Ponds and carry over to the Saranac Lakes, where extensive Forest Preserve lands around Middle and Lower to Saranac offer additional boating-camping opportunities. Or one can continue down the meandering Raquette another eighteen miles to Tupper Lake.

If these areas, these shores can be placed under a forever wild designation; if the waters can be zoned for canoes (and traditional Adirondack guide boats, if rowing again becomes popular), there will again be an opportunity to savor a wilderness environment along Adirondack waterways.

Every waterway imparts something of a wilderness atmosphere. The mystique of flowing water sees to that; so does the fecundity of plant and animal life that inhabits streams and lakes and their shores. That is why, I believe, it is so important to preserve the naturalness of our Eastern waterways. Except for a few mountain fastnesses, some extensive wetlands along our coasts, strands like Monomoy Island on Cape Cod, some remote islands and anomalies like the New Jersey Pine Barrens, waterways remain our only avenues into the dimension of wilderness experience. Only there can we find the natural antidote to the ailments of stress and overcrowded life. Perhaps we search for it as for a souvenir wherein the balsam scent of nostalgia lingers on. If we find a shred, catch a whiff, however, it refreshes and strengthens like a spring tonic. Some need large doses of wilderness for health and peace of mind, but for most of us, a little can do, though the more the better for us all.

"If we can only come back to nature together every year," wrote Henry Van Dyke, "and consider the flowers and the birds, and confess our faults and mistakes and our unbelief under their silent stars, and hear the river murmuring our absolution, we shall die young, even though we live long."

Unfortunately, we have long been determined to extirpate wildness as boys shoot hawks, considering it a vermin environment. As by the sight of a hawk or eagle soaring, we are thrilled by the nobility of wilderness, however, and are now moved to protect it.

In our national maturation, is the urge to kill giving way to the urge to enjoy and understand? We have already become the first nation in history not only to establish national parks but also to enact a law—the Wilderness Preservation Act of 1964—enunciating that wilderness is part of our culture, a legacy we should pass on.

The wild river, like the eagle, is an endangered species, particularly in the East where its last habitat of any size is in Maine. But here and there a stray lingers on to surprise and delight us. Sometimes it is a mountain stream tucked away in a roadless or protected area. The Dead and Swift Diamond Rivers in New Hampshire's Dartmouth College Grant are kept wild by Dartmouth's regulated management, though a road follows them. Indian Stream, in New Hampshire's once wilderness tip, is roaded too but could also be kept wild. Except for the headwaters of Israel's River flowing off the Presidential Range in New Hampshire, the only truly wild river reach in the Connecticut watershed is, surprisingly, a five-mile section of the Westfield's North Fork in Massachusetts.

I remember, almost with incredulity, a camping trip on the deep, narrow Batsto which winds through the forests of the Pine Barrens. Megalopolis glowed on the horizon, but we could reach over the side of the canoe and dip up a cupful of water which, though tinted brandy-brown by bordering cedar swamps through which the river runs, was as fresh and pure as waters from backwoods Maine. Wilderness has recaptured the Pine Barrens, once the center of colonial America's iron industry and patterned with towns, furnaces, and coach highways. Now it is a 650,000-acre expanse of forest amid America's most populous region. Conservationists hope to keep it that way, by augmenting already extensive state forests, fighting off a suggested jetport and new inroads of development.

I was similarly astonished by a trip down little Dragon Run that flows into Chesapeake Bay through Virginia's Middle Neck. There amid rioting vegetation huge cypress trees brooded over the cool silent flow, and sent their knees thrusting out of the water like goblin pilings. An owl took silent wing, and the strident call of a pileated woodpecker sounded through the forest like the call of some jungle bird. Pickerel swirled for minnows in the backwaters, where cardinal flowers and trumpet vines splashed occasional color against the green. We wondered aloud, around our campfire that evening, how long this small remnant of wilderness, this naturalist's Eden, would survive half way between Richmond and Washington.

If you drive approximately the same distance from Washington but in the opposite direction—northwest—you can, in less than three hours, be in an environment reminiscent of Wyoming. There in West Virginia the Cacapon River flows for forty miles through a virtual wilderness. You will see occasional camps, to be sure, and there soon will be more and more, and more, but the Cacapon, one of the Potomac River's cleanest tributaries, is the central thread of a nearly wild area of more than seventy square miles.

Wild itself as its winds, deeply incised in the wooded highlands buttressing Cacapon Mountain, the Cacapon is a favorite for whitewater canoe trips. Its waters pour over ledges and down bouldery chutes, emptying into long pools which have yielded impressive bass. Above the hemlocks that overhang the river's many bends, rise escarpments and talus slopes. As with much West Virginia scenery, these features lend a western character to the expected native Appalachian atmosphere. One awesome crag, Caudy's Castle, has legends of an Indian fight to add frontier flavor to the place.

There is nothing like the Cacapon anywhere around that region of the East. Preserve it? Hell, no! The Department of the Interior proposed placing the Cacapon in a National Wild Rivers System. The U.S. Senate agreed, and outraged West Virginians squalled like catamounts. The Cacapon had been let alone for 200 years. No one was going to buy their lands or take easements. "We'll do the protecting," they asserted. Three years later they were busy selling Cacapon-side lots. "One acre on the river . . . for people who appreciate true wilderness," one ad read.

The Cacapon wilderness, like the wolf, is to be shot and sold for its pelt.

More hopeful seems the reaction to protection needs of an eastern stream very similar to the Cacapon: Pennsylvania's Pine Creek. This prize of what is known as the "Northern Tier" of mountainy, forested, recreation-rich counties rushes for some fifty miles through a deep valley, carved in glacial times when an ice-dammed lake spilled over the mountain levee and began to cut down through it. Once Tiadaghton, "River of Pines," was the way of an Indian trail that crossed the creek eighty times enroute to the Genesee Valley. Later the creek bore lumbermen's rafts to the mills at Williamsport on the West Branch of the Susquehanna. But Pine Creek is in part a wild river now, despite a single-track railway that threads it. It is a wilderness experience for some 4,000 Boy Scouts and other outing groups who in Springtime take the run through this "Grand Canyon of Pennsylvania." As Walter Frederick Burmeister describes it in his two-volume river guide-book, *Appalachian Water*, "Pine Creek combines, in perfect harmony, spectacular scenery, clear water, and unspoiled country. There is a touch of the classic landscape about the magnificent gorge with its towering palisades, immense cliffs and symmetrical slopes." The nineteen-mile canyon, 800 feet deep in places, is largely in state forest and is overlooked by two state parks.

Pine Creek also has been recommended for protection in the National Wild and Scenic Rivers System, and is scheduled soon for special state-federal study. Landowners are interested, eager to do what is reasonable to protect Pine Creek's amenities. The most spectacular section is already mostly in state ownership. Along the lower reaches pollution problems being caused by existing developments are making landowners begin to question the wisdom of further subdivision of creekside lands. A special four-year study by the Pennsylvania State University School of Forest Resources is proving of great help. It is testing for pollution and other conservation problems in general, aiding people along the creek in a careful evaluation of their problems and possible solutions.

Led by Professor Peter W. Fletcher, students have painstakingly sampled Pine Creek water and have informed citizens of conditions and trends, as well as the nature of the scenic river idea. "It calls on us, as citizens, to take a hard look at what's happening throughout Pine Creek's watershed, and especially what's happening to its waters, banks, and valley walls," Dr. Fletcher wrote. In another article, entitled "Man in the Ecology of a Scenic Mountain Stream," he added: "As this story of research and extension continues to unfold on Pine Creek Watershed, it is hoped that rural people elsewhere, on other watersheds, will also begin to take a hard look at their own environmental problems, and begin to initiate whatever action programs seem appropriate."

Amen. The Cacapon folk were admittedly rushed, though after promising to do the conservation job themselves, they went right on with laissez-faire. Pine Creek people have formed a watershed association and are helping Dr. Fletcher's study learn the facts on which action can be taken. When the official scenic river study is made, it will likely find a knowledgeable, open-minded citizenry, concerned for their environment and willing to consider seriously the preservation of Pine Creek as a permanent scenic asset to its region, the East and the nation—a valley of wild beauty where the Red Gods' call can still be heard.

Crusade

This task is ours together. It summons our energy, our ingenuity, and our conscience in a cause as fundamental as life itself.

—Richard Nixon in a message to the Congress, 1970

U NTIL recently, America's Temple of Conservation was sparsely attended. Like Russian peasant women persisting in habitual worship, the "little old ladies in tennis shoes" (of jocular reference and underestimated effectiveness) faithfully made their devotions and gave their alms. A small dedicated professional priesthood kept the candles lit, the gospel preached, and the supplications laid before the government. Unlike Russia, the United States government was benign enough toward the Faith. It set aside a few new places of worship; and its leaders even attended services. But to most Americans conservation, while "worthy," was not "relevant." There were more satisfactory ways to spend money than to put it into that collection plate.

Today, the temple resembles a medieval cathedral, packed full. Even the square is crowded with singing multitudes, and they are wearing the white tunics and red crosses of crusaders. We have called for a holy war to save our environment. How earnestly this war will be pressed we do not yet know. Will it founder in political wrangling as the crusaders try to set sail? Will they be shot down by infidel arrows, or die in a desert of exploitation now too vast to win back? Will the belly dancers of copious consumption charm the fight out of them? Only time will tell. The movement to protect and restore the American environment has, nevertheless, the characteristics, good and bad, of a classic crusade.

For a long time we were content to let the saracens do their thing so long as they sent us plenty of silks and spices and perfumes to keep life luxurious and to mask their noxious enslavement of the water and the land. At length, however, we began to realize that they were polluting our Jordan; were bulldozing the olives off the mount. Shocked, angry, and scared, we began to listen to the old preachers and some new zealots as well who appeared like Peter the Hermit to galvanize our convictions.

So we have proclaimed the Great Crusade, and have enacted laws under which its banners can go forward. We have even opened the treasury wide enough to buy lots of white tunics, and a little armor and even a few swords (though we don't want to hurt the saracens too much; they might cut off our silks and spices).

There are all kinds of recruits donning the cross, as there were in the Middle Ages. Some are fired with holy zeal; some cynically join for a fight or to be seen on the right side. There are armies of naïve children, emotional adults, young people out for adventure, soldiers of fortune hoping for fame and glory. As in the medieval Crusades many courageous, conscientious men of substance are willing to take the cross even at the sacrifice of successful careers. Other lords, however, abide sullenly in their castles, afraid to shoot the heralds calling them to the colors, but otherwise hostile. After all, they own a substantial interest in those polluting silk and spice mills, and have just invested a bundle in Jordan River Shores. Slyer potentates pull the cross on over their heathen robes and join the march, though, come nightfall, they may slip secretly into the postern gate of a saracen stronghold.

As the crusade progresses, there is certain to be the usual amount of jealousy, struggles for leadership, and factional warfare—the usual energy-squandering side forays, the usual betrayals and sellouts to the enemy. Promises of money won't be kept; arms will be faulty, ships leaky. There will be some mighty battles and some proud castles taken and holy ground preserved, but the saracens will usually pretend to fall back, letting the crusaders' thirst do them in. No, there will be few casualties or prisoners, for, as Sir Pogo has said, "We have met the enemy and they are us."

Still, there is much hope, pointed up with some encouraging victories and strengthened by some promising campaigns. We do have, for example, the technology to cope with pollution, and a reassuring number of individuals have evinced willingness to pay the cost. We also have the antipollution laws, both federal and state. Some are new, and we are beginning to dust off some good old ones like the "bag-a-polluter" Federal Refuse Act of 1899 that gives half of the fine for polluting—up to $2,500—to the informer. To abate pollution there is both state and federal funding on an unprecedented scale, though still small compared with what is spent on other things. As a result cleaner river flows are becoming evident. The director of the Becket Academy canoeing adventures mentioned earlier noted that the Connecticut "is a cleaner river than when we took our first trip in 1968. We expect by next year to see much more improvement in the water quality." Interstate compacts are now in effect for the Deleware and the Susquehanna. The New England River Basins Commission is coordinating river management there, and the Hudson River Commission has with its persuasive expertise faced down would-be river despoilers.

Aesthetics are being more seriously considered in all planning, for example, in river basin studies by the Corps of Engineers. The studies are even listing rivers that should not be dammed, but protected as wild, scenic, or recreational streams. One wild stream, Beech Creek in Centre County, Pennsylvania, has been identified in the Susquehanna watershed, as well as several dozen scenic streams and recreational waterways (the latter having some inpoundment or diversion, perhaps, with more shoreline development permissable, but offering especially good recreation as they are). Similarly, a Connecticut River Basin study identified not only a wild river reach (on the Westfield) but also a dozen scenic stretches and more than a hundred recreational streams. Hundreds of particularly good fishing streams in the basins have also been identified for special care and management.

In the states, relinquishment of local sovereignty in the interest of regional resources is evident in emerging action to govern land use on a state-wide basis. New York has added a Conservation Bill of Rights to its constitution, avowing that it is state policy to protect its natural and environmental resources. In a number of states voters have repeatedly approved large bond issues to buy open space. They have also approved laws to preserve wetlands, and the careful delineation of flood plains is clarifying the legality of zoning to keep development from preempting them. In tune with the national concern for preserving free flowing waterways which resulted in the Wild and Scenic Rivers Act of 1968, several states have also undertaken scenic river studies, and have legislation to authorize scenic rivers enacted or pending. Vermont is thoroughly alarmed at the rate at which developments have been gnawing at its scenic beauty. "The increased capacity to organize capital coupled with an expanded technology has allowed hills to be leveled and valleys to be filled in Vermont as elsewhere," noted the State Planning Board. "The intrusion of incongruous commercial and residential uses on streambanks seems a real if unfortunate part of Vermont tradition, at least as judged by the many streams rendered unfit for viewing within cities, including the state capital. That this process continues in newly developing areas is known to all who care to observe."

With "stubborn optimism," however, Vermont has assumed that its citizens want development to conform with the basic characteristics of their scenic environment. The Green Mountain State has decided to guide land use through statewide authority. A special environmental board will regulate development and is preparing a comprehensive plan. The state recognizes that flood plains are natural extensions of rivers themselves and must be kept open. It knows also that conditions at the interface of land and water provide specific and important habitats for some of the state's more interesting and celebrated fauna. These shorelines are unique and fragile, not at all immune to damage from ill-conceived development. Vermont's Interim Land Capability Plan states firmly that "If aquatic habitats or the animal and plant systems within these areas are not to be intruded upon with the abandon of the past, development proposals for lands on lakes or ponds or along rivers and streams will proceed only after impact upon these values is shown to be minimal."

The state of Maine has taken a step that can conceivably do more to preserve Eastern rivers than any other kind of legislation short of actually establishing wild and scenic rivers systems, which its action may eventuate. In addition to establishing an Environmental Improvement Commission to monitor local conservation efforts and backstop deficiencies and failings of local government, the state has created a Land Use Commission. This will now serve as the planning and zoning board for the more than half of Maine which is in unorganized or deorganized townships and plantations. These form Maine's great wild heartland, through or out of which flow most of its finest rivers. Controlled in a very few large corporate or undivided ownerships and previously subject to no land use regulation, these forest lands are beginning to come under great pressure for development. Unbridled development not only could destroy much of Maine's wild beauty and the kind of outdoor recreation for which the Maine woods are prized but could affect the quality of the waters as well. The headwaters of 45 percent of Maine's waterways are in these unorganized territories, and in a state that is spending a quarter of a billion dollars for pollution abatement, it is important to keep clean waters clean. Recently, too, exploration of low-grade metals has raised the specter of open pit mining in the Maine woods.

The Commission and the land use guidance standards it is to formulate must prevent inappropriate uses, particularly near water, protect the water itself, and also preserve ecological and natural values. Riversides are among the lands to be designated as protection districts, free from development and therefore probably under permanent conservation easements, which the Commission is empowered to acquire. If the Commission's land use plans are well made and firmly adhered to in this vast eleven-million-acre domain, they could become cornerstones of a physical design for a state whose unspoiled waterways are among its finest treasures.

For one of its most popular rivers, the Saco, Maine has proposed a Saco River Authority, comprising the town and county governments, which would have an intergovernmental land acquisition authority to keep the river a regional amenity and recreation resource. Now the state has set up a Saco River Corridor Advisory Committee to develop a plan for the river, and residents of both Maine and New Hampshire have formed an S.O.S.—Save Our Saco—group that during one cleanup campaign recruited 6,000 adults and 12,000 children for the job. The organization intends to become involved also in the Corridor planning efforts. Most intergovernmental arrangements have, to date, emphasized only water resources. Maine's tossing of the ball to local jurisdictions in a region where they are cherished as kingdoms marks a new direction in the complex game of conservation-and-government.

One of the most impressive programs specifically for river protection is contained in the recommendations of New York's Temporary Study Commission on the Future of the Adirondacks. The Empire State, long so proud of the "forever wild" status of its Adirondack Forest Preserve lands, recognized that without drastic action they were doomed. Unguided development of the 3.5 million acres of private land in the Adirondack Park interspersed with the 2.25 million acres of State Forest Preserve lands would destroy the character of the entire park without immediate precautions.

"The private landowner of a lovely Adirondack shoreline

property may now, if he likes, build on its shores a movie theater or an amusement center or a trailer park. What is more important, he or his heirs, who will be concerned with inheritance taxes, are free to sell the shore front to developers to be broken up into 50 or 100 small building lots. And this is beginning to happen," the Commission pointed out.

Much of the private land is in large holdings. A third of the park is held by 626 owners, and thirty-two of them collectively control more than a million acres. These few can decide the fate of the park, and there are many small ownerships that could as well be detrimental. "The key to maintaining the park as a *lasting* entity," said the Commission, "lies in the avoidance of misuse by all landowners, large and small."

So the Commission recommended a special Adirondack Park Agency with land use regulation powers. That has been created, though with only interim powers and a mandate to develop a land use control plan for the legislature to consider. The Commission also called for a $120 million bond issue to buy land and also easements, which are seen as the primary means of keeping large private tracts—estates, clubs, and timberland areas—undeveloped and consonant with park objectives. Extensive wilderness and primitive areas are recommended as is a system of wild, scenic and recreational rivers that burst, crystal clear, from the Adirondack Park. "The enjoyment they afford within the Park and the benefits they bring to man after they leave the Park demand that they be protected," the Commission declared.

Patterned after the national system set up by the Wild and Scenic Rivers Act of 1968, the Adirondack system recommended would include 67 miles of wild rivers, including the famed Hudson Gorge and the Cold River that flows into the Raquette; 323 miles of somewhat more accessible but scenic rivers, including much of the Hudson above the gorge, the tributary Boreas and also a good part of the Cedar, the upper East Branch of the Ausable as well, and the Raquette between Long and Tupper lakes. The 528 miles of recreational rivers named include the rest of the upper Hudson, the Schroon, most of the Sacandaga (upper reaches are proposed as "wild" or "scenic"), and the rest of the Ausable in addition to the Bouquet and Saranac that also flow into Lake Champlain.

The riverscape protection recommended by the Commission is essential to the task of perpetuating the character of the Adirondacks, as is the protection of the lakes. Natural waterfront, already severely compromised along many Adirondack shores, will be the first resource to be seized upon for development. The record of New Yorkers' rallying to the cause of Adirondack conservation gives hope, however, that they will meet the financial challenge of the Commission's report: "If immediate action is not taken, many critical tracts will be broken up within five years and almost all of the large blocks of private forest land will be developed with second homes within less than a generation. There will be no Adirondack Park as we know it today." Already there has been encouraging private conservation action. The Nature Conservancy has purchased and holds for the state a tract of 13,000 acres, including three lakes of the Hudson headwaters.

Maine and New York have more impressive opportunities for river protection, but the Commonwealth of Massachusetts has made the most dramatic breakthrough to date in efforts to save the remaining beauty of riverscapes. In a study of its major rivers and tributaries the state counted nearly 250 dams, with many more proposed, and found some 14 percent of its stream banks ruined for recreation by urban-industrial blight. Another 5 percent is in immediate jeopardy.

But Massachusetts also found that more than 2,300 miles of streams still attractive and able to help meet an estimated demand in the state for more than thirty million days of streamside recreation annually. It even found wild stretches of the Westfield and Millers rivers, and long reaches of those and others like the Chicopee, Deerfield, Hoosic, Farmington, Nashua, and Scantic that are still largely primitive and beautiful. "An irreplaceable natural resource is represented in the relationship between a stream and its shoreline," warned the Department of Natural Resources. "Our streams and adjacent shoreline must be protected as entities in their own right."

The legislature listened, established a Massachusetts Wild Scenic and Recreational Rivers System and bade the Department get on with the job of designating the rivers, using compensable regulations, largely, instead of costly and politically aggravating land acquisition programs. As under its laws protecting coastal wetlands, the state will mark off for the system river reaches and protective strips of riverbank 100 yards wide and then will freeze their current use and development. If a landowner feels he has been damaged by this, he can take the matter to court. If he is upheld by the court and exempted from the regulations, the state can then condemn an easement or buy the land outright to protect the riverscape.

In many states, regional and county planning commissions are focusing local attention on the need for protecting waterways. Along the beloved Ottauquechee River, flowing through a beautiful notch, looping around the picturesque village of Woodstock and crashing through Quechee Gorge, regional plans recommend "critical" status for its banks. This means restrictions on development that may keep the Ottauquechee one of Vermont's loveliest small rivers. A rural community in Virginia is considering going further. Love and concern for a local river and resolve to protect it is nowhere more appropriate than in the Old Dominion county named Fluvanna—"Anne's River"—as colonists once called the upper James, honoring their Queen. They called another branch "Rivanna"—"Anne's Banks"—and the Rivanna River is Fluvanna County's pride and joy. It is a beautiful stream, secluded and inviting, the remnants of an old canal along it add historical interest and charm. Scenic river studies in the Commonwealth noted this. Fluvanna County has welcomed the thought of protecting its waterway, and local Boy Scouts are undertaking a trail along it. While other counties in the East fight off conservation in the name of their tax revenue base and their developer constituents, Fluvanna may quietly save Anne's Banks for posterity.

Human nature is apparently so constructed that it is always much easier to be against something than for something. And, amid the din of the crusaders' shouting, the protests and teach-ins, the lawsuits and injunctions, there is, strangely, often little opportunity, except through political support of conservation candidates and bills, for individual citizens constructively to aid the cause of conservation. Clayton Hoff of Wilmington, Delaware, helped to change that picture somewhat. Back in 1945, he organized the Brandywine Valley Association. Starting with a founding nucleus of people with impressive business and professional abilities it has grown to an organization of 2,000 members. It was the first of dozens of watershed associations now functioning along many of the East's attractive streams in a grassroots response to water resource care. Everyone lives in a watershed, of course, and when they are somewhat like-minded in their concern for that watershed, political boundaries can be crossed in a common effort. Watershed associations pass no laws, issue no directives; they simply provide information, analyze problems, find solutions, encourage right actions. They persuade. And, working in a small area where their members have influence, they are persuasive.

Through the association's efforts the state of Delaware created a Water Pollution Commission; Chester County, Pennsylvania, established a Soil Conservation District; 95 percent of the Brandywine basin's sewage and industrial wastes are now treated, 65 percent of the landowners in the valley have complete farm conservation plans, headwaters dams are planned for water supply, flood control, and recreation, and conservation workshops are sponsored at area colleges.

In his book on the Brandywine, Henry Canby remarked that "I have never known a river, except the upper Thames, to be held by those who knew it well in such affectionate regard." Unfortunately the regard was not sufficient to support a pilot plan by environmental specialists from the University of Pennsylvania to preserve the scenic amenities of the Upper Brandywine. Bad breaks, lack of grassroots leadership, misunderstandings, and fears of condemnation killed the plan.

On the other hand, affection for the Brandywine has flowered successfully in two other organizations devoted to the small green valley. Wilmington leaders established Forward Lands, a trust to acquire or receive lands in advance of the city expansion and hold them in an eleemosynary land bank for future public purposes. Residents around Chadds Ford, Pennsylvania, who fought the "Second Battle of the Brandywine" in 1967 to beat off industrial projects there, have founded the Tri-County Conservancy of the Brandywine to foster good care of the environment, its historic values and its artistic heritage. Of growing influence among valley residents as well as through the 200,000 visitors to its art museum each year, the conservancy has, with state and county help, developed continuous water quality monitoring stations. It hopes to create a mathematical model that can predict what land uses the waterway can and cannot stand and to develop criteria for managing small rivers which the Brandywine typifies.

The conservancy is working on an ecological restoration program, is helping valley townships develop protective ordinances and comprehensive land use plans, is active also in environmental education, and is registering historic sites and weaving a sense of history into the area planning process. The conservancy advocates the protection of the route following the creek as a scenic roadway, and hopes soon to have been given conservation easements on nearly all of the flood plains between Chadds Ford and Wilmington. The voluntary easement program is moving upstream as well, and may well succeed where the earlier effort failed. Ultimately the Tri-County Conservancy and the Brandywine Valley Association hope that the valley will be a classic example, applicable elsewhere, of good stewardship and appreciation of what a small Eastern waterway can mean in terms of beauty, history, culture, the quality of life.

Word of the Brandywine Valley Association's early work spread to Princeton, New Jersey, where the Princeton Garden Club had been badly scared by William Vogt's *Road to Survival* and Fairfield Osborn's *Our Plundered Planet*. Now the Stony Brook Millstone Watersheds Association cares for these picturesque tributaries of the Raritan which grace semirural New Jersey, draining parts of twenty-six communities and five counties. The entire Raritan Valley is covered by similar nonprofit organizations. The Stony Brook Millstone association works closely with the Princeton Open Space Commission, helps sponsor conservation education in the area, and guides real estate development where water and drainage are suitable. It has helped New Jersey toward a legally sound delineation of flood plains and local communities to write flood plain conservation laws. Through its own wise persuasion, it has held flood plain encroachments on the Millstone watershed to three.

In 1957 New Jersey recommended a $5-million reservoir on Stony Brook to store ten billion gallons of water. An association study revealed it would cost between $10 and $14 million and store only 4.7 billion gallons. New Jersey dropped the plan in favor of a water bond act. Development of a Leisure World for 50,000 people in the watershed would, in dry seasons, have put twice as much sewage effluent into the Millstone as its own dry-season flow. To avoid the dreadful consequences, the association figured out a way for the developers to use the effluent to fertilize their golf course, as well as to recharge ground water supplies by the use of a storm runoff collection system. Donations of open space resulting from association encouragement have created a Land Research Reserve, now used by universities and other institutions for such research projects as pesticide studies and water resource measurement. All in all, the association has created a climate where the various responsible public officials can sit down together to discuss mutual problems. And if any have not done their homework, there are informed citizens to help them out.

Watershed associations have also come to New England. Largest, with close to a thousand members (double that of ten years ago), is the Farmington, founded in 1953 and voice for twenty-seven towns in Massachusetts and Connecticut. The Westfield Watershed Association is of similar age and membership. They have industrial wastes and improperly used flood plains to cope with; are concerned with the placement and operation of dams and the nourishment of a recreation industry. They also fret about open space and encourage land conservation action by the town conservation commissions. In the Westfield watershed only a third of the towns have them, however, and some of those are inactive.

Over in western Massachusetts, the Housatonic River "means nothing to the town fathers," according to one member of the Housatonic Valley Watershed Association, and they think their zoning will suffice. So, with the help of the Berkshire National Resources Council's land conservancy program, the Association is sponsoring a four-mile scenic riverway down from the famed Canoe Meadows beloved by Oliver Wendell Holmes. "You can go from Holmes Run Bridge in Pittsfield to Wood's Pond in Lenox without seeing a man-made structure," a local resident explained, "and we ask ourselves why do we drive so far for a vacation when we could stay right here to enjoy our river."

Watershed Associations and similar inform-advise-encourage organizations of citizens are finding, more and more, that if a stream is to remain an amenity to their area, preservation of its banks is a necessity. Zoning controls can avert hurtful developments but do not keep the green belt which residents like those along the Nashua, only forty miles from megalopolitan Boston, realize will be a prime asset with which to keep life pleasant in their valley.

They are pushing for a river cleanup demonstration area. Well they should. The Nashua, along which more than a quarter of Massachusetts' paper is produced, has become a ghastly mess.

When I saw the river at Fitchburg, it appeared as if some giant from Mars had vomited into the stream. It was turquoise blue, with a pus-yellow crust on top. Once it was a lovely water, and it still is green-banked. The effort to protect its banks before river cleanup attracts development—to have a greenbelt from central Massachusetts to Nashua, New Hampshire—is showing progress. The Nashua Watershed Association will serve the region as a conservation trust. Groton citizens as well as the Groton School have given easements 220 feet back from the river. Lancaster has set up a special town committee to protect the river. The city of Nashua is buying 315 acres with a mile of riverfront under an interest-free loan from the Nashua Foundation.

The little Ipswich, remarkably unspoiled for a waterway practically on the outskirts of greater Boston and a favorite canoeing stream, is also getting help. Riverside lands have been acquired by the state, county, the Essex County Greenbelt Association and the Massachusetts Audubon Society, and a citizens' cleanup has also been begun, involving hundreds of people.

The Connecticut River Watershed Council has set up a Land Conservancy Program, a privately funded revolving fund to buy land in the basin for conservation. The program already has acquired some 1,300 acres, including two islands in the river, and hopes for larger projects that can protect stretches of the Connecticut's banks as well as key natural areas elsewhere. By means of purchasing lands and easements, the Great Meadows Conservation Trust is attempting to preserve the 5,000 acres of open lands right below Hartford that are so strategic for flood control as well as open space. The meadows, in the towns of Weathersfield, Rocky Hill, and Glastonbury, are being actively farmed for the most part and are in responsible private ownership for the present, but flood plain development restrictions alone cannot be counted upon to keep the meadows open if development pressures mount in future years.

It is this recognition that more is needed to protect scenery than mere regulation alone which has brought about the organization of land trusts. Usually related to town boundaries, they are proliferating in New England. There are reportedly thirty-nine in Connecticut alone. In New Hampshire, trusts have been established to protect the Souhegan, Piscataquog, and Nissitissit rivers, and Dartmouth College is sponsoring a community program for land and scenic easement acquisition in towns along the Connecticut River near the college town of Hanover.

Sometimes special-purpose organizations turn into what become the equivalent of watershed organizations and land trusts combined. The Penobscot Paddle and Chowder Society, an outing club which has long enjoyed the Penobscot for recreation, has now dedicated itself to protect the beautiful river from exploitation. There is great pressure on riparian owners to sell or lease development sites, and the Society is convinced that the Penobscot's beauty cannot long survive without permanent reservation of a scenic corridor embracing it.

The Paddle and Chowder Society has taken its cue from the Natural Resources Council of Maine, which has proposed a similar scenic corridor for the Kennebec. With the Kennebec's log drives soon to end, the Natural Resources Council of Maine realizes there will be a rush to preempt the riverside for developments—recreational subdivisions, resorts, commercial enterprises. Landowners will be pressured to sell out, and the rural charm of the valley will be lost. Working closely with local governments and state agencies, the Council hopes to obtain easements which can keep the land in agricultural and forest use under present-use taxation but leave the land on local taxing rolls and discourage "excessive" recreation use. Thus the Kennebec can be preserved substantially in its present character. Several large landowners, such as the Central Maine Power Company and Scott Paper Company, are reportedly sympathetic. Clinton B. Townsend, past president of the Council who has made a close personal study of the Kennebec, reports considerable interest in, even enthusiasm for, the concept of "a corridor plan which would be of benefit to *all* of the people, not simply to a few speculators and the lucky people who were able to buy a piece of land sold as if it were a piece of cake while the getting is still good."

The Lehigh River Restoration Association, of Pennsylvania, allied with the Carbon County Federation of Sportsmen, helped to get the Lehigh, privately owned in its entirety by the Lehigh Canal and Coal Company, back into public ownership. Through their efforts part of the old canal was restored, and cleaning up the severe acid mine drainage was begun. The coal industry gone, and with the conviction that outdoor recreation can be a major economic boost to the scenic region, they backed a state proposal for a Lehigh River State Park encompassing the river's wild canyon above Jim Thorpe.

Down at the other end of the Lehigh—at its confluence with the Delaware in Easton—public conservation aided by private philanthropy has also made a significant contribution to environmental quality. More than seven miles of the old Lehigh Canal were acquired by the City of Easton and established as the Hugh B. Moore Parkway, the name honoring the principal donor to the effort, the founder of the Dixie Cup Company. The old canal lands are being developed as a riverside park, a place of quiet beauty and history through what was long the none-too-attractive heart of an industrial town. Other communities have emulated Easton and now thirty out of the forty-six miles of the remaining canal are in public ownership for recreational use.

Whether in support of government programs or enrolled in private organizations, individual citizens are responsible for significant and heart-warming victories in the crusade for a protected environment. The victories are yet small, but they offer hope for larger successes.

To residents of Litchfield, Connecticut, the little Bantam River flowing through their rural, even semi-wild countryside and past a residential part of the village, is something special in their lives. To some it offers a micro-wilderness, a place for children to adventure. To others it is a place to remind a townsman of the country he once knew. Now two-thirds of the property owners along four miles of the Bantam have signed easements to keep strips of land along the river natural. There is to be no tree cutting, no signs, no digging of gravel, no buildings or roads, they have agreed. Yet none thinks he has sacrificed anything; in fact, some feel their property is enhanced. Anticipating that the Bantam would probably be intruded upon and spoiled for them all, they acted to insure its future beauty. "I enjoy the river now," one landowner said, "I hope that future generations will have a chance to do so also."

So felt neighbors of the Westfield River's North Branch. For five miles between Babylon and West Chesterfield it spumes through a narrow valley, delighting fishermen and whitewater canoeing experts. Except for a few mountain tributaries in the White Mountains it is the only true wild river reach left in the Connecticut watershed. Nature Conservancy members, assisted by the State, have now purchased nearly 600 acres along the Westfield, and hope for 120 more to preserve this unique wilderness. The Trustees of Reservations already hold title to the river's most spectacular feature, the West Chesterfield Gorge, a short distance below the wild valley.

The success stories of these small but important acts of preserving our Eastern riverscapes are often tales of patient dedication and down-to-the-wire saves that have filled communities with an exciting realization of accomplishment.

Along the Mianus River in Westchester County, New York, stand groves of ancient hemlock. The little river itself, some twenty-five miles long and one of thirty-two flowing through Connecticut to Long Island Sound, is unpolluted and undisturbed where it traverses a wooded gorge. For six miles, there is neither a habitation nor a crossing, and this only thirty-five miles from Manhattan.

Mr. and Mrs. Anthony Anable made this astonishing and delightful discovery for themselves while out horseback riding one day, soon after they moved from Manhattan to the Stamford,

Connecticut, area. The Anables fell in love with the valley, of course, but they knew that, unprotected, it could not long survive suburbia. They also knew that wishes alone would not save it, so they set out to own it, not personally but in an enduring trust. First, to make sure that theirs was not just aesthetic infatuation which scientific importance could not justify, they invited a group of scientists to evaluate the area. The response was enthusiastic. "We know of no other comparable tract of what appears to be virgin, or at least mature, forest anywhere in southwestern Connecticut or in fact in the entire New York City region," an ecologist told them.

Almost immediately threats gathered like storm clouds above the Mianus Gorge. A water supply reservoir project was going to flood it out. But Mrs. Anable and other friends of the gorge, backed by garden clubs and conservation organizations and armed with knowledge of its scientific worth, persuaded officials to lower the reservoir height and keep the area natural. Then came the real-estate crunch. The owner of the key tract to preserving the gorge, sixty acres along the river containing the old hemlocks, had an offer from developers. He was willing to sell to the conservation group but must know by New Year's Day. It was then Christmas-time. The Anables worked all Christmas week gathering support, typing up a contract, pledging their life insurance to help raise the down payment. They got it just in time.

After that local garden club women went to work in earnest. By June 25, six days before the rest of the $30,000 price had to be raised they were still $7,000 shy. They approached The Nature Conservancy which, drawing in turn upon foundation loans, lent the balance as well as its tax-exempt aegis to the project. Garden Club fund raising later paid off the loan and a growing allegiance to the project has raised further money for land and endowment.

Neighbors have given land as well (including the original seller who later gave ten acres more). Today the Mianus River Gorge Conservation Committee of The Nature Conservancy owns more than one and a half miles of the Mianus Gorge, and this Mianus River Gorge Wildlife Refuge and Botanical Reserve became first in the National Registry of Natural Landmarks.

Convinced that "you mustn't ask for money for something people don't understand," Mrs. Anable, a graduate botanist, has personally led hundreds of field trips through the gorge, finding 7–11-year-olds most responsive—most willing to listen and be inspired.

The Committee wants visitors "who really want to come, really want to find it," as Mrs. Anable puts it, and has marked the gorge with only a small sign. "People are angry at first when they have difficulty finding the gorge," she recalls, "but when we reply, 'You're the kind of visitors we want; you looked until you found,' they smile and their anger fades." The gorge receives about 5,000 visitors in a year. Eagle Scouts and other older boys interested in nature serve as junior wardens, some of them gaining a foundation of interest that has led to later PhDs. Trails have been constructed and a natural history exhibit as well, built with funds from a Garden Club of America award.

Even more important to the Committee than preserving a remnant of the old American East are the reactions of visitors who walk there. Alexander B. Adams, former president of The Nature Conservancy, made that point in an article on the gorge written for *American Forests* Magazine a decade ago. "The boy from the Bronx is noisy walking into the woods; on the return trail he is silent," Adams observed. "The biology class from a neighboring high school sees that the wilderness is more than an illustration in a textbook. The bird-watcher, swinging his glasses upward as he catches the sound of an unrecognized song, feels free of the pressures that have haunted him all week." He continued: "The preservation of the hemlocks at Mianus Gorge is not only a triumph of aesthetics over practicality, of scientific needs over the physical requirements of our civilization; it is also an adventure in human values, in giving people an insight into the world from which they came and the peace that can be found in rediscovering it."

In southern New Hampshire a little river called the Nissitissit rises in Potanipo Pond and flows southeastward for 9.2 miles, crossing the Massachusetts border to join the Nashua River at Pepperell. There would seem to be nothing in particular along the Nissitissit to command your special attention; no virgin forest, no dramatic geology. If you pause on one of the bridges crossing it, you might simply remark on what a pleasant, peaceful, secluded, clean, natural little river it is. You might well wish you had an hour to spare and your fishing rod along, or perhaps your canoe and a picnic lunch. It *invites* you, shyly, perhaps, but unmistakably. And it has invited townspeople round about to keep it the way it is. They know that this little vein of clean clear water with ferny banks and tall pines behind makes life especially delightful in the towns of Brookline and Hollis, New Hampshire, and Pepperell, Massachusetts. They realize, also, that it is only forty miles from Boston.

Once the natural world was encountered in every dimension of living. Today it is a fourth dimension which we can all-too-seldom find and enter. Canoeing down the Nissitissit on an autumn afternoon with Jeffrey Smith, a town selectman of Hollis and treasurer of the Nissitissit Land Trust, I realized as never before what a little river can mean to human enjoyment of the earth.

We found ourselves in another world. Although we sensed the usual traits of the modern-day existence—the sound of cars on a nearby road, a jet trail overhead—they were no longer relevant. Our world was one of maples more brilliant than stained glass; of the south-song of goldfinches in high branches, of limpid moving water with a turtle in the shadows. The scarlet berries of the black alder seemed to glow like coals amid the dark greenery of the river bank. A soft puce hue had supplanted the green coloring in the foliage of the dogwoods, and their berries were ripening from white to blue. Soon we glided into the sunlight of a marshy reach, where royal ferns offered up their autumn spores. The arrowweed blossoms had passed, but the leaves sparkled in the sun. Ducks would soon be circling down for the seeds of the Pondweed. The water wound silently round bends of sedge. The river seemed fuller as we rounded a quiet bend; ahead we saw the cause and mustered our strength of push across one of seven beaver dams we encountered in that brief-long afternoon. Below it, the Nissitissit flowed along banks lined with tall white pine. It was shady-quiet there, and cool. Cinnamon fern, interrupted fern, and sweet pepperbush greened the forest floor. Then sunlight splashed again, where the river broadened and deepened into a splendid swimming hole. Something flashed on its surface; then another, and a third. A dozen in all. I forget the species, but the genus was beer can. A roadway had come to the river's edge and man's usual offering to nature had been made.

At twilight that day, I canoed down a lower section of the Nissitissit. The evening chill had silenced the katydids, the day birds had finished evensong, but the misty river seemed silently expectant of the night drama that would soon rustle along its banks or flit down its darkening surface. The only sound was of an occasional riffle, and soon that was still in what seemed to be an unusually slack and full reach of the stream. I realized that the bases of the tall pines growing beside were now inundated, and the trees would eventually drown.

Before long I found why. Man had consumed what he considered a small part of the Nissitissit. It was just enough for a dam, light green cinderblock walls, and a cottage commanding the stream. Man is master here, it proclaimed; the Nissitissit a slave to his weekend will. And if a thousand trees die, so be it. A river has no right to a life of its own.

The Nissitissit Land Trust hopes to keep at least a part of this small river as natural and free as Jeff Smith and I had seen it earlier that day—free to be enjoyed over and over again in some harmless, refreshing way with flyrod, or binoculars, or canoe.

The trust has come a long way toward doing so. Nearly four miles of the river have so far been secured in town or state ownership or through easements. A large part is owned by the Beaver Brook Association, established there to offer a place where children can learn about that "fourth dimension" of their life.

The Nissitissit is an exceptional stream, but there are many, many Nissitissits throughout the East, some not so clean or pretty, perhaps, but offering in a corridor of micro-wilderness a chance to give megalopolis the slip for an afternoon and exercise that serendipity we call recreation. Thoughtful people have already safeguarded a few like Lisha Kill Preserve in Schenectady County, New York, Ten Mile Creek, near Albany, the Miller Memorial Tract along the Hunt River in Rhode Island, all administered by The Nature Conservancy, and Bartholomew's Cobble on the Housatonic in Massachusetts, owned by the Trustees of Reservations. More than two miles of the Kennebec riverfront at Skowhegan are preserved by the Somerset Woods Trustees and the trustees of adjoining Coburn Park, alleviating disgraceful conditions farther up the gorge.

Stewart Udall has reminded that "Few of us can hope to leave a poem or a work of art to posterity; but, working together, we can yet save meadows, marshes, strips of seashore and stream valleys as a green legacy for the centuries." As our crusading zeal for a better environment spreads to more minds and hearts, we remember Justice Oliver Wendell Holmes's saying that "A river is more than an amenity, it is a treasure." And we ask ourselves and each other, "What are you doing for *your* river?"

Hear the Fishes

Poor Shad! Where is thy redress?
Who hears the fishes when they cry?

—*Henry David Thoreau in*
"A Week on the Concord
and Merrimack Rivers"

E VERY two hours, from dawn to dusk, June through October, Biologist Jim Fletcher inspects the salmon trap in the Whitneyville Dam on the Machias River four miles above Machias, Maine. The day I watched him, a handsome male fish of 6½ pounds was in the trap. Gently, Jim and his young assistant held the salmon with wet gunnysacking, placed a plastic tag in the dorsal fin, and released him above the dam.

It is all part of a program of research, river improvement and stocking through which the Maine Salmon Commission, aided by the Bureau of Sport Fisheries and Wildlife and National Marine Fisheries Service under the Anadromous Fish Restoration Act of 1965, hopes—perhaps vainly but steadfastly nonetheless—that a little of America's once glorious salmon fishery may become a reality again.

Down on the Connecticut River below Hartford, Connecticut, State Biologist Bill Jones rows a zigzag course slowly upstream. Earphones are on his head and complicated electronic equipment in his boat. He is listening to his shad.

The fish, swimming somewhere below in the Connecticut's dirty and, in some places, heated water, transmits a tiny radio signal from a capsule transmitter inserted in its stomach. The signal, which can be heard a half-mile away, is slightly different from similar ones emitted by other transmitting shad, and Bill knows just what course his is taking, and how fast. How the shad, running upriver to spawn, cope with their polluted environment adds to the information with which Connecticut, like other Eastern states, hopes to restore the bounty of that succulent and tussly migrant, which could be the premier sport fish of the urban East.

It is difficult today to conceive of the piscine plenty which early-day Americans found awaiting their nets and hooks. The Delaware River Basin once produced more than twelve million pounds of shad annually. It has been said that during an early-day shad run on the Susquehanna River, a man could cross the water on snowshoes. One sweep of a net could bring in 10,000 fish. Atlantic salmon were once similarly plentiful in New England rivers. America's salmon wealth was noted by the Vikings, who of course knew the fish in European waters, and Adrian Block dined on salmon when he discovered the Connecticut River in 1614. "Shad, bass and salmon more than half support the province," an eighteenth-century Connecticut historian recorded.

"It is hard for Americans who have never seen an Atlantic salmon, either in the market or the river, to realize that once they were as numerous as the salmon are now in Alaskan or Pacific Northwest waters," Anthony Netboy remarks in his recent book on the Atlantic salmon's life and fate in Europe and North America. "Every suitable coastal stream from the Ungava Peninsula to the Housatonic River proliferated with salmon. . . . At times this fish was a drug on the market in some localities in the Colonial era and was used for fertilizer!"

Netboy titles his United States chapter "The American Disaster": "No nation," he writes, "has frittered away its salmon wealth so completely." Dams were the basic cause of the disaster, blocking the salmon and the shad, and alewives as well, from their ancestral spawning grounds. Overfishing with nets and weirs that trapped most of the runs aided the near extirpation. These migratory fish had lived in harmony with wilderness America since glacial times. Now came progress.

A dam built in 1798 at Hadley Falls on the Connecticut blocked that greatest and longest of the New England salmon rivers, up which the silver hordes swam and leaped for more than 300 miles, and the dam cut off the shad from half their spawning area. Dams at Bristol, New Hampshire, and Lawrence, Massachusetts, choked off the Merrimack. Similar obstacles thwarted Maine's salmon and shad runs.

An Indian chief from Maine's Sebago Lake region walked to Boston to protest when, in 1739, the first dam blocked the Presumpscot River that once abounded in salmon, shad, and alewives. The governor ordered a fishway, which did not work, and the Indians, who loved the river, went to war. Today ten dams now block all fish runs and inundate nearly all the Presumpscot riffles that once provided spawning and nursery areas for salmon. Pollution has destroyed all fish habitat in the lower river. The fish runs, like the Indians, are gone.

The Connecticut, where, in the late eighteenth century, several thousand salmon could be taken in a single net haul, was devoid of the beautiful fish within twenty-five years. (Saybrook fishermen who caught a stray salmon a century later did not even know what kind of fish it was!)

A few communities, like Machias, Maine, recognized the danger early and passed laws prohibiting total blockage of the river, but dams proliferated, and burgeoning, arrogant industry ignored the laws and the fish. What fishways were built to provide passage for the migrants were usually improperly constructed and useless. One Massachusetts corporation, faced with a state ordinance requiring a fishway, fought it all the way to the Supreme Court until, beaten at last, the industry graciously built an expensive structure that didn't work.

In Maine, the salmon that somehow surmounted or circum-vented the dams often found their spawning beds choked with sawdust from the lumber mills, or scoured useless by annual log drives. Young salmon—smolt—coming downriver on their first journey to the sea wandered confusedly in the river impound-ments until they died or were eaten by predatory pickerel. Those not loath to dive to underwater outlets faced death in the hydro-electric turbines through which they had to pass. The number of Maine's rivers inhabited by fishable populations of salmon dropped from thirty-five to three. Shad, which once yielded yearly catches of three million pounds, are now seldom seen.

Pollution also has destroyed anadromous fish runs of enormous value. "Pollution (together with numerous dams) in the 120 miles of river from Berlin, New Hampshire, to the river's mouth has virtually destroyed natural environment for all the important fishes," a federal fishery specialist told an Androscoggin River conference recently. "Consequently, no appreciable fishery of any kind is left in the main stem of the Androscoggin downstream from Berlin." A New York assemblyman, protesting that shad runs were curtailed by the lack of water released from headwaters reservoirs, was told by the Delaware River Basin Commission:

Many people have quite naturally associated the death of shad with low flows observed in reaches of the upper river. This is not correct. The shad are not present this year because they cannot survive the pollution barrier in the lower Delaware River in the area between Philadelphia and Chester. . . . The migrating shad are presently bottled up below the pollution's barrier, and we do not expect that many of them will survive this year's upriver migration.

We have carefully investigated all possibilities for a short-range solution to this problem, including physically transporting the fish through the pollution barrier, but conclude that there is no physically feasible short-range answer. Even if the gates on the three New York City dams were opened wide it would not provide sufficient fresh water dilution in the lower river to enable the fish to pass on safely upstream.

The proposed pumped storage electric generation project at Storm King on the Hudson may roil and ruin the main spawning area of the striped bass, which seeks that brackish river reach for the species' major breeding area. The pumped storage plant at Northfield on the Connecticut River may affect the river's current periodically and frustrate migrating shad and salmon oriented to water flow. The nuclear plant at Vernon will, at times of low water, require much of the Connecticut's flow for plant cooling. What of the fish then?

"Still patiently, almost pathetically, with instinct not to be discouraged" (as Thoreau put it) those which still can perpetuate their runs at all revisit their old haunts, and, despite all the problems, there is hope that at least some measure of America's former bounty of anadromous fishes can be restored. If so, the programs will bring an increased knowledge of river environments and of what protection and management they require to be whole again, beautiful with the fish-life they can nurture and sustain.

People as well as shad have been patient. Four hydroelectric power dams on the lower Susquehanna have completely blocked that once-great shad river and, in the words of National Geographic Society writer Ralph Gray, the fish "circled dumbly before the mystery of concrete." The power companies had to pay only $6,500 a year to compensate for not building fishways. Now Pennsylvania has upped the payment to $25,000. The three Susquehanna states have agreed on a fish restoration program and first steps toward a fishway at Conowingo Dam are beginning.

The Connecticut, where attempts to restore salmon date from the 1870s, has been singled out for special effort. The basin states, together with the federal agencies, have launched a cooperative program to bring shad back to their original ultimate range to Bellows Falls, and salmon at least as far up as the White River in

Vermont. A hand-operated fish lift at Holyoke, Massachusetts, began lifting 100 shad a year over the Hadley Falls Dam. Now the lift has increased to 45,000. Thousands still die below the dam, however, and the goal for the lift is a million fish per year.

For salmon in the Connecticut, the days of a commercial catch are gone for all practical purposes. However, the fish are far more valuable as sport trophies than in the market place, being worth probably $200 a piece in revenue to communities where they are caught, and far more in the spiritual benefits to those happy souls who catch them. Salmon are difficult to rear, and there are heavy losses during their early life. Fisheries experts are not sure how successful a run they can recreate in a river where salmon have been gone so long. There are problems, too, of imposing salmon fishing on existing angling activities. But they feel they can fulfill their aims even under existing conditions, and new fishways and abated pollution will help greatly. Experimental stocking is already in progress. Good headwaters habitats are proven, and their goal is a Connecticut salmon run of 40,000. That would produce a 7,000-fish annual catch, which compares favorably with Canadian salmon waters.

Maine, the only state in which residual Atlantic salmon runs still survive, offers the greatest hope for a program to restore a substantial sport fishery for salmon to the Eastern United States. The Saco, the Androscoggin, and the Kennebec have been written off: there are too many dams, too much pollution. Spawning areas have been damaged, and there is danger that trash fish like carp now existing in the lower sections of the rivers would use fishways to invade precious trout waters of the interior. However, in the East Machias, Machias, Narraguagus, Dennys, Pleasant, and Sheepscot, relict salmon runs have continued despite the barrages, and the Penobscot, Maine's premier salmon resource, still provides an occasional fish for anglers at the Bangor Pool.

Some stocking had been carried on as early as the 1870s when the second oldest United States hatchery, Craig Brook near East Orland, was converted from trout to our only federal hatchery devoted principally to Atlantic salmon. In 1948 Maine's Atlantic Sea Run Salmon Commission was created and charged with the restoration of a substantial salmon fishery. Successful stocking and fishway improvements on the Narraguagus and the Machias Rivers proved it was feasible. A fishway on the St. Croix, tributary to the St. John, has opened it to salmon for the first time in a century, and if pollution can be cured, that once-great salmon river may again be famous. Restoration has begun on the Aroostook, another St. John tributary, on the rivers with remnant runs, and the Orland and Kennebunk as well.

In summer now, the kids of Machias, Maine, will likely have, in place of the usual baseball bat or mitt, a salmon rod clutched across the handlebars of their bikes. They may be heading out to fish Munson Pitch or join several distinguished older gentlemen who cast expertly from the rocks below Whitneyville Dam. (There's no generation gap among fishermen.) Down at Cherryfield on the Narraguagus a local sportsmen's club sign politely asks you to fish slowly downstream to make room for the next expectant salmon angler. Like as not you will see him, dressed in his fishing togs, snoozing in his out-of-state car, waiting for his particular magic hour on the stream.

To an angler who measures his sport in how close to the catch limit he comes, there is probably no way of explaining the enchantment of fishing for salmon with the fly. The quest for *Salmo salar*, "King of the Sport Fishes," is as for some piscatorial Holy Grail. Undaunted by time, energy, and, often, expense, infinitely patient and expectant, the angler for Atlantic salmon follows the run seasons northward, through Maine to Canada, each stop a bare chance to do battle with His Silver Majesty. "Great" salmon fishing can mean not a trophy taken but merely the holy salmon seen.

If the Machias River continues to improve and if the river basin is protected as the near-wilderness environment most of it now remains, it may be able to provide a significant wild river experience for both fishermen and canoeists. Some sixty miles in length, it drains a circular chain of five Machias Lakes which offer an unusual opportunity for a wilderness canoeing-fishing journey. The river's West Branch, flowing out of Machias Lake and the Sabao Lakes, adds its water to the main river a third of the way down its course. Water in the upper reaches can be thin, a round trip via the West Branch would be arduous, and one would have to contend with whitewater pitches like Holmes' Falls. There are lumbering operations, of course (dams on some of the lakes help to steady the flow of the salmon river), but the whole region is in a single ownership which, if managed for wilderness as well as timber, could make the Machias an epitome of north woods canoeing adventure, and a recreation asset of high-quality "Down East" in Maine.

The Penobscot has the greatest potential as a salmon water. It is the largest river wholly Maine's and the second largest in New England, gathering in its 350-mile course the waters of 625 lakes and ponds and more than 1,600 streams. And at least in its upper reaches, it is easily Maine's most beautiful river, partaking of the wild majesty of Mount Katahdin and Baxter State Park which its two branches enfold.

The Penobscot's East Branch, flowing out of Grand Lake Matagamon, and roadless for a stretch of nearly thirty miles, leaps and thunders in falls and precipitous pitches as it courses beneath the rampart of Traveler Mountain: Stair Falls, Haskell Rock Pitch, Pond Pitch, they grow in size and violence, until Grand Pitch sends the East Branch plunging down a twenty-foot precipice. Below vicious Hulling Machine Pitch and Bowlin Falls, however, the river quiets to a different wilderness world of deep bends and oxbows, leading one on in an atmosphere of silent mystery, before occasional rapids again break the placid mood.

The West Branch, rising north of Moosehead Lake, courses through rolling northwoods country and connects huge lakes: Seboomook, Chesuncook, Pemadumcook. Between the latter two, however, it brawls like its eastern brother, spuming over ten falls as it flows beneath the huge bulk of Mount Katahdin itself. Below Medway, where the two branches form the main Penobscot, it picks up the first of its beautiful big tributaries, the rapid Matta-wamkeag; then farther downstream at West Enfield, the Pisca-taquis and Passadumkeag come in to swell the river to majestic size on its way between many delightful islands to tidewater at Bangor.

This is the river that added its name, almost like that of a subspecies, to "salmon" on the dinner menus of nineteenth-century America. From 1873 to 1890 the annual commercial catch taken from the lower river averaged nearly 12,000 fish, but it soon dwindled to less than 5,000; then to 1,500. In 1947, the last year of weir fishing, the take was 40 salmon.

Six dams across the Penobscot plus worsening pollution were responsible for the fishery loss. Fortunately the Penobscot dams are low. Not only could a few fish get through but also fishways were feasible. Now all six have such devices, and stocking plus trucking of adult salmon to spawning grounds is slowly building up the salmon population. Had the pulp and paper mills on the Penobscot been located close to one another, they long since would have had to clean up their own pollution. They were, how-ever, spaced far enough apart to allow the river to recover suf-ficiently to serve the next downstream industry. By a citizenry and industry unwilling to recognize waste treatment as an essential of civilized progress, the Penobscot was degraded with a waste load equivalent to the sewage of all the people of Maine, New Hamp-shire, Vermont, and Rhode Island combined. In 1965, the state legislature set Penobscot water quality standards which are suit-able for fish, with a 1975 target date.

With fishways provided, pollution controlled, headwaters spawn-ing areas still in good condition and water flows steadied by formal agreement with dam operators, the Penobscot may be suitable for a significant salmon fishery once again. Fisheries people have their fingers crossed, however. There is no known salmon run in the world where fish have to negotiate multiple fishways, and the Penobscot experiment is being watched worldwide. "Whether we can restore a self-maintaining salmon run in a river which has been devoid of salmon for over a decade is something that must be proven," says biologist Alfred Meister of the Salmon Commission. "We feel that we can, but it is still a hypothetical question." Maine hopes for a salmon run of several thousand, yielding a rod catch, perhaps, of 15 to 25 percent. Most will probably be taken in the lower river, including in the once famed Bangor Pool, rather than in the headwaters, which the fish reach late in the year. Moreover, the West Branch will not be opened to the fish because of its own fine landlocked salmon fishery.

If the Penobscot and other programs are successful, modest though they now must be in view of all that must be cured or overcome, the next generation can sense along our Eastern rivers an inkling of what they were like two short centuries ago. Even the foul Merrimack is slated for a salmon restoration program— presuming its successful cleanup.

It is exciting to imagine traveling along the upper reaches of the Penobscot, the Connecticut, the Housatonic, too, those still beautiful waterways alive with the ten-pound leaping silver of *Salmo salar,* the true salmon, which, unlike his distant Pacific cousin, lives on after spawning to go back to the sea and return again. Imagine, too, the lavender-silver tide of ten million shad teeming the rivers in springtime when the "shad bush" blooms, offering the angler sporty 3–6 pound prizes minutes away from megalopolis. Out of the knowledge and concern gained and fostered by fishery restoration work may come a public caring and love which our Eastern rivers have not received since white men landed on these shores.

A boy who canoed the Connecticut once told me that his most vivid and delighting memory was of the shapes of fish moving, gliding under the water. Their graceful presence gave the river's flow a double life. When fishes cry no more but flourish in our rivers once again, perhaps we shall be encouraged to realize what they can mean in our American life.

Fishing rods used by perceptive people have ever been keys to conservation, and angling, particularly for our fresh-water fish species, has brought Americans close to their rivers and streams in appreciative ways. "Who can catalogue the pleasures which cluster round the angler's pursuit?" wrote Genio C. Scott a century ago in his *Fishing in American Waters.* "It is he who follows the winding of the silver river, and becomes acquainted with its course. He knows the joyous leaps it takes down the bold cascade, and how it bubbles rejoicingly in its career over the rapids. He knows the solitude of its silent depths, and the brilliancy of its shallows. . . . He can salute Nature when she laughs." Fishing has long been extolled as the contemplative man's recreation, and the title of Herbert Hoover's little volume, *Fishing for Fun and to Wash Your Soul,* sums up that extra "why" of angling expressed in beautiful ways by countless angler-writers. Fresh water fishing in a land where it was largely free became our preeminent outdoor pastime.

"Boys may go out," said schoolmasters one magic day in spring.

"Go forth from your countinghouses, your mephitic offices, your workshops," exhorted Scott, "for it is the opening day of the trouting season!" And Americans went out, go out, farmer and urbanite, schoolboy and president, to waterways where they find the pursuit of happiness is very likely to be a successful one. How easy it was to go out and get good fishing in the era one might date as "B.D."—"Before Despoliation." Scott remarks that it would be difficult to find a stream within 100 miles of New York where one could not find trout.

A sorry lot of "trout water" most are today! The old sordid story of pollution and destruction applies. Headwaters were logged off, soils washed away, watersheds lost their capacity to hold water, so that once-steady streams fluctuated too much for fish to thrive. Waters warmed beyond trout tolerance, and warm water species of fish invaded them. Pollution stifled the aquatic life on which trout depend.

We found in the East a paradise of trout waters and promptly began relegating them to history. The results are evident today even in mountainy West Virginia, presumably and in appearance one of our troutiest Eastern states. There are only about half-a-dozen fair-sized streams there where rainbow trout can now exist in the wild and a couple of hundred little native trout brooks. They survive as such only because the hot time of year and the low water period do not quite coincide, and also because they are remote or protected.

Greed and ignorance also took a heavy toll. Fishermen amid the early day plenty caught fish to their heart's delight. Genio Scott speaks of anglers on Pine Creek in Pennsylvania catching 30–50 pounds of trout in a day. Alfred Street, writing of the Adirondacks in 1860, fished for trout in the Cold River (now tepid) and "soon scores of the speckled fellows were flopping in our boats." William Chapman White outlines the Adirondack debacle in his recent *Adirondack Country:* "As trout fishing was practiced the goal was big fish, but that quickly degenerated to fish of any size. One sportsman wrote in 1873 that on an Adirondack trip he had caught one hundred and thirty-five trout for a total weight of nine pounds, and added, 'I return from the woods refreshed in spirit.' He must have had quite a spirit, that he could be refreshed by a mess of fish of average weight less than an ounce, but he was not the only one."

Many of the glorious fishing places were not actually productive habitats. They were merely unfished, and the anglers were skimming the cream either careless or confident of the waters' endless bounty. Many an Eastern trout stream still deemed 'good' can produce only a quarter of the fish poundage of a stream which biologists would praise as trout habitat. When the fishing deteriorated, or else to provide more variety, all kinds of experiments in fish culture were perpetrated on our trout waters. Bass, perch, and other competing fishes were introduced by accident or by design. In some places, of course, they have proved a boon. Some of our rivers were never great trout water anyway. As water quality in other streams slipped irrevocably below trout habitability, the hardy and prolific warm water species which require little management gave the increasing throngs of fishermen continued sport. Today, rivers like the James, Shenandoah, and Potomac, the Susquehanna and the Delaware are among the great bass streams of America. He who has happy fish fights with the mighty and truculent bass may wonder why all the fuss and money is spent on what often is phony trout fishing.

Historically, trout in the East meant *Salvelinus fontinalis,* the Eastern brook trout (actually a char) that is so beautiful, sporty, and delicious and which lives in such beautiful places that the fish has become the most beloved of our Eastern game fish. Now he has had to be reinforced with hardier cousins, the European brown trout and the Western rainbow, which can stand warmer, less-pure waters, and more fishing pressure. But trout, whatever the genus and species, remain the sine qua non for many anglers. This has had some unfortunate results.

In fishing as with so many other things, our American tradition presumes and demands plenty. We expect to catch fish not as a prize or privilege but as a right. When the fishing declines we call for stocking. Had fish-culture been more refined in the past and fishermen more understanding, judicious stocking might have restored many a trout fishery to its optimum carrying capacity. With more and more fishermen, measuring success only in terms of the weight of their fish baskets, optimum carrying capacity was regarded as scientists' hokum, however. What was wanted—demanded—was fish, and if a man caught too few, that was not *his* fault. It was obviously because of a depleted fish population. Put in more, the anglers ordered, the duffers' political voice being as effective as the experts'. Stocking would mean luck for everybody. Simple.

Now stocking can be beneficial in two important ways. If done scientifically on the basis of thorough stream research into how many pounds of fish a given stream and its food supply can support, stocking a heavily fished stream can maintain its proper quota of healthy, acclimated trout. Also, spring stocking when flows are full and cold can, for a month or so, turn damaged or naturally poor streams into recreation assets. Trout are inexpensive, costing about a dollar a pound to rear, and five hundred fish, probably paid for out of fishing license monies, can mean a lot of man hours of recreation and result in economic benefit, too.

Yet opening day now is often touched with pathos as well as happiness, for the anglers who crowd our degraded eastern streams are playing make-believe. Too often we must now pretend that our streams are pure and that the trout we catch are their wild and wily natural denizens. We would rather not remember that the hatchery truck put them in just an hour ago; that there are scores of other fishermen vying with us to harvest their share of the crop which their license fees and other public funds have purchased. We would rather not think, either, that, come June, the stream we wade in our splendid fishing togs will be but a scummy seep wherein only a few hardy suckers or sunfish can survive.

One is loath to be overly critical of this often harmless fraud because the anglers *are* getting out into the fresh air to enjoy the natural world once again. Perhaps it is worth the deception if only to let us jaded urbanites be refreshed under the spell of springtime along a river. Moreover, since many of our waterways are now so poor, an early spring planting of trout, to be caught out before the water dwindles and putrefies, is about the only fishing use we can make of them. Even where the trout waters are good, stocking is needed to bring people, for people bring money, and beautiful yet unhandy places like north-central Pennsylvania, with no local industry to underwrite their economy, are relying more and more on recreation.

Pine Creek, Pennsylvania, source of Genio Scott's fifty pounds of fish a day, is still a noted trout stream thanks to nearly 200,000 fish planted in the watershed each year. My own first glimpse of Pine Creek was the sight of a fisherman backlit by wading through the mists of morning. But the trout I caught later that day amid the wild beauty of the "Grand Canyon of Pennsylvania," had hatchery pallor about his gills. He too was a "city fellow."

I wonder, though, what all this pretending we do nowadays may do to the American psyche. Like actor cowboys in TV westerns, we seem to playact experiences in the out-of-doors that, earlier in our national life, were genuine. Could such delusions be harmful? Stocking often is. Some streams—a good many, I am happy to say—are still excellent natural trout water, capable of sustaining a resident population of trout that reproduce themselves. Such streams have a natural carrying capacity and a natural yield. To overcrowd the capacity or expect too much of the yield is to play havoc with the natural balance of the stream. Yet the angler unable to catch fish there blames not his own lack of luck or skill but the stream, and pressures the Fish Commission for heavier plants of catchable fish. Soon the whole stream balance is awry, just as your house would be if somebody suddenly shoved fifty strangers into your kitchen and bedrooms.

The stream becomes a "put-and-take" proposition, a fish pound. The fish are not given a chance to acclimate and reproduce, even if the water is suitable. Moreover, hatchery-bred stock do not have that hardihood the wild strains have inherited over countless acclimatizing generations. The wild ones may be weakened by hatchery mates. The voracious angler must be served, however, for to him happiness is measured in pounds of fish flesh, not in terms of experiences along a stream or the beauty of a wild fish.

The difficulty of finding solitude, beauty, and trout that are natural inhabitants of their cold clean water increases all the time as more fishermen with more time and better roads march on the waterways. Who has not seen the annual spring newspaper photograph of scores of men standing shoulder-to-shoulder in a single New Jersey stream? "What they don't catch they step on," grumbled a New Jersey angler.

But there is hope to save some natural trout fishing in our Eastern streams; a little of what to fishermen is a true wilderness experience, even though civilization may be close by. State fish commissions are trying, within the limits of their public's demand for fish. A small, struggling but growing angler's group called

Trout Unlimited is helping. Organized first in Michigan and now with fifty chapters, eighteen of them in the East, its purpose is to encourage careful management and protection to preserve and enhance our remaining natural trout fishing opportunities. One of Trout Unlimited's directors, Ben Schley, summed up the idea and the problem in a recent article, "Quest for Quality Fishing":

Despite a rich background of literature and legend and a recognized code of behavior, fishing for trout may soon become a thing of the past unless management philosophies and practices are revised. Sure, there will always be trout fishing—count on the managing agencies to see to that—but there's more than a little bit of difference between trout fishing and just catching trout.

A trout fisherman will tell you that his sport must offer a challenge, a test of his skill, his knowledge, and his equipment under strictly laid-down ground rules against the native cunning and wariness of a wild and beautiful creature in its native environment. He'll tell you that enjoyment of his sport depends upon a measure of solitude and natural beauty and freedom from the frantic competition so common to today's existence. And he will tell you that he wants to fish for trout that behave in a natural manner and look as nature intended them to. He'll say he must have a touch of adventure and suspense in his fishing experience; he doesn't want things too easy.

Why then do we continue to manage many of our prime trout fishery resources in such a way as to seriously damage or destroy them?

Surely, even the most optimistic fishery administrators can't expect our dwindling trout streams to supply unlimited recreational opportunities for a constantly increasing population. Yet today we are still managing some of the world's great trout waters for hordes of fishermen without the slightest regard for many intangibles which may be worth far more than other values currently used to evaluate the economic worth of the sport—catch per hour of effort, cost per pound of fish in the creel, returns from plants of hatchery fish, all measurements directly tied to the catching and killing of fish. Did anyone ever measure the suspense involved in floating a fly over a rising trout, the solitude and beauty of a wild stretch of a mountain stream or the sudden sweet anguish of the too-quick strike and resulting broken tippet, or the wealth of previous fishing memories stored through the years? Don't you think it's time we tried?

We are trying, in fact, at least a little bit. A few of our very finest Eastern trout waters are being managed by state and federal fisheries administrators or by riparian landowners for a sustained yield of indigenous wild fish, and thereby to foster the ideal that fishing is not merely a taking of fish, but a happy sacrament. Other good trout waters, though stocked, are managed in ways respectful of their natural characteristics and capacities. The stocking programs seek only to maintain optimum fish populations without overcrowding and disrupting the stream's system.

Up on Gray's Run, flowing out of Pennsylvania State Forest lands into the West Branch of the Susquehanna, Boy Scouts and sportsmen's club members put in 40,000 hours of work to improve the stream habitat so as better to support a natural trout fishery. Pennsylvania's Spruce Creek, which appears at first glance to be just another run-of-the-mill rural watercourse, is a magnificent trout producer because riparian landowners take care of the watershed and limit fishing pressure. A mile-long privately owned reach of productive Letort Spring Run near Carlisle, Pennsylvania, has thrice produced the state's largest annual brown trout trophy and once yielded a ten-pound four-ounce runner up for national honors. Yet the stream is not stocked. Anglers are permitted to fish if they abide by landowners' regulations, and, according to one owner, "We do what is best for the stream. Instead of hauling in truckloads of trout, we put in truckloads of gravel for spawning beds." A number of states have restricted some prime trout waters to fly fishing only, in order to limit the toll of fish taken. Fly fishing enjoys much wider popularity than in the past, but there are experts with the worm and spinning rod who resent the implication that their form of sport is less skilled or honorable.

State fish and game departments are often accused of responding too rapidly to luckless voters' demands for more stocked trout. On New York's famous Beaverkill, however, the state maintains a no-kill section of the stream as a natural fishery.

New York state has also designated "Trophy Trout" waters where the only fish which can be killed are of trophy size. The West Fork of the Ausable in northern New York is so designated for 2.2 miles. It enjoys a popular acceptance—so much so that, even with the restriction to trophy kills, the fishery depends on put-and-take programs of stocking. Moreover, its attractiveness to anglers has put excessive pressure on other parts of the Ausable, both on the West and East Forks.

The Ausable is one of the most beautiful little rivers in the East. It rises in the High Peaks region of the Adirondacks and splashes down through wild lands and picturesque farmed valleys to Lake Champlain. The mountain views from the narrow valley of its East Fork above Keene are glorious. The West Branch, swelled by the Chubb River, outlet of Lake Placid, is a meadow stream at first, then plunges wildly through Wilmington Notch beneath the shoulder of Whiteface Mountain. Below Wilmington it brawls, wide and bouldery, along a course that is classic fly fishing water. The branches join at Ausable Forks, and the river, just before its mouth, enters Ausable Chasm, a privately owned tourist attraction notable not only for beauty but also for the careful preservation and display of its geological and botanical features.

On more than one listing the Ausable has been called the "Best Trout Stream in the East," and in a 1965 *Field & Stream* article of that title, Arthur Glowka termed it "a stream for everyone."

"For those who want to take their chances in tough water, there are long, fluming rapids for the adventurous. For those who have mastered the art of fine tippets and tiny dry flies there are the raptures of long shimmering riffles and deep quiet pools.

There are plenty of bulging slicks and fast water for streamer and nymph experts. Then there are the miles of slower water suited for bait fishing and spinning," he wrote. The Ausable's water conditions are also superb for trout—cold and stable, with good spawning and nursery streams tributary to it and plenty of cover and food for trout. But "everyone" has made the Ausable a put-and-take proposition, with 125,000 yearling fish stocked each year.

If any river in New York, indeed the East, should be an example of what constitutes the glory of a top quality Eastern American trout stream, it is the Ausable. And as a scenic amenity for New York's most magnificent piece of country, its scenic qualities, like those of the upper Hudson, should be strictly protected. New York fishing easements along much of the West Fork are for access alone and offer no protection to the riverscape. Now subdivisions have arrived, and those inevitable commercial enterprises that distract the gaze and extract the coin once our eyes, having been lifted unto the hills, return to their roadside bases.

The Battenkill has been another name for fishermen to conjure with. Rising in the Green Mountains of Vermont and flowing southwestward to join the Hudson River in New York, it is everything one imagines a trout stream to be: beautiful to look at as it winds through lush meadows and alder thickets under the benign watchfulness of big gentle mountains; beautiful to fish in, too. It is so productive and well balanced that New York has found stocking to be needless, and New York anglers get enough sport to keep them from badgering the Fish Commission into upsetting the ecology with stream-packing plants of hatchery fish. Although anglers' pressure is heavy, the tyros are unable to deplete the Battenkill of its wily brown trout, while the experts who enjoy the catching above the keeping of trout release much of what they catch.

Vermont fisheries people have more difficulty in convincing their limit seekers that stocking may be unwise. The American Museum of Fly Fishing tried to lease some 2½ miles of the Battenkill in order to build natural trout fishing. Oral agreements had been reached when local fishermen took amiss the proposal for a small fishing fee to pay for a fraction of the special management on the theory that Americans do not respect things that are free. The locals had been used to fishing the Battenkill for free, and this, they were convinced, was some type of rich men's scheme. The leasing arrangements collapsed. Nice as it is, the Battenkill is still put-and-take, though state biologists will admit privately that there are already too many small fish for the habitat to support. "Things will have to go downhill a lot farther before anything can be done," one angler remarked sadly. As for preserving the Battenkill's beauty as a community asset, even zoning is anathema. There is nothing to keep trailer parks off its banks, yet local people feel that since they have never had any protection problems before, they need expect none in the future.

The museum has not given up, but has gone elsewhere, and has secured lands along three miles of the Lamoille River in northern Vermont, another fine natural trout stream. Known as the Ten Bends, this protected reach of the Lamoille will become a laboratory for management techniques to maintain maximum quality and health in a naturally fine trout stream.

To ask a fisherman not to keep his catch is going against the grain of human nature. After all, that is the original purpose of fishing. Juliana Berners, earliest of angling writers in England, observed nearly 500 years ago that, "If a man take fish, surely then is there no one merrier in his spirit." But Dame Juliana made no mention of killing the fish, and on the Rapidan River in Virginia one feels merrier when he has caught and then released a wild "brookie" back to its cold clean Rapidan pool. It is as if one has lifted a rare sparkling jewel from its case; then gently replaced it on the velvet.

The upper Rapidan, which flows through Shendandoah National Park and a tract of Virginia State Game Lands, has been designated as a fish-for-fun stream. Barbless hooks only are permitted, and no fish may be killed. All are wild native brook trout save for a few brood rainbows Virginia has placed in one reach to give anglers a chance at a big fish. It is another method of keeping quality fishing under the increasing pressure of recreation seekers, and, despite the fact that it means an empty creel, it is surprisingly popular. Leaving his creel at home, the angler goes forth to enjoy the stream and the day and the sight of one of earth's most beautiful creatures.

I did not believe there was wild fishing left in Virginia to speak of until Ben Schley took me to the Rapidan one spring day —nor that there was a stream so beautiful. Down near Fredericksburg, where it flows into the Rappahannock, it is a good-sized little river, and a good bass fishery, too. Up in the park it is really just a big brook, but one you would like to hear splashing in your dreams. Its watershed protected since the park was established in 1935, the Rapidan seldom varies much in volume or temperature, and in springtime, with the trillium, saxifrage, and wild geraniums spangling the woodlands underfoot, it is the perfect place to celebrate the end of wintertime's imprisonment. Big hemlocks shaded the water course where we fished. A jumble of grey lichened boulders hemmed the rushing stream that plunged white from pool to shady pool. Where the rocks were submerged, the deep green of moss color accentuated the glinting crystal flow. In 1929 a president of the United States came to this small paradise, and built a fishing camp where the Rapidan's Laurel Fork and Mill Fork join. Herbert Hoover built carefully, so as to disturb the environment little, and there brought his family, friends, and official guests to catch a trout and a respite from Affairs. The camp is still there, used by government officials and their families, and we walked in to see it, Ben and I, as do many park visitors. Under the little bridge to the camp Ben spied a trout. "Look," he called, and I hurried up, but the only shimmery thing I could see was that ubiquitous spoor of the American angler, the flip-top from a can.

My treat came later that afternoon from a superb little pool where a trout came to my fly and, still fighting gamely, to my hand. It seemed as if all the life of the falling waters and all the brilliance of the spring woods had combined into the life I briefly held and released. The Western rainbow trout's name speaks for itself; California's golden, too, its radiance indescribable. But to me the wild brook trout of the East is most beautiful of all. Orange fins edged pure white, belly red and gold, azure ringing the crimson spots upon its sides, it is the glory of Eastern American waters. It is a rare sight now, for there are few Rapidans left, and hatchery stock are pale copies indeed of the brook trout of the wilderness.

"I wish there was a resource like this close to every population center, so the people could see a sight like that," mused Ben. "But to have one requires an adequate reproducing trout population, and that in turn requires a quality environment." Poor America cannot afford that, it would seem.

Would you believe that there is such a resource, in fact, three of them, near the largest population center in America? They are on Long Island. "There is not within any settled portion of the United States another piece of territory where the trout streams are comparatively so numerous and productive as they are throughout Long Island," wrote Genio Scott in 1839. "It is scarcely possible to travel a mile in any direction without crossing a trout stream.... The value of the Long Island trout streams to New York City is inestimable, for each one of them is approachable by railroad in a few hours ... they are above price."

They are numerous no more, of course, but three that remain are still as productive as any in the land. Yes, they are above price. Daniel Webster must have thought so when he left his church pew one Sunday in 1827 to cast for and catch the world's record brook trout—fourteen pounds, eight ounces, while minister and congregation cheered. Martin Van Buren witnessed the catch, which was duly entered in the church register and a weathervane made from its outline.

The river, which flows into the Atlantic, was called the Little Connecticut then. Later, and now, it is Carman's, named for Sam Carman who kept a tavern where fishermen lodged, and New

York sportsmen bought it up and made it the Suffolk Club. Another group of well-to-do New Yorkers regularly came to "Lif" Snedecor's Tavern on the nearby Connetquot to catch the lunker trout that lived in the mill pond and the stream or ranged up from tidewater below the dam. They formed the Southside Sportsmen's Club. Eventually they amassed a 3,500-acre fishing and shooting preserve along three miles of the river. A third club acquired the best of the Nissequogue, that flows to Long Island Sound. They called their club the Wyandanch in honor of that famous old Long Island Indian sachem.

These three miracle trout streams seem to appear from nowhere, welling out of the glacial gravels and flowing quietly, gin-clear, over gravelly beds through forests and wetlands, to empty into small ponds and then the sea. Starwort and valisneria wave beneath the cool and constant current, and big dark shapes with white-edged fins materialize from the shadows to feast on aquatic plenty. They float a moment deep in midstream and then are gone. The clubs all had trout-rearing facilities to augment the natural reproduction sufficient to offset the catches, and, in the 1880s, sent as much as 3,000 pounds of surplus trout to market in a year.

The Southside's huge, rambling shingled clubhouse is what many a fisherman or hunter dreams of coming home to after a happy day along the river or in the field. It is classic—redolent with old-shoe comfort, and with the quiet, sometimes whimsical good taste of gentlemen of the old school, whose means and status may be guessed only by the maker's names on the hand-made shotguns and flyrods in the racks, and whose identity is reflected only in small polished brass name-plates on their individual lockers.

In the original tavern room, so wide it must have been an architectural showpiece in its day, stout rocking chairs surround the massive Franklin stove that once graced the John Jacob Astor house in Manhattan. Ancient commodious leather and oak furniture which wives and office decorators must once have banished with a vengeance now invite infinite repose at Southside. Photographs from the eighties, Currier and Ives prints, and sporting pages from the *Daily Graphic* adorn the walls. There are antique bottles behind the bar a draft from which would have made Daniel Webster smack his lips, and the members' lockers nearby hint of more modern elixirs of equal quality. Beyond the wind gauge, the row of fish baskets waiting for the morn; past the locker room with its rod racks and smell of waders hung to dry, is a dining room for gentlemen who knew Delmonico's in its halcyon days. Chafing dishes gleam against the oak paneling and huge coffee cups line shelves above the iron-bound fireplace. An American eagle commands the mantel, while on the dining room table a Tiffany silver trophy, the sides of its sculptured trout inlaid with copper spots, commemorates a live trout exhibit of 1884. In the far end of the building, where clubrooms have a framed-print, country-seat decor that would be a credit to the state of any squire's lady, a special case holds ivory poker chips, each engraved with a leaping trout, with which an evening's sport may be doubly artful.

This venerable club (which some state authorities reputedly regard as a fire trap and want to tear down) should be the Museum of American Angling. It reveals a dimension of our cultural past as interesting and delightful as the many other types of historic buildings we have preserved the better to appreciate our heritage. I make that recommendation advisedly because the Southside Sportsmen's Club is already in public ownership. So is the Wyandanch Club. Both were bought with special bond issue money for open space by a State Conservation Department which knew that otherwise those resources "above price" inevitably would succumb to Long Island development despite the love and wealth of their owner-members. As yet unprepared to take over the management of the properties, the state leased them back to the clubs after purchase, so for the time being they are still private preserves. They are in trust for the future, however. How well that trust will be administered remains to be seen.

The old Suffolk Club on Carman's River, more recently a

private shooting preserve, was also purchased, by Suffolk County, and the 600-acre preserve is operated as a county park. So ingeniously is the fishing managed that all types of anglers have both fun and success without damaging the fishery, which is carefully augmented with just enough stocking to keep it up to a proper, healthy par. In a forty-two-acre lake in the river, the county allows bait fishing for an unlimited number of bluegills and for three trout per day of twelve inches or over. The upper reaches of the impoundment and lower part of the river above it are for both fly and spin fishermen with a three-trout, twelve-inch limit. Above that, it's fly fishing only for three trout eight inches or better, but a good fly fisherman can enjoy catching and returning forty or fifty fish in a day. Access roads and parking are designed so that only three cars will fit each fishing reach, and fishermen can avoid the shoulder-to-shoulder sport encountered along so many other trout waters near cities.

The tale of these three Long Island miracle streams is a happy one to date, but all is not bright. Although some 85 percent of the watersheds are protected in the reserves, there is such greed for land on the island that the remainder, including headwaters areas, may be developed and damaged. Recharge basins are being developed along the island's highways to catch and return water underground, but so many other areas are being sealed over and such heavy demand is being made on Long Island's water table that it may dwindle. Moreover, although the gravels filter out bacteria, they cannot remove the nitrates, phosphates, and detergents that go into the ground with sewage effluent. These can upset the ecologic balance of the streams.

There is strong local interest in environmental protection, however, so perhaps the watersheds will be successfully defended and preserved. If so, then what about the quality recreation now existing so near megalopolis? Can it too be perpetuated, or will it disappear under a mass of picnic tables, camping grounds, and hordes of fishermen? Along the Connetquot, the Nissequogue, and Carman's children can see clean clear water and the graceful shapes, some shadow, some fish, that help to give river gazing its enchantment. Life blooms and hatches in the streams, and on the banks and in the woodlands and wetlands close at hand. There is an opportunity for environmental education such as teachers dream of. And those children, grown, can come back again to cast a fly, catch beauty, and share the sacrament which nature offers so generously but which we so rudely and irreverently spill and spurn.

White Water

*Count that day lost whose low descending sun
Sees no fall leaped, no foaming rapid run.*
—From Henry Van Dyke's "Little Rivers"

AT Hopeville Canyon in West Virginia, the North Fork of the South Branch of the Potomac River has cut 200 feet down through contorted layers of limestone and shale. It is a gaunt wild place, reminiscent of the West, and roaring water is the dominant, the overwhelming sound. So I was quite startled when, wandering there to enjoy a sun-warmed springtime solitude, I heard voices amid the shout of rapids. Half-a-dozen paddlers in kayaks and canoes shot around the bend like a school of bright minnows, embroidering the white water with their sleek red and blue and yellow hulls.

I waved, expecting them to disappear quickly downstream, but they did not. Instead they began to play in the rapids. Entranced. I watched what was, in a way, a boat ballet. After dashing down the heaviest part of a chute, half-buried in spray, the paddlers would turn neatly into an eddy; then glide up with the eddy's reversed current until their bows were fairly pinned down and held by the water plunging over the rocks. Suddenly nosing out, with a downstream brace on their paddles, they would make a steeply banked turn into the torrent and come shooting down once more. Where there was a long pitch of current they would tack up across it, with their craft deflecting the thrust of water so that it ferried them from one side of the stream to the other. They could do this heading up or down, and back and forth they would go, working upriver for another run or else just zigzagging for practice. No tumble of water power seemed to daunt them from turning in its midst, banking on beam ends, to come sailing down the white slope. They were like swallows on the wing, dolphins on high seas, salmon braving cataracts. Then, like seals, they rolled—over on one side and up on the other. It was the survival trick the Eskimos learned ages ago. These boaters were practicing it half in fun, half in training for the time they might upset unexpectedly. Then a roll would obviate the necessity of bailing out, being swept down river, perhaps for a considerable distance with the risk of injury, and with the discomfort and strain of dragging the boat ashore for dumping; in all a wet, cold, exhausting business.

The boats I watched making these maneuvers were not the river running craft I was used to—the long graceful, stately canoe of American tradition with its wannigan or pack-basket amidships and its woodsmen at bow and stern. These were small shiny lozenge-shaped affairs, made of fiberglas and completely decked over, with only a round hole for the paddler's body. The boatmen could roll because they were virtually sealed into their craft. An impervious sleeve, secured by elastic around their waists and the cockpit combings, kept water out. Moreover, they could grip fast to their craft below decks by means of leg braces—straps or protuberances against which they could press their thighs and knees like horsemen and make man and boat into one. All were armored against the water, mailed in wet suits, with life vests that looked like puffy surcoats. Crash helmets gave them a further knightly air. One even had a crest of ribbons.

The kayakers sat in their boats, their legs extended under the fiberglas decking. Powerfully they wielded double blades with a simultaneous push-pull coordination of arms, backs, and shoulders. The canoeists, paddling alone in a craft of kayak size though with a canoe's higher bow and stern, knelt in center cockpit and wielded a single bladed paddle. With their bodies farther above decks than the seated kayakists, they looked like some kind of water centaurs, and their torsos writhed and flexed as they leaned far out or forward to brace and stroke. Though they lacked the kayakists' double-bladed power, they were more agile. They could lean farther out to grab a bladeful of water and spin into an eddy. They almost never changed their grips on the paddles—it lost time and stability—but deftly twisted arms and shoulders to switch from side to side as maneuvers demanded.

This is the sport which may well become, in popularity, the skiing of the late 1970s and 1980s. Each year the number of white-water enthusiasts and spectators at races doubles, and the sport has become an Olympic Games event. Each year there is consequently more interest in the good whitewater reaches of American rivers, more information about them in guidebooks and chamber of commerce literature, and more concern for preserving these resources. Once they turned the wheels of industry; now they power the physical and mental flywheels of human recreation.

To commit a canoe to singing waters is an activity as old as the Indians. It can be as filled with gay daring and abandon as were the voyageurs, as rugged and muscular as were the raftsmen of logging sagas, as calm and philosophical as was Thoreau's immortal week on the Concord and Merrimack rivers. Canoeing can be a Sunday idyll complete with guitar and cooler. Essentially, however, canoeing is journeying into wilderness. Whether that wilderness is the backwoods of Maine or comprises merely the green banks of a suburban stream, it takes us back to enjoy reacquaintance with the natural world. Indeed, there is no outdoor recreation save walking that can bring us in as close touch with that world. As woods and fields, even mountain fastnesses give way to roads and houses, the riverways yet can provide secluded lanes to nature. Often they are, as they always have been, the only routes into deep trackless wilderness where even the hardiest hiker is daunted.

"The way of a canoe is the way of the wilderness and of a freedom almost forgotten," Sigurd Olson has written. "It is an antidote to insecurity, the open door to waterways of ages past, and a way of life with profound and abiding satisfactions. When a man is part of his canoe, he is part of all that canoes have ever known."

Olson also said, "As long as there are young men with the light of adventure in their eyes, and a touch of wildness in their souls, rapids will be run." The zest of white water, the thrill of tugging current, the wild exhilarating ride, testing eye and nerve and reflex, demanding skill with paddle and knowledge of the dynamics of flowing water, these are perhaps the supreme joys of canoeing and among the greatest physical pleasures to be derived from a river's challenge. The fisherman, like the naturalist, knows the life of the river and that life's many moods. The bank walker and river gazer as well know its aesthetic beauties. But the canoeman knows the character of the watery element itself: the surge and power of it, the twists and eddies of its currents. With experience, he can say with Mark Twain that a river becomes a wonderful book. He can read it. He can pick out the V-shaped main channels, where current is deepest and safest, avoid stony shallows, and "holes" into which rapids sometimes plunge. He knows which humps of water are stuffed with rocks and which are mere waves. He knows also what an eddy can do for him—and to him. He has learned the consequences of broaching on a rock or of leaning upstream and letting the rapid paw his upstream gunwale. And since he has capsized, as all whitewater boatmen have many times, he knows that whitewater means not only a ride but also, perhaps, a wrestle to retrieve his craft from tons of swirling pressure.

Throughout its history, and prehistory, whitewater boating, despite its thrills and the dares and disports it encourages, has usually been a serious business. To Indian, voyageur, lumberman, it has been a necessary way of getting through to the trading post with precious furs, through for help or with provisions, down river to beat winter and reach home. To those who had the ability to navigate whitewater, woodsmen and guides mostly, it was a working skill, the object of admiring awe by all who lacked such experience.

The prudent, skillful running of whitewater will always be an honorable tradition of outdoor acitvity wherever river trips are made. Aside from the thrill of the bucking, dodging ride, there is essentially the need to get safely through with a whole craft and whole skin. On a river trip, when the canoe is heavy with gear and provisions, a mishap in rapids can spoil an outing or even precipitate disaster. Consequently, whitewater skills are of utmost importance, as is sound judgment of when to skirt heavy water, or let discretion rule valor and carry around rapids altogether. A wrong decision or a bungled maneuver can result in discomfort, distress, injury, even death. Experienced wilderness voyagers never willingly take chances. They take their pride not in the caliber of rapids run but in dry duffel, an unscathed canoe, an ongoing journey. Despite the flowering of whitewater sport, many experienced canoeists stick to their less maneuverable, more vulnerable open craft, refining skills to the point where they can mince down heavy rapids in a laden canoe without taking in a gill of water. On New Hampshire's Ammonoosuc River one spring I watched a pair of canoes do just that. Battened into their special whitewater steeds, the fleet of decked canoes and kayaks charged into the heaviest waves, which soaked the paddlers despite their armor, yet with equal skill though far less derring-do, the old hands in the open craft also came through and without a drop of water shipped.

When the skills of paddling and maneuvering in rapids are applied in craft especially designed for the purpose, however, whitewater boating becomes delicious sport for its own sake, de-

manding the utmost in alertness and alacrity, instant cool judgment, and galvanic action—all the qualities which an athlete
most prizes and in which he glories. Though the young and strong
excel, of course, the sport is not only for the few with prowess
but, much like skiing, for young or old, large or small, male or
female, all who are willing to learn and practice and enjoy. In a
way it is like skiing sitting down but with one huge difference:
the element under you is not a motionless plane but a churning,
living complex force. And often it is around you and above, as
well as beneath. Whitewater boating is flying in water.

Safety precautions at races are usually elaborate, including life
guards with rescue ropes posted at all difficult places. Notwithstanding that and the fearsome-looking accouterments—the life
vests, crash helmets, flotation arrangements in the craft, tell-tale
patches on their hulls—whitewater boating is reasonably safe and
sane provided one has judgment and training. Indeed, there has
not been a fatality in any formal whitewater event in America so
far. The whitewater fraternity has vowed to keep that record and
has schooled itself sternly in prudence as well as boating skills.
Nothing so affronts a whitewater enthusiast as to be regarded as
an irresponsible daredevil or lumped with fools who go over
waterfalls in barrels. It is well that even the most self-confident
boaters have this attitude, not only for their own sake but for the
reputation of their young, fast-growing sport, because the public
is still ignorant of it and, being ignorant, afraid. Club members,
by and large, know far more about good practices and boating
safety than do the public protectors—the police and fire departments, park and forest rangers, fish and game wardens under whose
purview such activities often fall. They need and want whitewater
education. New England canoeists were filled with consternation
not long ago when some Housatonic River Valley citizens had a
bill introduced in the legislature to ban canoeing on the river.
"Reckless foolishness," they had concluded after pulling out a
good many inexperienced canoeists who had come to grief in

what is not, to those who *are* experienced, a difficult stream. Such hysterical action is like banning skiing in, say, Vermont, because every year there are some injuries on the slopes.

As in all strenuous outdoor activities, there have been many river crackups and drownings of overventuresome fishermen, of showoffs who cared even less than they knew, of untrained kids whose adult leaders allowed them to try to lark through treacherous rapids. The foolish mishaps of others are the crosses the whitewater fraternity has to bear. And so it sets out to teach. At local training sessions, boat club members will pound into you the folly of boating alone on difficult or untried waters. Being sure you are a good swimmer, they will insist that you be adept at a "wet exit": able, when capsized, to pull off your spray skirt from the cockpit combing and drop out into the water. They will insist that your boat have adequate flotation and grab loops at each end and that you learn to maneuver your swamped craft immediately to shore before tumbling down too many rapids. If they ever see you swimming on the downstream side of your boat, you will catch pure living hell, for a water-filled boat, sweeping down stream under tons of pressure can pin you against a rock, perhaps to drown. If you mean to race, you will have to learn to roll, for otherwise a spill puts you out of the running. Club members will, with unending patience, stand by to roll you up, when in scheduled pool, pond, or river practice you flounder upside down under water, completely disoriented. They will show you how to sweep out with your paddle, using it as a lever to bring you up again, with a twitch of hips, to proceed on your way.

They will teach you all kinds of strokes, and that a paddle held out and sculled on the water is the firmest brace you can ask to lean on. You will quickly learn never to lean up-current for it will instantly flip you over, but rather to lean down, way down, bracing on your paddle as your agile craft banks round. You will learn to cross almost straight over the most raging torrent using its own deflected power to push you like a sailboat tacking into the wind. Most of all, they will teach you not to fight the water.

You can't. Instead you learn its nature and let it help you. Then its power becomes your joy.

It is ironic that an aboriginal American boating activity has recently come to flower as a sport by way of Europe. Canoeing was, of course, very popular in the East in the late nineteenth and early twentieth century, and many cities had canoe and boat clubs which indulged in river cruising and perhaps a little discreet rapid-running. Then, diverted by that marvelous new toy the auto, we relegated canoeing largely to boys' camps and resort areas where there are lakes. Imaginative Europeans, however, determined in the 1930s that an adaptation of the Eskimo kayak, constructed so as to fold up and be transportable in a couple of large knapsacks, could provide excellent cruising sport on Europe's fine and plentiful riverways and canals. The fold-boats were not particularly maneuverable, but they were very riverworthy, and in addition to recreational cruising, racing them was formalized as a sport.

The Europeans capitalized upon another American development, fiberglas, and foldboat makers came out with fiberglas craft. Tough and moldable into all manner of hull designs, fiber-glas invited designs emphasizing maneuverability. As a result slalom racing became the supreme test of whitewater skills, and the best practice as well. As in slalom skiing, gates, consisting of two vertically suspended poles, are hung at strategic places in the rapids, and one must pass his boat cleanly between them in a watery form of human croquet raced against the clock. Sometimes you pass through forward, sometimes backward, having had to spin around in the midst of some awesome chute of water. Some gates must be charged upstream. It is exhausting, exacting fun, with never an opportunity to hesitate and think things over. Judgments, reactions, must be instantaneous, precisely executed, right.

The art of slalom course hanging requires a thorough understanding of whitewater. An expert course-hanger can make a babbly brook into a course to frustrate experts, or a raging torrent into a snap race. It all depends on precisely where in the infinite variety of chutes and eddies, rocks and "holes" of plunging current he hangs his gates, and what directions he gives for threading them. The proof is in the running, of course: if no experts can run the course cleanly, it's too difficult; if novices make all the gates faultlessly, it's too easy.

Whitewater racing was imported into the United States in the late 1950s. Americans, familiar with canoes rather than foldboats, at first used the former, with plastic or canvas decking attached. Fiberglas brought about a host of new designs, many derived from European models of Czech or Yugoslavian origin, and hence referred to as basically "Czech" or "Yugo." But America innovated as well as copied. John Berry and Bob Harrigan of Washington, D.C., designed a two-man cruising classic they called the *Berrigan.* Up in Boston, Bart Hauthaway, long-time designer of small boats, became a whitewater convert and successful racer and designed and produces a line of craft that have been adopted for commercial production also by the Old Town Canoe Company. John Urban, also of Boston and author of a whitewater manual, designed another popular craft, and there are scores of others. Every year, as molds are traded for home boat-building in garage or cellar and as designs are duly criticized or admired, new variants come forth designed to be a wee bit faster or more agile than the other guy's.

There are three general design categories for whitewater sport boats. Cruising craft are maneuverable but steady and comfortable, not built for speed but merely for a fun day, though whitewater events usually include cruising class races and often even standard canoes enter and can win. The slalom boats, having a bowed keel, or "rocker," are built for extreme maneuverability, and many can turn 360 degrees with a single paddle stroke. Boats built for downriver or, as it is often called, "wildwater" racing, are designed purely for speed. Thin and almost V-hulled, some are so tippy that only fast forward movement or a braced paddle keeps them from capsizing, and their turning ability is poor. Consequently their use demands long-range judgment of what course to take. There cannot be the quick and drastic course corrections possible in a slalom craft.

Each design category of boats includes both kayaks (referred to as K-1s) and single and double canoes (C-1s and C-2s). The C-2s encourage astounding achievement in partnership, bowman and sternman functioning together—in time without any communication other than an empathy which can be counted upon even in an upset and roll-up.

Because it is a young sport, whitewater boating has an intimate and fraternal spirit still. Even at a major race the faces are familiar, and the greats, near-greats, past greats, coming greats are well known among the participants. And they are young, too. The patriarchs of whitewater boating are scarcely fifty now, and the coming champion may be the teenager you just passed carrying his kayak up the path to the starting line.

Not that there are no grizzled oldsters with cool eyes and still-bulging muscles. Indeed, until recently an octogenarian raced in down-river events in Vermont. But breadwinners and family men find it hard to spare time for the conditioning that racing requires, and they tend to confine their sport to cruising or training youngsters. Nevertheless, many will go out for a couple of easy slalom races each year just to keep skills sharp. There's nothing like competition to restore confidence and put precision into whitewater maneuvers that may save the day (including the picnic basket) on some Sunday outing.

There are plenty of women in whitewater racing. They love the sport, and are very good at it, and compete in special K-1-W races. There are also C-2 races for couples. Often the woman paddles stern, with her partner's brawn employed in the bow to veer the craft to the best course.

Considering all the people involved and the many newcomers each year, the whitewater crowd keeps amazingly good tabs on how experienced the would-be race entrants may be, and many events are open only to experts or advanced intermediate paddlers. I don't suppose the high command of whitewater racing in the American Canoe Association has a computer yet, but it knows who can make the race and who cannot, and the clubs, of course, all help.

As more and more information about whitewater resources is gathered and disseminated through guidebooks, an internationally recognized classification of stream difficulty can be applied to advise boaters. Class I and II rapids are easy, though the latter could well hang up a novice and are termed "medium." Class III is "difficult," requiring maneuvering experience. Though the passages are recognizable (not always easily), there are rocks, eddies, and numerous high irregular waves. Class III is about as much as an open canoe can stand, and spraydecks are needed to avoid the likelihood of shipping water. Class IV and V, with their difficult passages, powerful current, dangerous rocks, and boiling eddies, are for decked boats and expert paddlers only, and require reconnoitering before they are run. Class VI rapids are the nearly impossible and extremely dangerous, the very limits of navigability. The difficulty and danger of rapids vary greatly with water height, of course, and optimum levels for boating must also be known. A pleasant little Class II in fairly low water may turn into the devil's caldron after a rain, though some rocky reaches that are tricky in medium water smooth out with added flow.

The best season for boating, naturally, is early spring, when streams are brimming. Spring runoffs make hundreds of otherwise dinky streams into exciting, challenging whitewater runs. But then it is raw and cold; hands get numb; wet suits are needed; and a dunking is to be dreaded. This is the greatest disadvantage of the sport. A great advantage, on the other hand, is that an eighth of a mile of rapids, even one good pitch, can keep you excitedly busy and happy all afternoon, practicing runs, ferrying, getting good exercise while entering into the joy of running water. Whitewater people have their favorite rivers, of course, and will travel far to run a classic reach. But there are hundreds of good whitewater opportunities handy over much of the East that can give unending pleasure so long as they are free-flowing, clean, and accessible.

One whitewater favorite is right in the middle of Wilmington, Delaware. Brandywine Creek, which once attracted Wilmington's industry, now lures hundreds of contestants and thousands of spectators to the oldest slalom race in America, first run in 1953. This is sponsored by the Buck Ridge Ski Club of Upper Darby, Pennsylvania, now better known for boating activities than for skiing. As I walked down through Brandywine Park to watch the event one warm April noon, a brawny-armed sixteen-year-old kayaker from Pennsylvania was whirling through the last of twenty-two gates in the course, as compatriots cheered him on. Upstream, other spectators were encouraging a canoeist who struggled, inch by inch, upstream against the current to work through one of the earlier gates. Two girls in their canoe tried turning too close to a rock and fetched up on it, flipping over. One scrambled atop the rock while the other rode the canoe down to a pool below. Soon afterward a kayaker capsized. Four times he tried to roll up, each time the crowd groaning in sympathy. Finally he gave up and bailed out to sympathetic applause. There was cause for cheers a few minutes later when a youngster pushed his single canoe up through a vicious chute to inch through a gate; then lunged into a quick ferry across the rapids, slewed around in their teeth, and shot down through another gate. A ten-year-old, clad for the race, stood on the bank looking downcast. "How you doing?" I asked. "I'm wet," he replied with a quick grin. "Thing that bugs me, though, is that I had to miss so many gates. . . . Hey, nice brace!" he called to a friend who had just stood his kayak on edge to turn into the central chute of water.

Another major Eastern city, Richmond, Virginia, will have accessible a very challenging reach of whitewater in its heart with James River Park developed, offering access to the river's fall line rapids, long monopolized by industry. Recently, Virginia canoeists who are trying to keep the proposed Salem Church Dam from flooding out their beloved Rappahannock River established an annual slalom race at Kelly's Ford Rapids near Remington, Virginia, to dramatize how enjoyable a recreation resource the river can be as is. Kelly's Ford Rapids can be tough even in summer, as I once found out to my sorrow in an open canoe, and their caliber for a slalom race matches their scenic charm. The first racing event brought out a wide variety of entrants, from University of Virginia paddlers, all energy and muscle, to housewives who wielded their paddles with as effective aplomb as they would their dust mop or gardening spade.

Washingtonians have several whitewater racing areas nearby. The Seneca Breaks of the Potomac twenty miles above the city offer, in addition to a pleasant cruising area, a slalom course beside of the old C & O Canal towpath that can be made suitable for both beginners and experts. Most of the canoeists in town, plus hundreds of visitors, assemble below Great Falls for the annual Potomac Whitewater Race seven miles downriver through Wet Bottom Chute, Difficult Run Rapids, Yellow Falls, and Stubblefield Falls. Little Falls, just above the District of Columbia boundary, is for experts only. The sharp turns and powerful sucking currents there can make running those rapids a deadly folly for the inexperienced.

At the upstream end of the Potomac watershed, two areas are famed among eastern whitewater people. The annual Petersburg, West Virginia, Whitewater Weekend offers wildwater, cruising, and slalom races on the North Fork of the South Branch, the region of Hopeville Canyon. Over on the North Branch above Cumberland, Maryland, a tributary, the Savage River, flows down a continuously steep gradient of seventy-five feet per mile for nearly five miles, providing one of the wildest wildwater races in the East.

When March sends snowmelt roaring out of the Alleghenies, Pennsylvanians head for races on Stony Creek, south of Johnstown. There spectators brave flying snow to watch a four-mile run that gives winterbound wildwater racers a first chilling test of spring. The Red Moshannon near State College does the same for the many college and high school competitors thereabouts.

Then in April comes one of the largest racing events of the season, on Loyalsock Creek at World's End State Park. Coursing through a deep and beautiful canyon, swirling under a high cliff, then spilling down a dam chute to more rapids below, the Loyalsock offers a long and exciting slalom course, and has been the site of wildwater races too. Where a few rugged individuals perched on the rocks there to watch the first races of the mid-1960s, thousands stand six deep now, with Sullivan County and state park authorities and the Wildwater Boating Club of Central Pennsylvania teamed up to provide hospitality for the occasion.

When spring water levels are too low, Pennsylvanian white-water enthusiasts and their neighbors will turn to perhaps their favorite run: the Youghiogheny River in the Ohio River drainage system. There a two-mile river loop in Ohiopyle State Park brings paddlers back within a quarter mile of their starting point, and water releases from Youghiogheny Reservoir provide good sport all season. Or, they may go to the upper Lehigh, whose spectacular canyon, thirty miles long, is being made into another state park, and where the Francis E. Walter Reservoir provides releases of water for special boating weekends.

Although most whitewater folk are staunch conservationists who prize natural conditions, some are apt to be ambivalent when it comes to dams. It's nice to be able to arrange for an assured flow of water, and thus count upon a perfect whitewater outing even in summer's low-water periods. The dam people—the Corps of Engineers, power companies, and water resources boards—make lots of brownie points with the boating public by graciously acceding to requests for such special releases. Such favors are obviously limited by water supply requirements, however, and as whitewater sportsmen increase, the dam people will not be able to accommodate them all.

The Kayak and Canoe Club of New York has, since 1964,

sponsored an increasingly popular race on Esopus Creek in co-operation with the townspeople of Phoenicia, where a railroad provides access along a fine stretch of rapids. It is scheduled in June, when many other streams have fallen too low for good boating. The Catskill Mountains give the popular trout stream a good flow, and water from Schoharie Reservoir, diverted into the Esopus by tunnel from the other side of the Catskills, is sometimes added if New York is feeling generous with its water supplies.

New Yorkers are proudest of their Upper Hudson, even though its water is generally too low for boating after early June. Throughout May it offers as heavy and challenging rapids as any in the East, however, and at North River a Hudson River Derby includes not only a giant slalom race but an eight-mile wildwater race from North Creek to Riparius. The greatest Hudson thrill of all is too hairy and inaccessible for racing, but is sought out by experienced cruising groups, often supported by rubber rafts. It churns and thunders through ten miles of gorge above North River, accessible only by dirt road to a starting point near the Indian River confluence and by a few trails. Even when water levels are minimal, there are pitches to challenge any canoeman, and when high, the force of mighty water piling into six-foot waves can flatten a seated kayaker back on his deck.

Although cold weather grips their country even longer, New Englanders seem to get out on their rivers as early as anyone. Members of the Ledyard Canoe Club at Dartmouth, where winter is a fact of life for most of the college year, practically break ice on the little Mascoma River, their nearby training area near Hanover, New Hampshire, and they hold races there in mid-April.

The surprisingly wild and beautiful little Salmon River, which flows into the tidewater Connecticut, offers a March race for all grades of paddlers. Snow may still mantle the rocks when the Appalachian Mountain Club holds slalom races on the Farmington River at Tolland State Forest near New Boston, Massachusetts. Heavy rapids at Tariffville Gorge on the lower Farmington offer another racing site popular later in the year.

In another early spring race on the Westfield River not far away, canoeists compete on a course that involves two portages around dams. This, of course, is a race more for open canoes than whitewater craft, and many novices enter it as a lark. Spectators groan for them when, lacking the skill to navigate, they drift helplessly down on a rock, or, wallowing down half-filled with water, their canoe sinks slowly beneath waves. Cheers go up when a couple of lively kids leap out, dump the water, and bash on. The Westfield races now attract so many onlookers that the rural highways are clogged for miles, and a sheriff's posse of mounted troopers is needed to help state police cope with the crowds.

Climax of the spring racing season is on the West River near Jamaica, Vermont, where National Canoe Slalom Championships plus other races have been held since 1958. Plenty of kayaks are also around for regional races, both slalom and downriver, held in conjunction with the canoe slalom. A state park provides camping for the hundreds of contestants and their families, and a riverside trail provides vantage points for race watching.*

Vermont's West River is beautiful, wild-looking, and roars through a green canyon with water the Corps of Engineers' Ball Mountain Dam provides for the racing. At the Dumplings, a clutch of huge boulders around which the water foams and thunders, the boaters must meet the supreme tests of slalom racing. In a race I watched there, the canoes slid backwards through Gate 10 of the course, whirled around in the midst of the raging rapids, and darted obliquely through 11. Disappearing be-

---

* Kayak Championships, slalom and downriver, are held annually on a rotation plan in the East, Rocky Mountain area, and West. The slalom and downriver championships are not held in the same area in the same year, thereby giving each area a championship race two out of every three years. Canoe Championships are now held in the East only, because there is not yet enough competitive canoeing activity in the West. When more activity is developed in the Western areas, the canoe championships will undoubtedly go on a rotation plan.

hind a Dumpling, they turned stern down again and shot backwards through 12. Another reverse in mid-torrent put them in
position to thrust through 13, drop just below 14, and turn to fight
upstream through it. Then they backed into the main channel
again and headed on.

One temporary victim of this watery obstacle course was a
rangey fifteen-year-old, shivering in a waterlogged sweatshirt,
whom I overtook as I walked back down the trail after watching
other racers. "We dumped about halfway down, my brother and
I," he told me, declining the offer of a coat, and I figured him for
a still-green partner to an older paddler. Yet he seemed not in the
least chagrined by the upset. "We're twelfth in the country in
C-2s. We're coming along. My brother's great in lighter water but
he's not quite big enough yet to handle this stuff."

"And how old is your brother?"

"Twelve."

I looked again at the churning river, reviewing my own gaping
inabilities after long canoeing years. "Twelve!" I muttered to
myself. "Godspeed to him and whitewater boating, for that kind
of spirit and training, and for that partnership of brothers."

After the Esopus races, the event in the lower Farmington's
Tariffville Gorge, and one on the lower Delaware, the action
moves north to the Saco and Androscoggin in New Hampshire
and the Kenduskeag and Dead rivers of Maine. Though named
for its slow mid-section, now doubly deadened by being dam-
flooded to form Flagstaff Lake, the wild and beautiful Dead has
in its lower part the longest reach of continuous rapids in New
England—sixteen miles of Class III and IV whitewater, including
a thirty-foot waterfall. Access is long and roundabout, but the
lower section near the confluence with the Kennebec is a popular
whitewatermen's rendezvous. One wonders what the shades of
Benedict Arnold's men, who detoured these rips on their horrible
march to Quebec, may think of laughter in that valley of long-ago
ordeal. Their spirit pulled them through, so no doubt they'll

bless the Dead River country for offering pleasure, now, instead of pain.

The season's advance does not mean that whitewater racing is confined altogether in the north. There is racing on the Kittamagundi Creek in Maryland, on Spring Creek in Pennsylvania, where the Wildwater Boating Club provides a permanent slalom training course for all boaters. There are racing events in late season on the upper Susquehanna in New York, a return to New Hampshire's Androscoggin, and a final go at the White near Hanover.

Not all the racing events are whitewater, however. There are those which, though they involve river navigation and its problems, are tests of straight paddling strength and endurance over long courses—twenty miles or more. Races on the Susquehanna at Tunkhannock have become famous, and a similar event is held on the Shenandoah, as well as on the Androscoggin and the Charles.

The river boating activities I have been discussing are really athletics, of course—formal competitions. The vast majority of the canoeists who are enjoying the rivers of the East, however, are the cruisers: those who go off for a day's outing, a weekend camping trip, or a vacation voyage. They are already legion and continue to grow in number. It would be interesting to poll all the outing organizations and businesses in the East for a fair estimate of such river use, but by the time the statistics were gathered they would be irrelevantly out of date.

The Appalachian Mountain Club and its several chapters now schedule more than 250 canoeing outings, including races and training sessions. There is a rental fleet of close to 300 canoes on the Delaware to supply people who do not bring their own for weekend use, with bookings made long in advance. Estimates of canoeing use of the Delaware have run as high as 25,000 canoe days per year. In the Washington, D.C., area some 2,000 canoes are sold each year and several hundred are for rent. More than 5,000 club and family members go paddling as well as 10,000

Scouts. One part-time but dedicated renter of canoes maintains a fleet of 100. "I could rent out 500 if I did not care about overcrowding our rivers," he commented. "If you make it too easy, you get people who are either unappreciative or unqualified."

Whether it be an expedition down the Allagash or a Sunday afternoon on the local creek, a race or a languid float, the joy of running water is entering into more and more American lives. We are finding that Paul Brooks' words are true: "Quick or smooth, broad as the Hudson or narrow enough to scrape your gunwales, every river is a world of its own, unique in pattern and personality. Each mile on a river will take you further from home than a hundred miles on a road. You will see more in an hour than a motorist will in a week." With this realization will come, I am sure, a deepening love for our Eastern rivers, a keener awareness of what they can mean as amenities in our landscape and as avenues for our recreation. They are our most important parkways—water parkways—the most convenient, the most natural, often the most beautiful. Through enjoyment of them we shall perhaps recognize how important they are, water and banks, as community assets, and will insist that they not be walled off with houses, cluttered with debris, fouled with wastes, or drowned by dams. Aldo Leopold once mused in discouraged vein that "Perhaps our grandsons, having never seen a wild river, will never miss the chance to set a canoe in singing waters." Boatmen, like fishermen, know how precious is a live and winsome waterway. As their whitewater craft proliferate on our waterways, they will not, I trust, let Leopold's words come true, but instead will help preserve and hand on the riverine beauty of America.

Scenic Rivers

A measure of the beauty, the allure, the adventure that is the unique quality of clean-flowing water should be retained in every section of our land.

—*Stewart L. Udall and Orville L. Freeman*
in "Wild Rivers"

IN a century of conservation action to protect scenery and natural wonders, forests, sites of historic and scientific note, and, more recently, sea and lake shores, America forgot about its most popular scenic and recreation resources—its rivers. Great and small, they gleamed throughout the American landscape, offering a pleasant vista, a swimming hole, a fishing excursion. So they were taken for granted, serving when needed, too common for care. Protect them? Why? Rural America treated them gently and, if industry dammed, polluted and scarred some, that was its privilege. After all, industry was progress, industry was king. Industry paid the wages, owned the river banks, and could have the river. Anyway, there were always more.

To a nation entranced with engineering solutions and mastery, moreover, leaving rivers alone for esthetic, recreative or scientific purposes was absurd. Like horses, rivers were most useful when fully harnessed. Optimum development of a river would come when it was transformed into a chain of impoundments. Though there might be arguments of the cost-benefit ratios of dams, few questioned the wisdom of building a dam at all. When they did, it was to save some superlative scenic splendor: California's Hetch Hetchy Valley or Colorado's Echo Park.

But a fight to stop a dam at Bruces Eddy on the Clearwater River in Idaho was different. It was one of the last and largest free-flowing tributaries of the heavily harnessed Columbia watershed, and people loved it just for being what it was: a wild, scenic, clean, cold, trout-filled American river flowing free. During the 1950s and early 1960s conservationists fought an epic battle against the dam but lost. The dam was authorized in 1963 and is under construction. The fight convinced one concerned official, however, that the time had come for a new national policy toward rivers, identifying and protecting some in their natural condition, and thus balancing what had been a one-sided program of river development. The official was in a good position to implement this idea, for he was Stewart Udall, Secretary of the Interior.

As he nursed the idea along, other river plights and proposals reinforced his conviction. Missourians were suggesting National Park System status for their beloved Ozark float-fishing stream, the Current. A dam proposal threatened to flood out Maine's legendary Allagash, its wilderness seclusion was being breached by permanent logging roads, and national or state protection for it was being urged. Missing, Udall realized, was a nationwide program to determine which rivers should be harnessed and developed and which should be left in their natural state so that future generations might know a heritage so significant in the development of America's character. He realized, too, that the climate was right for such a suggestion, what with the nation already earnestly debating a Wilderness Bill and increasingly concerned over environment. Together with Secretary of Agriculture Orville Freeman, whose Forest Service controlled many pristine rivers, Udall in 1963 fielded a Wild River Study Team. It sought out scenic river reaches at least fifty miles in length along clean or cleanable rivers fifty feet or more in width, with no major dams. Although it was a crash study, timeliness made up for the inevitable shortcomings and oversights, and it came up with some 650 rivers which appeared to have unique qualities deserving protection. Seventy-three were recommended for preliminary consideration. The Eastern rivers among them were the Allagash, the Ausable, and the Cacapon, the upper Connecticut and Hudson, the James and the Mullica, the Penobscot and Potomac, the Shenandoah, and the Susquehanna. Later the upper Delaware and Pine Creek were added to the list.

The Wild Rivers Study gave the two cabinet officers the backup they needed to suggest to President Johnson a fresh frontier of conservation action—protection of scenic rivers. And the president, in his State of the Union Message of 1965, declared the time come "to identify and preserve free-flowing stretches of our great scenic rivers before growth and development make the beauty of the unspoiled waterway a memory."

As on any frontier, the going was hard and slow—and it still is. Few people interpreted "wild rivers" (as the concept was first called) as broadly as did Udall. Most thought the term meant wilderness and protested that their rivers were not wild at all. Later the generic term became scenic rivers, and three categories were recognized: wild, which meant wilderness; scenic, which were still largely undeveloped; and recreational, which, though altered and developed, still had significant amenity value.

Then there was the problem of scenic easements, by means of which a national scenic rivers system was to be effectuated.* Scenic rivers were not to be linear parks, totally in public ownership, though some land along them would be needed for access and public use. How much easements would fetter and frustrate the riparian landowners was a big question. Many wondered if a protective strip of riverside land designed for Western streams was too broad for the East.

As Congress mulled over scenic river bills in several sessions,

---

* The Wild and Scenic River Act of 1968 calls for a protective zone of 320 acres per mile, with a maximum of 100 acres per mile acquired in fee. Condemnation is forbidden when half the lands are already publicly owned or in incorporated areas with adequate zoning in force.

the scenic river ideal, like motherhood and the flag, merited praise, but when it came to the nitty-gritty of whose river was to be taken out of the development mart, that was another story. All the bills had two categories of rivers to be treated: "instant" scenic rivers declared so by the law, and a study category of those to be looked at further. This meant a freeze on river development of up to fifteen years, and nobody with plans for a nuclear power plant, a dam, or a subdivision in his hip pocket wanted that. So many a fine waterway disappeared from the scenic river rosters being considered. To oblige conservationists and the Department of the Interior, West Virginia's senators acquiesced to putting the Cacapon and Shenandoah in a bill which passed the Senate. West Virginians in whose opinion a quality environment must never interfere with property rights and laissez-faire howled with rage. In short order they had those two beautiful and threatened rivers knocked out of any further consideration whatever and they now seem doomed to be streets through shacktown.

As it turned out, no Eastern waterways at all were named immediately to the National Wild and Scenic Rivers System. The Congress prudently decided to get the concept established with the least controversy, by sticking to Western and Midwestern rivers which either were already largely in public ownership or for which there was overwhelming support. Named for study, however, were the Upper Delaware, Pine Creek, and the East and West Branches of the Penobscot, all excellent choices much revered for their free-flowing beauty. The Upper Hudson, involved in interstate compact negotiations and other studies and within the Adirondack Park boundary, disappeared from the legislation, though of all Eastern rivers it seemed the most logical first choice. (Governor Rockefeller promptly recommended it for addition to the study list authorized by Congress, the Federal government has since reidentified it as a potential addition to the system* and it

* Potential additions also identified are New York's Beaverkill, Maryland's Pocomoke, and Virginia's Rappahannock. Mentioned again, too, are the Mullica, Cacapon, and Shenandoah.

is likely to head State scenic river protection efforts.) The James was left for Virginia to study. The Susquehanna also disappeared to the angry sorrow of Representative John Saylor, Pennsylvania's tower of conservation strength in Congress and an original sponsor of scenic rivers legislation. There were too many developmental goodies planned for the Susquehanna, and if a congressman wanted a river in his district deleted from the bill, out it came. Some key state officials in Pennsylvania had doubts about the usefulness of easements anyway; it was hard enough protecting state-owned lands, and buying up a substantial part of the Susquehanna seemed out of the question.

If you have seen the Susquehanna, you know what it means to its region. The very name conjures up the romance of the American landscape. Robert Louis Stevenson, seeing it from a train in 1879, wrote that "when I had asked the name of the river from the brakeman, and heard that it was called the Susquehanna, the beauty of the name seemed to be part and parcel of the beauty of the land. As when Adam with divine fitness named the creatures, so this word Susquehanna was at once accepted by the fancy. That was the name, as no other could be, for that shining river and desirable valley."

The Susquehanna's branches flow through scenery so exquisite as to defy any but poetic and artistic expression. From Liverpool to Maryville where the river breaks through the Appalachians and sweeps down, mile-wide, island-studded, toward the gold dome of Pennsylvania's capitol, the Susquehanna has a majesty unrivaled by any river in the East save the tidal Hudson. Not even the railroads and superhighways that line its banks can tarnish the glory of that reach of rolling river except to blanket it with the incessant racket of their traffic. I have read that the Susquehanna is much wider and shallower than it was two centuries ago because of erosive land uses along the way. That may be, but it took a huge bed to carry down the glacial melt of an ice sheet which once loomed across north central Pennsylvania. It excites the imagination to think how mighty the Susquehanna must have been in glacial times. Mighty it is still, though but a bony memory of the Pleistocene.

The West Branch, entrenched in mountains, is remembered by all motorists who travel Bucktail State Park to see the valley in flaming fall. It is a park which does not protect the river, however, and Pennsylvania can only hope that the valley will stay as attractive as it is. Nothing is planned to keep it so.

It is along the North Branch of the Susquehanna, however, from Tioga Point near Athens to above Pittston, that Susquehanna beauty most fully flames. Even as glimpsed from the highway, it is clearly the central scenic feature of the Endless Mountains. Boating upon it, however, is one of the supreme aesthetic experiences to be enjoyed in the East. I could not believe the river was more than "pleasant" until, with George Harter one still bright morning in autumn, I floated down a few of its miles from Wysox to Tunkhannock. Mountains were outlined dimly in autumn's haze, and a boatman drifted silently in the distance. Each hundred yards of river travel subtly changes the composition of mountain and meadow, grove and glen, until, after a few miles, one's mind gains the deep refreshment that is obtained from a leisurely tour of some great gallery of art. Save for an occasional riffle, the water is slow—no challenge to a whitewater boatman, certainly—yet voyaging through such ever-changing beauty offers an equivalent though different exhilaration. No wonder the Susquehanna was thought fit for a queen.

The log village, Asylum, built on its banks in the vain hope that Marie Antoinette might escape to America, was surveyed from a huge natural marker, Standing Stone, stuck by the glaciers in the river's edge like a giant thunderbolt to amaze Indian and settler and Boy Scout alike. Such details along the Susquehanna are as satisfying as are the distant vistas. The layered flagstone cliffs are cracked and fissured by ten thousand years' thawing, and at Wyalusing Rocks they tower 500 feet above their river. Sandstone has been worn by millennia of wind and water into smooth shelves inviting a lunch stop. Fossils are to be found among the riverside cobbles.

On my Susquehanna outing, the bronze oaks and deep green hemlocks along the river escarpments heralded a hunting season that would soon send boatmen sculling silently along in search of ducks. Already the air was chilly, but fishermen were still out on that finest small-mouth bass stream in Pennsylvania. They hoped, too, for muskellunge, first planted in the Susquehanna in 1959 and now caught as large as twenty pounds.

Even through the half-urbanized Wyoming Valley, where the landscape is scarred with the residue of coal mining and the Lackawanna drains in its orange acidity, the Susquehanna remains attractive, its banks still partly open and farmed or forested behind low dikes. A scenic gorge below Nanticoke could make a splendid Susquehanna River State Park despite an existing power plant and railroads. The reach from Tioga Point to Pittston, however, should be high on the national list of protected scenic rivers. Indeed, it could be a national park—not in the sense of our present park system, where the lands are bought up, but rather in the English sense of a region protected through planning restrictions, where property is privately owned and worked and life goes on as usual. Only harmful acts and uses and developments that degrade the environment are forbidden, and where this creates a burden on residents they are reimbursed for the extra work or expense in keeping the area beautiful.

Although planning commissions exist, there is no protection for the beautiful Susquehanna, even though it is the only major water resource for recreation in the entire region, and its principal scenic element. Pennsylvanians well know the assets of the Endless Mountains region and its shining river. It is a "land of promise," a Bradford County Planning Commission brochure exults. "From border to border, its rolling mountains and rich valleys combine into a landscape which is both aesthetic in appearance and bountiful in its provision of valuable open space for the many uses of man," the brochure continues. "One finds view after view, disclosing beautiful wooded mountains, rustic farms and picturesque sweeps and curves of the Susquehanna River. The countryside is impressive, rarely equaled for its fine natural detail. It is a land of historic trails and winding streams, imprinted indelibly in the hearts of residents and visitors alike."

"Approximately thirty-two million people live along the Atlantic Seaboard between Boston and Washington," the brochure notes, "and many existing recreational areas are being filled up. Bradford County—in the land of the Endless Mountains—can help to provide a recreational haven for some of these people in its beautiful, untarnished rural setting."

And all without even zoning to protect this paradise! The Town of Athens cherishes within its museum the relics of Indian and colonial times. But its greatest treasure, Tioga Point, perhaps the most historic focal point along the upper Susquehanna awaits only the decline of agriculture and the extension of a sewer line to be vulnerable to suburban sprawl.

As a water resource, the Susquehanna is Pennsylvania's greatest glory. Its tributary the Juniata has wrought an equal beauty on a smaller scale through farmland and defile. Some call it the most beautiful river in the state. In New York there is comparable charm along the Chenango, the Unadilla, and the upper Susquehanna itself. The Susquehanna Compact offers no land conservation powers to protect the river scene, but perhaps people will heed the recommendations of the Federal-State Susquehanna River Basin Study Coordinating Committee. Its report proposes management of the Susquehanna's finest reaches, the Juniata's also, as "recreational" or "modified recreational" streams, with not more than ten and twenty percent (respectively) of the shorelines developed. The best of the Susquehanna's West Branch is proposed as "scenic"—no more than five percent developed.

If any Eastern river constitutes a stronger, more influential element of regional landscape than the Susquehanna it is New England's Connecticut. In fact, few rivers in the nation offer the opportunity to more people for enjoying a beautiful and whole-some total environment. From its source near the Height of Land that divides it from the St. Lawrence drainage to its long estuary below Hartford, the south-flowing river in its north-beckoning valley forms a great natural parkway, undesignated, unmanaged, unprotected but there. It beckoned the pioneers and it beckons today's recreationists seeking the Green and White Mountains which slope down to it.

Throughout New Hampshire and Vermont, the Connecticut is the central presence in the landscape through which one journeys. Its valley fields are emerald, pricked out with glimpses of a trim farmstead or a white steeple beyond the elms. It holds the eye and imagination even when there are dark, alluring hills on either side and blue peaks thrust up beyond. Farther south, in Massachusetts and Connecticut, the river, though larger, seems less commanding. Its stately reaches are half hidden in broad bottomlands and bustling townscapes it has created and encouraged.

Many sections of the Connecticut commend themselves to particular admiration. There are delightful riffly bends below Wells River. Mount Ascutney looms majestically above the river's course below the roaring, rock sluiceways of Hartland Falls. Green hills tumble about the river at Brattleboro, and the Connecticut's cut through the Holyoke Range in Massachusetts is a renowned scene. But the Upper Connecticut, flowing between Coos County, New Hampshire, and Essex County, Vermont, is most beautiful of all. That is personal opinion, of course, but it is borne out in an elaborate analysis by eminent landscape architects of what makes scenic beauty along the rivers of the East. The Upper Connecticut passes all the tests with few peers. The variety of surrounding landforms, of vistas near and far, is exceptional. When one has passed Monadnock Mountain near Colebrook, the Stratford mountains become the impressive backdrop. Then one glimpses the Percy Peaks, a pair of high granite cones so smooth and symmetrical as to seem unreal, yet having a beauty unique among Eastern mountains. More immediately in view is the green wall of Pilot Range that seems to block the valley. The river edges southward around it, and soon, far up the valley of the tributary Israels River stands the blue grandeur of the Presidential Range.

Upper Connecticut River riffles have been authoritatively called the finest rainbow trout waters east of the Rockies. And the fast water is balanced by long meanders looped around velvet hayfields. There are wide beaches for basking, and fishing holes where big bass lurk and schools of perch widen young eyes with excitement.

Although the Connecticut remains a beautiful, sovereign presence throughout the New England heartland, few monarchs have been so enslaved. Sixteen dams have harnessed all of its falls and rapids except two. Half of the river's length above tides is now slackwater. The dams, all either directly or indirectly used for hydroelectric power generation, so regulate the river that it flows largely at man's command. At Turners Falls no water runs in the river's bed at all except during floods. At other places, when dams shut down to refill reservoirs for power needs, the proud Connecticut shrinks to a trickle, and this most frequently happens on weekends when fishermen and boaters turn thoughts to a river outing.*

As noted earlier, the Connecticut has been grossly polluted, and the riverscape has received last consideration, as usual. Recreation facilities have been fitted in where they least conflict with other developments, and therefore are sure to meet fewest needs. There has been little interest in preserving the waterfront of this great New England community asset, for immediate financial gain has been the only measure for its use.

Fortunately, some New Englanders came to realize the river's plight and its potential. The senators of Connecticut, Massachusetts, New Hampshire, and Vermont sponsored a study bill, enacted by Congress in 1966, to consider preserving the natural

* The state of Connecticut has now enacted a law empowering its Water Resources Commission to regulate minimum water flow in rivers and streams that are stocked with fish by the State.

beauty and historic heritage of the river valley for recreation. "What we do in the next decade will be decisive for the river's future," said Secretary of the Interior Udall, who was directed to make the study.

His comprehensive report, *New England Heritage,* issued in 1968, had something for everybody to do. It proposed a national recreation area of three units, one at the river's mouth, another at Mount Holyoke, and the third protecting the upper Connecticut as a scenic river. Recommendations for state action included Connecticut parks at Windsor Locks and protecting the Glastonbury-Wetherfield-Rocky Hill meadows. Both parks would serve the Hartford region, and the latter would safeguard bottomlands which not only provide precious open space for the Hartford area but which also are worth as much in flood protection as all the existing flood control works on the Connecticut Basin combined. Massachusetts was urged to effect a joint industry–state plan for recreation at Turners Falls, as well as to increase greatly its parklands at Mount Tom. For Vermont and New Hampshire an interstate park around the Moore and Comerford reservoirs was suggested, as well as a much-enlarged New Hampshire park around the Connecticut Lakes. Also recommended to the two states was a Rogers Rangers Historic Riverway, from Comerford Dam down to Charlestown. Commemorating Major Robert Rogers' famous French and Indian War trek to save his successful but starving rangers, the riverway would also protect, through state and local programs, the second most beautiful reach of the Connecticut.

The Connecticut River report had many other suggestions as well: a trail, tourway, and much that local governments and private landowners could do through zoning, easements, and land trusts. Though broad brush in approach (too broad brush, many grumbled), it seemed a superb orchestration of conservation action.

Unlike the Connecticut and Susquehanna, impressive scenic corridors, geographical presences which command admiring attention, the Delaware comes almost as a huge surprise when one glimpses it from the heights above Sparrowbush, or suddenly finds the road dipping down to its lower reaches at New Hope or Washington's Crossing. Only its central section flows through a "great valley" and that may be flooded out.

Yet the Delaware, 200 miles long above Tidewater and flowing around nearly a hundred islands, is the most important river in the East for recreation and scenes of high quality close to some sixteen million people in the very heart of megalopolis.

If I had to choose a single "finest" canoeing stream in the East, I think I would name the Upper Delaware from Hancock to Port Jervis. It may not be the most challenging; in fact with the exception of three or four tricky places, it is easy. But it is lively all the way. Even the pools have life and movement, and there are always the white teeth of rapids gnashing in the distance, growling that they will give you a hassle but then laughing as they send you flying downstream to the next excitement. Augmenting the natural rifts are eel traps, built no doubt upon ancient fish weirs. You must look sharply for the gaps in the barrage through which to shoot down in a shower of spray. Skinners Falls, a rocky two-step rapid below Cochecton, is a particularly beautiful place on the river and a favorite challenge to canoeists, who often linger there for an hour or two, carrying up over the rocks and shooting the rapids over and over again. Others, not so expert, come floating down beside their overturned craft, paddles, picnic and other paraphernalia floating along beside them to be retrieved from the calmer water below. The rapids at Shohola can swamp you with waves, as I learned to my sorrow one chilly fall when the river looked more like a chocolate milkshake than the clear waterway I had learned to enjoy. The narrow chute at the junction of the Mongaup creates waterpower to be reckoned with even in normal levels, and often one must back-ferry around the inside of the chute to avoid engulfing waves.

The Upper Delaware remembers its Catskill Mountains origins: no billowing farmlands here, no broad velvety meadows (though a narrow cornfield may border the river occasionally), no cozy farmsteads and white New England villages. Below Equinault, Barryville, and near Port Jervis, escarpments loom above the river, and all along dark ridges border the valley as if nudging the river to a faster pace. When you are traveling it by canoe, the valley's extensive woodlands, the river's bouldery shores, and the cool water's powerful flow lend the Delaware a north woods air. Once in your canoe you feel transported, somehow, to Maine, though you have driven little more than an hour from Manhattan.

The upper section of this part of the Delaware—that between Hancock and Callicoon—is one of the finest areas for big trout in the East, if you know where to fish for them. Small-mouth bass are the river's most famous game fish, celebrated (as were the Delaware's exciting rapids) in some of the early writings of Zane Grey, whose riverside home near Lackawaxen is now an inn and museum. Walleye are also a prized game fish in the river, and the annual runs of shad as far up as Hancock provide some of the sportiest fishing of all.

There is a serious water fluctuation problem caused by releases from Pepacton and Cannonsville reservoirs on the river's branches. Slugs of cold water let out to meet downstream flow requirements raise hob with the ecology of the river, anglers complain, and riparian landowners have begun to collect on claims for water damage along their shores. Despite this, however, and because of its delights and convenience, the Upper Delaware has become the most popular canoe trip in the East, and this is the stretch named for study in the Wild and Scenic Rivers Act.

It seems to be the Eastern river most likely to receive such protection. Not that the valley is without do-nothing local governments or vociferous opponents to such "taking," who place their private plans above the welfare of the Delaware riverscape. Yet there are also thoughtful residents of influence along the way who realize that the Delaware's destiny as a scenic, recreational river so close to so many users requires the most careful planning, protection, and control. They want the Delaware as is and feel it will be profitable that way, too. Give way to the river, they advise

both industrial and residential interests, and let it adorn its region
with woods and wildlife and dancing water down the generations.

A different Delaware with a far different destiny flows through
its handsome valley from Port Jervis to the Delaware Water Gap.
It is a slower, more stately river there though not without its
pleasant riffles. The long ridge of Kittatinny Mountain rises to
the east in New Jersey, and the hill country there is reminiscent
of New England. On the west the valley is backed by a low
escarpment forming spectacular waterfalls that attract many
tourists. The valley itself, however, resembles that of the Susquehanna, somewhat pastoral as well as wooded in character with the
river a broad silver avenue through the green and gold of its
fields. It is especially beautiful as viewed from the Appalachian
Trail atop Kittatinny Mountain. From there one can compre-
hend as from no other vantage point what the river has wrought
in the landscape and what it means to the environment.

But nearly all of this forty-five-mile reach seems destined to be
turned into a 12,000-acre lake formed by a multipurpose dam
authorized at Tocks Island above the Delaware Water Gap.
Around this lake is to be a 60,000-acre National Recreation Area,
offering quantity outdoor recreation to the millions cooped up in
nearby urbs and slurbs.

To destroy that splendid river for a reservoir seems a pity,
however. The river itself is large enough to provide almost all
the kinds of recreation that water can provide, except sailing, and
the pleasurable lessons in natural history it can provide far surpass
those of a fluctuating reservoir. The rocks along the river's edge,
sliced smooth or wonderfully pocked by erosion, the variegated
stones from ten thousand sources whence ice and water have
fetched them are worth our perception. One afternoon as I canoed
around Wallpack Bend, one of the most beautiful and secluded
sections of the Delaware, I saw a deer standing motionless in the
shallows ahead. Behind me came the roar of a power boat. The
boatman shot past me, sent the deer into frantic flight and, seem-
ingly satisfied by the rout, blasted back upriver again. I could not

help but wonder if this was a symbolic prelude to the "recreation" of the Delaware Water Gap National Recreation Area. Would it serve to enrich the human spirit through intimate contact with the natural world, or would it merely let millions park their trailers and rev their engines; inveigling them to miss or ignore the subtle beauties of the Delaware in their play with powerful sophisticated toys?

I wished that in such a beautiful part of New Jersey and Pennsylvania close to fifteen percent of the United States population there could be a National Recreation Area of hills and woods and streams for roaming and retreat, and with the Delaware left its own natural recreative self to grace the valley. Perhaps there will be, for the validity of the big reservoir idea is being strongly questioned. The National Park Service has acknowledged the worth of a "natural systems" recreation area around the river. It would be ideal for providing opportunities for environmental education.

No matter what its precise purpose and character might be, any grand recreational reservation established on the Delaware will place the rest of the river in jeopardy. Individuals and commercial interests attracted by the recreational development will quickly consume the rest of the riverscape if nothing is done to plan and control its use. As the Bureau of Outdoor Recreation has pointed out in an excellent report on the Delaware River's islands, it will be folly for federal, state, or local governments not to protect the rest of the Delaware.

The recreation area is, of course, named for the single most impressive feature along the entire river, the Water Gap, one of the mid-Atlantic region's great natural spectacles. Below Schellenburger Island and the mouth of Brodhead Creek the river bends left and has cut more than 1,400 feet down through the Appalachian spine. There on Mt. Tammany can be seen the great arching bands of rock of which the heights are constructed. The gap is impressive even from the highways that thread it, but most impressive from the river. Unfortunately sound pollution along

Interstate 80 does much to break the solemnity of that awesome geologic epic.

The seventy-seven miles between the Water Gap and the rips that form the fall line at Trenton and tidewater compose, in one respect, the most surprising and significant part of the Delaware. For it is apparently the least recognized for its tremendous importance as an environmental asset right in the midst of a populous, recreation-starved region. Not that there is absence of recreational use, or of cottages or boats along it. New Hope is the center of a bustling riverside summer resort. Rapids like those at Foul Rift and at the Lambertville wing dams challenge the whitewater boater. The bass and shad provide good fishing, for the water is of fairly good quality despite the dirty Lehigh's contributions. The river banks are generally green and pleasant despite an occasional town, summer colony, or ogrish power plant squatting at water's edge. If any river in the East should be made into a linear park this should be, if only to provide open space. All the surrounding states have mentioned open space needs in this area, and Bucks County, Pennsylvania, has recently augmented parklands along the Delaware. Also, the Delaware Canal on the Pennsylvania side and the Delaware and Raritan Feeder Canal on the New Jersey shore are public recreative properties and help to protect the river's edge for many miles. But much more is needed if this portion of the Delaware, so convenient and attractive, is to adorn in future years the renowned green countryside still sandwiched between New York and Philadelphia.

Of all the major scenic rivers in the East, Virginia's James is most surprising. The fame of its historic tidewater region, and the infamy of its disastrous floods notwithstanding, it is the least remembered as a major scenic element in the bucolic landscape of the Old Dominion. Local folks refer to it in neighborly fashion as Big Jim. Even its stature as a major league small-mouth bass river is little recognized. Few persons outside the valley share in the lore of the James.

Yet, from the Jackson–Cowpasture confluence near Iron Gate

that forms the James to the water gap below Glasgow, this king of
Virginia's rivers flows through some of the finest scenery to be
found along any Eastern waterway. It ranks with the Ausable and
Connecticut, Shenandoah, Penobscot, and Androscoggin. Like the
others, however, its water quality is impaired by paper mill wastes
that turn the James foamy and coffee-black. The river winds
under cliffs, with Rich Patch Mountain looming vast and blue
above it. Beyond the defile at Eagle Rock, its meanders are
incised in forested bluffs, and below Buchanan it laps the base of
the Blue Ridge, passing near Natural Bridge to be joined by the
Maury at Glasgow.

Then begins the longest and most spectacular water gap of any
along the Eastern Seaboard. For fifteen miles the James bores
through the mountains. Near the upper end of the gap the Blue
Ridge's steep forested slopes tower nearly 2,000 feet above the
river, which for four miles rumbles in white rapids down Balcony
Falls. Under the mountains, amid the rapids, it seems a wild and
lonely place despite the nearness of railroad and highway. Lonely
too is the vine-clad weathered monument to Frank Padget, a slave
who in 1854 gave his life in a noble effort to save victims of a
James River freshet. Balcony Falls is the only reach in the gap
where the river is free-flowing now, however. Seven dams, many
dating from the days of the James and Kanahwa Canal and since
converted to power or industrial use, have stilled the James in
pools between Glasgow and Lynchburg. Power lines have added
their scars to the scene. Yet the long pools, secluded and forest-
edged, are not unattractive, and the Blue Ridge grandeur remains.
It is fortunate that it is not yet commercialized, and a wonder that
Virginia and its counties have not done something to recognize
and protect this outstanding scenic and recreational canyon.

It is a wonder, too, that no one has seen what a slight expansion
in the boundary of Jefferson National Forest might do to protect
the upper James. Like the boundary of George Washington National Forest along the Shenandoah, the Jefferson line is the
river for most of the way down the James from Eagle Rock through

the water gap to the vicinity where the Blue Ridge Parkway crosses it. Little land has been bought along the river inside the boundary but there is authority to do so, and if the boundary were extended beyond the far bank, the most beautiful part of the James could be preserved.

Lynchburg has relegated its James to industry and railroads, but below the city the river soon regains its rural character. Onward to Richmond the James is truly the forgotten treasure of Virginia. You scarcely know a river is there until you glimpse its broad ledgy purling course, find the highway suddenly elevated and crossing a broad bottom on its way to a river bridge, or come down to one of the old ferries that will take you across by pole power.

The piedmont James is edged for a while by picturesque bluffs, but below Wingina the country flattens and the river itself becomes the entire scene. When distant views no longer captivate the river traveler's gaze, the river's infinite variety of detail fills that scenic lack almost completely. It offers a world of water patterns curling over boulders, of weirdly metamorphosed rocks, of islands, and of trees. My most vivid memory of the James is of leaning against a maple bole twelve feet in circumference and, as twilight came, watching the water patterns behind a lacework of willow foliage. Kingbirds performed their aerial pirouettes barely an inch above the water surface as they pursued their insect prey, and the first fireflies of evening winked among the high branches overhead.

Between crossings, the James is as solitary as a wilderness waterway. Only the C & O freights rumbling by occasionally behind the screen of trees remind one that civilization is near. Until the weekend brought out some fishermen, the only human beings Kip Dalley and I saw during a three-day June float trip from Bent Creek to Bremo Bluff were a few farmers at work in their fields. Except for the few settlements along the way only three or four houses could be seen. Big Jim just muttered to himself down mile after forgotten mile of green-edged river. Were it not for the rocks, and shallows and rifts that demanded some navigation, I could have been rafting with Huckleberry Finn a century ago. I hope Virginia keeps the James that kind of green aisle to serenity. The piedmont James, though not scenic in the montane sense, can offer memorable outing pleasure, and it ranks, in its own way, with the more spectacular upper section. Agriculture, inconvenience, floods have guarded the James to date, but Virginia will soon have to pay attention to this superb resource. Planning Commissions along the way are beginning to, and the Virginia scenic rivers study of 1969 recommended not only that a segment of the upper James receive scenic river designation but also that the whole river be accorded special attention as a major resource of the Old Dominion.

States as well as the federal government at last are beginning to take action to preserve rivers. Virginia, Maryland, and Massachusetts have taken inventory and passed authorizing legislation. New York and Connecticut are preparing to, but it is late in the game. Studies take a long time, and political action following them up takes even longer. Often it has to be attempted over and over again. Because waterways are such powerful attractions to developers, to industry, to road and dam builders, any scenic protection they are to receive must, at least in the East, come in a hurry. Few can count on more than a very few years, perhaps five or six, to get the job done, and the obstacles to it are depressing. Along the Shenandoah, for example, the Forest Service has been hobbled by Administration fiscal policy from buying land offered for sale within authorized national forest boundaries. Virginia's Commission of Outdoor Recreation thought it had a good chance to make little Dragon Run the Commonwealth's first scenic river. There seemed to be little competition for its undeveloped banks, the lower stretches largely in cypress swamp, and two of the three county governments were at least tacitly in favor of protecting the waterway. But at the last minute some landowners set out ferociously to kill the proposal. State conservationists were shocked and dismayed to see opposition build up overnight to the point where the chances for scenic river status seemed slim indeed.

The situation proved even worse along the beautiful Maury and its upper section, the Calfpasture, just reprieved from a pumped storage hydroelectric scheme. Landowners were rabid in their opposition and were backed by local water and health authorities who wanted dam building opportunities to remain for storage and flushing. Even on Craig Creek, proposed for dammation, the local landowners regard scenic river status as only the lesser of two evils. Virginians do not yet understand the scenic river idea, and, moreover, seem not to trust their state government. All that the Commonwealth can do now is try to maintain the status quo through zoning and donated easements. There is no money to buy rivers.

There may be little power to do it either. After authorizing the Commission to acquire any real property of interest it considers necessary or desirable to protect a scenic river, the Virginia Scenic Rivers Act adds that "the Commission may not exercise the right of eminent domain." Although other state agencies may be able to act instead, it is doubtful that Virginia will be able to preserve any scenic rivers until the day when riparian owners, many of them developers, voluntarily sell or grant easements on their waterfronts.

Nation's River

W E collect experiences as they come; we recollect them as we please. Memory is our library of them, from which we can draw out those we like best for re-enjoyment again and again. Unlike a library, however, where topics are usually separated into volumes, memory permits us to form our own anthologies of experience, combining and recombining them as fancy dictates, either in kaleidoscopic contrast or subtle blend.

My own memories of the Potomac River are such a blend, though my library is comparatively small. I am not a true "river rat," numbers of whom are on the Potomac every weekend, some almost every day. Their mental archives of pleasurable experience must be enormous. I only savor the river occasionally, as one might go to the theater or dine out, but my memories are satisfying all the same. They start in childhood with my first perch brought wriggling over the seawall railing along Washington's East Potomac Park, and they lately include the canoeing gold medal won with no contest when Maurice Sullivan and I, admitting our agedness, found ourselves the only entrants in a senior division race. (Our time was nevertheless respectable, pride hastens to add.)

I like to remember a Sunday morning in springtime at Harpers Ferry, when the Potomac bloomed white—spring beauty and shadbush on the banks, rapids in the stream. A passing freight, rumbling out of the railroad tunnel, moaned a reminiscence of the town's bloody, flood-torn past. But a church bell gainsaid the train's sad call, and sunlight flooded the towering mountainside as we sailed down the rapids and under the bridge, Art Hendrick and I, so happy to be outdoors and a-fishing once again.

I remember many Sunday afternoons in summer at the Seneca Breaks, only twenty miles from Washington. At Pennyfield Lock you can put a canoe in the canal, restored in that section, and paddle the two miles up to Violet's Lock. The lively breaks contrast with the placid canal that skirts the cliffs of Blockhouse Point. (A park at last, it commands a grand view of the river and is a Sunday afternoon destination in its own right.) At Violet's Lock, you can launch in the river and go sailing down the rips to your starting point. They are zestful enough to require a deft paddle, yet not seriously risk the picnic basket prepared for a suitable lunching rock.

It is always a question which of the channels gurgling through the river's island maze you should choose. If you venture over near the Virginia shore, you can canoe down what once was part of George Washington's Potowmack Canal. It seems a wilderness stream now, with huge beeches and chestnut oaks, centuries old, growing on the rocky escarpments above it.

Sunday evenings in summer, I remember, are inviting times to wade the breaks for bass. Usually, however, such recollections are of birds more than fish: the great blue herons; the egrets and the young little blue herons that look like them; ducks wheeling; swallows skimming. Save for the sound of water, it is a silent place. The splash and laughter of humanity comes from above the breaks where the motorboats can play. But from mussel to muskrat to blooming mallow and willow thicket, the breaks have their own full complement of life.

Although some may say that autumn is a sad season, it has always been an exhilarating time to me, especially on the Potomac. The sun was back-warming, but spice was in the air the afternoon I floated down through a mosaic of fallen sycamore leaves along the shore of Terrapin Neck toward the longitudinal ledges known as the Horsebacks. The water was low, and I let the canoe bump against the rocks as I fished the clefts and pools and riffles. Up on the C & O Canal towpath a troop of Boy Scouts laughed by, and I resolved to take a bike ride down it the following weekend. One tends to think of a towpath walk as a spring outing. After all, that is when one longs to get out again; see the returning birds and up-springing flowers. That, too, is when conservationists gather in hundreds to commemorate in an annual one-day hike, the long trek by means of which a devoted group convinced government and press that the canal is far more precious as a place to get away from cars than as the right-of-way for another parkway. This escape route back to nature is equally delightful in the fall, however. Though the black walnuts on the towpath make you or your bike stumble, you hope then that you may find a luscious pawpaw the raccoons and opossums have somehow overlooked.

Autumn more than any other time of year has an old-time feeling about it, when you expect to scent wood smoke and crushed apples, and the historic canal seems an appropriate route to be following. There is nostalgia for an era and a way of life gone by (though the old canal days were rough, bustly, matter-of-fact and often ugly).

Sometimes the canal's beauty broods like the old man I once saw standing on a canal bridge gazing at the weedy bed. He knew the canal and the railroad back when, and still wore his trainman's vest and watch.

"How are you?"

"Not so good."

That's what the huge old canal stones in the locks and aqueducts seem to say, though they were laid with matchless skill and cemented with sweat and sometimes with blood. They were too tough for Jubal Early's Confederate raiders to demolish. But freshets have crumbled many of them down. The government, which has owned them for thirty years, has so far done little to preserve them except to cut the trees and vines that slowly were prying them apart.

The Potomac Valley is ideal for winter walking, too, but my own winter memories are of floating down the river's placid piedmont reaches when the sycamores' stark trunks were matched with icy edgings along the riverbank. I would hope to surprise a mallard or the grand flotilla of Canada geese that used to be there every winter. On one such day, less than twenty miles from the Capitol, my only company on the river was a solitary muskrat trapper.

Best of all I remember a camping trip through the Paw Paw Bends. The moon, still untrodden then, rose full and red, and cast its age-old spell over the two boys, Gordy and Andy, whom we had brought along on our adventure. Sully, my own contemporary and a trained naturalist, told us the why and how of the contorted layered cliffs that loomed above us, named the wildflowers we admired, gathered us poke salad for supper and made our evening fire with his fire bow. The spring bird migration was at its highest, and the woodlands piped with music.

"Hear that redwing calling 'Okaree'?" asked Gordy as we relaxed after a lunch. He knew his bird calls almost as well as Sully, and discussed ornithology eagerly with the naturalist. "I like to lie on my back and look up through the silver maples," Gordy mused, stretched out under a big one. "They're beautiful, and that's the way to watch for warblers." Another three-note bird call sounded, this one silvery-clear. "I wonder if anybody heard that field sparrow," Sully asked musingly. "It's a lonesome song."

But it was beautifully appropriate to that most remote, secluded part of the mainstem Potomac, enfolded by great green mountains. We had seen but one human, a solitary canoeist, during the day, and at evening had tramped an old trail to ask camping permission. The landowner was gracious toward a group who, he realized, appreciated his quiet domain of forty years. "You get where there aren't any houses and you lose yourself in time," he said. That evening, when our beached canoes were mere silhouettes among shadows and our campfire sent its smoke to mingle with the mist, time dropped away, and we could sense the river magic our times try so hard to dispel.

Yes, indeed, the Potomac, like all rivers, is a river of memory and a river of history too. It remembers Michael Cresap's trading post and young George Washington's command at Fort Cumberland, James Rumsey's steamboat, and the soldiers, blue and gray, who crossed the river and bled in it.

Before all that, the Indians knew another history, told in Algonquian. The migrating birds have had their history all along. So have the seeds, floating, blowing down the valley, and so have the rocks, rising, worn, rising, worn. All rivers have such history, some more in certain periods than the Potomac. It has a special history, however, for the Potomac is the river of the capital. Having influenced the location of Washington, the Potomac has ever since watched a flow of national policies and events and, reflecting the marble majesty of Washington the city, the faint shadow of Washington the man, it has become a symbol. Like England's Thames, France's Seine, Rome's Tiber, it has come to mean something special in the American cultural heritage. Consequently it has a national stature disproportionate to its rank as a waterway.

When rivers became a matter of deep concern in America, the Potomac seemed a logical place to begin caring for them. It was logical not only because of the Potomac's location and historic status but also, paradoxically, because, although rich in history and memory and familiar to all who have governed the United States, it had largely been forgotten. George Washington's vision of it as a major corridor of transport and commerce never came true, and after the canal life along it died away, the river was known best to small boys, fishermen and cows, and the trains rumbling by. Cleansing and protecting it seemed, by comparison to other waterways, a relatively simple and noncontroversial matter—a large but attainable goal. To be sure, industry had fouled it in the Appalachian stretch of its North Branch, and Washington had turned its upper estuary into a sewage lagoon. Otherwise, however, it was and is a scenic, recreational river, polluted, but not badly so, and almost entirely forested or farmed. Below Appalachia, industry has intruded only at three places, and subdivisions, though well started, have as yet committed only a small portion of the riverscape to suburban character. Its recreational variety and capacity are enormous. Moreover, it is the scenic centerpiece of a large section of the East, a fast-growing section that happens to be the back yard of the nation's capital.

So if any river in America can be a model of cleanup; of protecting scenic and recreation values; of regional environmental design, it is the Potomac. The resource problems are relatively uncomplicated; the options are open. The federal government already has a stake in the valley along the 184 miles of the C & O Canal, in Washington's parklands, at Harpers Ferry National Historical Park and in extensive national forests. The Potomac is under the very nose of Congress and the Administration, and its status as the national capital river commands nationwide interest.

In view of this, it is astonishing that conservation of the Potomac has been marked by nothing save wrangling and lassitude. The engineers have wanted dams and the conservationists have been dead against that. It took fourteen years for them to get the C & O Canal lands augmented recently as a still-meager national historical park. Meanwhile, pollution has worsened and water and recreation needs have mounted.

But with a conservation breeze stiffening the White House flag, President Johnson in 1965 ordered a once-and-for-all interdepartmental task force to study the total Potomac resource: not only water supply, flood control, pollution abatement, and erosion control but also protection of scenery, and recreational development, including fish and wildlife and historical features. The Potomac Basin states also aided the effort, and set up their own study of a proposed Potomac Basin Compact under which an interstate-federal commission would ultimately manage the river.

Like General Braddock's redcoats, marching up the valley to save the colonies in the French and Indian War, a brave battalion of planners and technicians filed off up the Potomac. Drums rolled, fifes squealed, conservation banners fluttered proudly. Sweethearts from the conservation societies blew kisses and waved their handkerchiefs. Hopes ran high; the Potomac would be saved. But behind every tree up that river lurked political Indians from the forests and Frenchmen from the towns, their quivers full; their muskets charged.

The Department of the Interior, which coordinated the study, ruled out the long-controversial proposal for a big dam on the main stem of the Potomac near Washington, one which would have flooded out some thirty-five miles of valley, including a stretch of the old canal. Instead, the task force compromised on dams on upstream tributaries. Although some were supported locally, this solution disappointed both the Army and District of Columbia engineers who wanted an efficient site near the city, and also conservationists who wanted no dams at all. The erosion and siltation people recommended small headwaters dams and stricter antibulldozer law enforcement to control erosion from the myriad near-city construction projects. But some had to admit that the best efforts probably could only keep the often-brown Potomac from getting siltier. The antipollution experts were more promising and received more support, inasmuch as they were backed by a tide of national concern and strong new clean waters laws. Of course, when federal money was not forthcoming, there were, and are, many mutual recriminations over who is basically responsible for doing the job. Nevertheless, the Potomac is scheduled for cleansing.

For the first time in history a river basin study gave full time and attention to scenic and recreation values. The landscape and recreation planners had opporunity to take inventory of the scenic and historical recreation resources existing in the basin, examine their potential, and design a wide range of proposals for federal, state, and local government action and private initiative as well.

The task force realized especially that if the still largely uncommitted riversides could be preserved as open space, a major principle of regional landscape design might be established. It could, indeed, be an influential national model. With the riverscapes preserved, generation after generation in a region predicted to have nearly ten million inhabitants within forty years could count upon the Potomac drainage for continuing beauty and pleasure. Homes and businesses could be designed around and carefully fitted into such protected resources, and the Potomac Valley would have high quality as a place to live and work. Everyone would benefit, landowners and industrial employees as well as recreation seekers. A pattern for riverscape conservation in America could thus evolve.

The government planners had blue-ribbon concurrence in the idea. As a control study against which to measure the federal effort, Secretary of the Interior Udall, who headed it, had invited the American Institute of Architects to pick a special Potomac Planning Task Force of its own to study the Potomac independently and recommend ideal guidelines for stewardship of the Potomac Basin. This committee of eminent architects, planners, and engineers recommended stream valley protection so far-reaching and comprehensive, so thoroughly influential over the entire Potomac environment, that Udall in publishing their report could only thank and praise them without commitment. He did, however, say that "How—qualitatively—we live tomorrow, will largely be determined by our present ability to convert the insights of this report into inspired realities."

The Potomac Planning Task Force called for a Potomac National Landscape, with all perennial streams of the watershed, their banks back at least 500 feet, and all land viewable from the river within a mile and a half, subject to sufficient controls to keep the water and land clean, useful, accessible, recreational, and handsome. Ecology, the group urged, should be the guide in development decisions.

The government planners could not be as comprehensive, but worked, rather, on specific proposals they considered feasible for local, state, and federal government units to act upon. Nevertheless, the planners came up with a conservation cornucopia of ideas for protecting the basin's amenities so as to design it for handsome growth and pleasant living in harmony with its many natural and historical attractions. They confirmed the importance of two already-proposed scenic rivers, the Shenandoah and Cacapon. Moreover, they identified a major potential national forest recreation area, around the Shenandoah River forks, within an hour and a half's drive of Washington, and a 50,000-acre potential primitive area, embracing the Cacapon River, within two hours of the city. They pointed out opportunities for a dozen exceptional state and regional parks and wildlife areas, mapped 2,000 miles of Potomac Basin trails including a 500-mile-long Potomac Heritage Trail up the valley. They focused attention on a thousand miles of proposed parkways that could help tie the region's attractions together into a meaningful travel pattern; tried to encourage interest in giving special protection to historic townscapes and landscapes; and gave guidance on how private enterprise could seek assistance in conservation and recreational planning.

The principal suggestion was to protect the mainstem Potomac from the Appalachians to tidewater in a green sheath of parkland. It would be, in effect, a king-size stream valley park, serving the fast-urbanizing region as Rock Creek Park served the City of Washington in protecting a central lifeline of beautiful green breathing space the people could count upon for outdoor pleasure. As a central element of environmental design, it would enhance the quality of life and development in the whole basin.

The proposal was first called Potomac Valley Park, but it was really more a recreation area than a preserve, spacious enough ultimately to sustain a predicted thirty million visits a year by recreationists of varied interests. Rather than insisting upon absolute protection of all wildlife, as in parks, hunting would be one of the recreational pursuits, dear to the hearts of Maryland and West Virginia sportsmen. Yet an important parklike purpose was scenic and historic preservation, especially of the C & O Canal, which would be an integral part of the reservation. So it came to be called, simply and evocatively, Potomac National River. It was to be a model, a demonstration area, a prototype of what riverscape protection could mean to a big valley and its people.

As finally perfected, the proposal was to include nearly 70,000 acres of land in Maryland, Virginia and West Virginia, and would reach from Washington, D.C., 195 miles to Cumberland, Maryland, mountain terminus of the old canal. More than 10,000 acres were already publicly owned, largely in the C & O Canal National Monument and in state and local reservations. An additional 41,000 acres would be purchased along the river's edge to keep it green and accessible, and in big recreational nodes of land consisting of some of the river bends and other areas of exceptional recreational usefulness. The balance of the national river would be protected by means of easements, and other controls short of public ownership. State and local governments were invited to acquire and administer any parts of the national river they wished to have, making the project a cooperative one. And if adequate zoning were enforced, that method of control was suggested as a alternative to some of the purchasing in places where public use was not of paramount importance.

Averaging about 600 feet in width on each side of the river the national river would require about 175 acres per mile, along each river bank—forty percent more than the 125 acres per mile normally needed for a parkway. The green sheath of national river lands would, however, be narrow where scenic protection needs were minimum; wide where recreational opportunities and scenic values were great. The easement idea gave room for residential and even industrial development within the national river, under scenic controls. Indeed, one of its purposes was to demonstrate how residential, commercial, and industrial development in a river valley can proceed in harmony with the processes and amenities of nature, perpetuating them for continuing enjoyment rather than consuming them to satisfy short-term demands or for short-term profit. Every national river recreation site, every building, road, sign, as well as every private development, would, it was hoped, be a good, influential example of how modern America can innovate and grow in pleasing, successful harmony with nature and in appreciation of an historic past.

Already served by major highways and by railroads, the national river was eventually to have fifty-seven major development centers along the river, some as large as several square miles, for camping and day use, and to preserve natural areas and historic sites. Developments would ultimately also include 375 miles of trails and nearly 200 miles of bridle paths, some 300 individual campsites for hikers, towpath cyclists, canoeists, and fishermen. There would be nearly fifty centers for group camping, and these could serve as environmental education facilities, an important purpose of the proposal, as well as for school, church, and other group outings.

The quality and variety of recreational opportunities which the national river could afford were far more impressive than the quantity. The Potomac seemed capable of offering almost the entire spectrum of outdoor activities. In the Paw Paw Bends area, backed by Maryland's Green Ridge State Forest, a near-wilderness environment could be enjoyed. This was also true, astonishingly, close to Washington both above and below Great Falls, and on many of the river's islands, some of which are very large. On the other hand, there are huge bends and broad bottomlands where thousands could come to enjoy outdoor pastimes. Behind the old canal diversion dams, some now converted to run-of-river power generation, are slackwater reaches for boating. Other stretches offer the free-flowing riffles beloved by fishermen and cruising canoeists. The Potomac corridor is a natural hiking way, and the canal towpath has already been designated by the Boy Scouts of America as an historical trail. Though the traditional duck and squirrel hunting along the river marge is somewhat limited, the farm and woodlands nearby have considerable potential as upland game habitat.

And for the more passive but deeply satisfying types of recreation derived from studies of nature and history, the Potomac Valley is a treasure trove. Its archeology has scarcely been mapped, but, withal, sixteen out of the twenty-two themes into which the National Park Service divides American history and prehistory can be interpreted along the river. The premier historical feature, of course, is the C & O Canal, and restoration of its crumbling works was given first priority in plans for national river protection and development.

Almost everywhere, the Potomac riverscape offers aesthetic pleasure to all who behold it. One may marvel at its gaunt grandeur in Mather Gorge below Great Falls or at Harpers Ferry. It gleams through the big trees on Blockhouse Point. It has majesty at Point of Rocks, serenity at Whitings Neck. From the highway overlook near Great Cacapon, West Virginia, and from promontories in the Paw Paw Bends, one can thrill to that special, creative splendor with which rivers baptize the landscape.

The Potomac National River became the first recommendation to emerge from the Interdepartmental Task Force study and be officially adopted by the Administration. And it was perhaps the most complex conservation project the National Park Service had ever faced. Few, if any, have involved such a scope and variety of recreational and educational opportunities, or would be so influential in setting standards of quality in the growth of a region. Few were suggested that would have such diverse and tricky management problems. The proposal involved more than 5,000 separate parcels of land in three states, twelve countries, and five incorporated municipalities, all in a fast growing, changing region. And the land requirements alone would be more expensive than any other park or recreation area proposal ever advanced to that date by an Administration. By the time the real estate appraisers had updated fast-changing land values for the national river, the price tag for land alone was more than $90 million.

The Potomac study, in setting a precedent for riverscape conservation that could have nationwide, even worldwide, influence, had indeed followed Daniel Burnham's famous advice: "Make no little plans. They have no magic to stir men's blood, and probably themselves will not be realized. Make big plans, aim high in hope and work." And the newspapers liked to use the adjective "vast" in describing the Potomac National River proposal. Actually, it was not as large as the already established Ozark National Scenic Riverways and other river, seashore, and lakeshore conservation proposals similarly linear in character. Its cost was startling because of the double standard under which conservation projects have always been judged vis-à-vis other public expenditures. We blithely spend hundreds of millions of dollars on projects which have only a brief life of usefulness, but throw up hands in thrifty dismay when we are invited to spend a far more modest amount to protect a resource of the ages. Twenty miles of the Shenandoah River, for example, could have been preserved for the life of the nation in scenic river status at the price of one and one-half miles of interstate highway. Even for the "grandiose" Potomac National River, the average amount of money now spent on a mile of interstate highway could buy two miles of Potomac riverscape—for good. But many felt America could scarcely afford that kind of extravagance.

Well, big and costly or not, the Potomac National River proposal did stir men's blood. The planners had made a strategic error back in the early stages of the Potomac study, when ideas were jelling. They should have spent a year or two getting acquainted with Potomac Basin folks, with the grassroots, addressing civic meetings and county boards, asking questions, sounding out opinions, trying out ideas. They should have prepared the ground; planted the seeds of conservation ideas, and helped them to grow in native soil. They had not the time, money, or mandate for that field-office, extension-service approach, however. The conservation army of the Potomac was on the march. So they did what they thought was the next best thing: they put all their ideas into a "for-instance," "what-do-you-think-of-this-idea," "try-this-on-for-size" book. It was a great big handsome book, twenty inches long and eighty pages thick full of pretty pictures, green-tinted maps, and broad-brush conceptions, and it scared the bejeesus out of a lot of people.

For few bothered to read the clearly stated disclaimer that this was nothing more than a bunch of ideas thrown out for public study, comment, and improvement; that this was something for the citizenry to chew on as preferable to talking to them in vague generalities about "saving the Potomac." The citizens of the basin, at least a lot of them, took one look at the big book, believed it to be a pat plan of what the government was going to do, and promptly went into orbit.

To the question asked by the report, "What do you think of these ideas and how can they be improved?" the answer was, "We're against them!"

The planners were stunned. Surely in all that cornucopia of conservation opportunities there was something exciting and worthwhile to merit enthusiastic support. Yes, there was one. A major riverside park proposal for Mason Neck on the tidewater Potomac went over successfully as a state-regional-federal project with strong local conservationist support. Bald eagles lived there and were in danger of being driven out by a planned residential community. Other riverside park suggestions, however, were filed with thanks by states with empty treasuries and growling land-owning voters. The public (some of whom, possibly, might even be black) should not be allowed to have prime resources that otherwise could be made into profitable, taxable developments.

By means of loud snarling and congressional coolness, Virginians in the Shenandoah Valley cowed the public relations–sensitive Forest Service sufficiently to dash hopes for a Shenandoah recreation area that could have been that agency's prime showcase for

quality recreation near Washington. West Virginians simply ignored the Cacapon wilderness area. After all, they had just
knocked the Cacapon River out of the scenic rivers law entirely,
so that was that.

Sensing that the main conservation thrust of the Potomac Study
would be along the main stem, however, the West Virginians and
their western Maryland allies thereabouts girded for serious action. Like Committees of Correspondence and Committees of
Safety formed to oppose the redcoats, they organized Land and
Water Protective Associations. Signs nailed to trees announced
meetings to "Hear all about the big Potomac Land Grab." Fire-
brand orators harangued them, alleging that the green tint which,
in the planners' big book, indicated suggested county zoning near
the river actually meant the Feds were going to confiscate large
portions of the counties. Someone even started a rumor that an
entire town might be moved, and many were certain that people
would be peremptorily moved out. After all, back in the 1930s the
government did just that up in what is now Shenandoah National
Park.

What a lot of West Virginians and Marylanders really wanted
was not recreation (they had enough of that for their own use and
who wanted city people up here anyway?). They wanted industry.
Some Marylanders believed that the federally owned C & O
Canal walled Maryland off from its river, cut off access to
river water and so scared off industry. Think what a national
river will do to drive off industrial prosperity, they implied. This
well-perpetuated myth was in part based on the fact that an ex-
plosives plant once moved a planned site across the river at a time
when the C & O Canal route was being considered for a parkway
right-of-way, for such an industry cannot safely locate near routes
of heavy travel. Also, the canal towpath was managed as a trail,
off-limits to motor vehicles, and this ticked off local sportsmen
who used to drive it at their convenience. That the industries
which have located near the canal have gotten their water access
without difficulty, gladly cooperating with the Park Service's land-

scape requirements along the canal; that there is a law guaranteeing such access; and that the canal is for the most part the only
public access to Maryland's river, which otherwise is hedged with
"no trespassing" signs—all were conveniently overlooked. So was
the fact that industry now likes to locate where employees can
find pleasant living, and a recreational Potomac would certainly
be an attraction rather than a deterrent.

In addition to the industrial boosters, there were, of course,
the real estate developers. They blended well into the ranks of the
old-time farmers and the retired refugees from the city who opposed the national river, though sometimes one could detect
the shiny shoes of a speculator sticking out from beneath the hastily
donned overalls.

In any proposal involving large amounts of private land in
thickly settled areas, it is necessary as well as right to employ
every possible means to soften the impact of a public project on
the communities it will affect, blending it as slowly and comfortably into the local way of life as possible so that it becomes a
boon, not a blow. Accordingly, there were provisions in the national river plan for using easements, life tenancies, sell-back and
lease-back arrangements, encouragement of agriculture, and private conservation activities. Commercial enterprises to supply the
needs of visitors were to be left for the benefit of private enterprise both in and adjacent to the national river. There were large
areas within the boundaries where residential and even industrial
development could go forward under scenic controls. To allay
local governments' fears of tax revenue losses, the Park Service
had an economic study made. Its findings were impressive: within
a decade, the national river was predicted to generate nearly $35
million of new income annually for the affected counties, and far
more later. Total annual tax revenue losses of less than half a
million dollars would be offset by an increase in assessed valua-
tion in the counties of nearly a billion dollars. These findings,
however, came too late for publication, and as for the other sugar
coatings to what many upriver folk regarded as a conservation

horse pill, it was still too big to swallow. Potomac Valley people just wanted the status quo. "Mr. Secretary, we don't want you up here," said a woman, wagging her finger under Udall's nose.

The upriver opposition did not mean that there was not also substantial grassroots support for the national river concept. It stirred men's blood positively, as well as negatively, to know that the Potomac might be dedicated to all the ideals of environmental stewardship about which the nation had been talking so earnestly of late. In the Alleghenies at the western extremity of the proposed national river, there was need for recreation to improve the dreary old industrially blighted life and landscape and provide a new economic interest as well. The counties near Washington were experiencing all the horrors of urban sprawl and sopped-up open space, and, unlike their more rural fellows, knew what the government was talking about when it said there was dire need of reserving green space and recreational lands.

But the corps of conservationists that might be expected to swing solidly behind the federal effort was badly split by other battles. One contingent was committed to fighting Potomac dams to the death. "We aren't interested in a Potomac park until the dam matter is killed once and for all," said one of them, titularly a parks man. Conservationists, like most people, have more fun being against something than for something. Another battalion of them was off fighting a parkway proposal in the Allegheny Mountains which ten years hence might, if authorized, run through some prized back country. There were many local issues around Washington and on the Potomac estuary—bridges, pollution, indutsrialization—that drew off other energies.

In addition there were the proponents of a Chesapeake & Ohio Canal National Historical Park who wanted that first. The government had acquired this finest relic of America's canaling era in a deal with the B & O Railroad in 1938, but, after restoring twenty miles of the canal near Washington, did nothing with the rest until the early 1950s, when it was suggested as roadbed for a parkway. To dramatize the value of the old canal as a place to get

away from roads, along a green serene walkway through history, a
doughty group led by Supreme Court Justice William O. Douglas
hiked the 184-mile length of the towpath. They won their point;
the parkway plans were dropped, but that was about all. Despite
annual one-day hikes to promote the canal's value for recreation;
despite bill after bill to add 10,000 more acres to its meager 5,000
and make it a national historical park, the canal property lan-
guished. The Senate obligingly passed legislation twice, but the
concept was difficult to map, even see, and Congress didn't. Besides, as already noted, a popular park along the Potomac might
thwart a big dam being advocated. President Eisenhower tried to
help things along by designating the canal property a national
monument, thereby making it a full-fledged unit of the National
Park System. That angered some Congressmen, however, and it
did nothing to beef up a thread of federal land so thin that in
places it comprised only the canal bed and towpath. There was
no room either to accommodate the public or protect the historic
setting. And there were never more than token funds for maintenance of an historic property that needed millions in restoration work.

It was unfortunate, to say the least, that two worthy conservation proposals so interdependent and complementary should in a
sense have become rivals, a situation aggravated to some extent by
partisan politics. Many proponents of a C & O Canal park felt that
the national river proposal was an impossible dream, a scheme too
grandiose and controversial for success. Although they approved
of it as a concept, they did not want their smaller proposal jeop-
ardized, and they urged a different strategy: first establish the
national historical park in Maryland; then build on that. Some
even favored a bill that would merely change the name from
monument to park, sidestep landowner opposition by adding only
a token 1,000 acres, and hope that the new designation would
wheedle out of Congress a bit more money for the crumbling
relic. Udall loved the old C & O Canal and wanted to do right by
it, but he declined to report favorably on the canal park bills,

frankly admitting his was a tactic to focus attention on the larger issue of the Potomac riverscape, which he felt was far more important. This, of course, irritated the canal park sponsors and proponents and strained relations with some old friends. Some accused Udall of wanting to bury their beloved relic under recreation, even though the Administration gave top priority to canal preservation, for the national river proposal merged the canal administratively with the larger project. A few, egged on perhaps by landowner friends upriver, vowed they would actually fight the river proposal until the canal park was a reality.

Udall knew that preserving the canal alone could not possibly do the job of environmental protection and design for which the Potomac offered such a meaningful opportunity. It would not begin to provide sufficiently for recreation. Furthermore, it was doubtful if the Congress, deluged with conservation proposals, could reasonably be expected to put in more than one lick at protecting the Potomac before development pressures precluded any large open space effort along the river. Udall wanted it to be a good lick that would preserve the riverscape. With the iron of Potomac conservation hot with national interest, it was not the time for halfway measures in creating a great model of scenic and recreational values for the entire country.

Despite the schism among conservationists, the national river proposal went forward with high hopes. And it was the Secretary himself, having pored over maps, thirty feet long, spread out corner-to-corner in his huge office, who indefatigably, devotedly, became its principal apostle. I doubt if any Secretary of the Interior has given so much personal time and interest to a single project. He knew what the national river could mean as a grand design for environmental stewardship and recreative living, and he gave himself to it unstintingly. He knew every aspect of the proposal, not only the philosophy behind it, but the details, too, and rarely did he need to turn to an aide for even the smallest statistic. Virtually unassisted, save for a couple of staff men to carry maps, he would explain the proposal to Congressional delegations, conservationist conclaves, citizens' meetings. Sometimes he was on his feet for hours at a time, patiently explaining, answering questions.

So important did Udall consider the opportunity that he recommended it midway in the Potomac Study, and cracked it out as a final recommendation well before the study report was issued. The President backed it fully, commending it to Congress in 1967 and again in 1968, when he said, "We can achieve a new concept in conservation—greater than a park, more than the preservation of a river—by beginning this year to make the Potomac a living part of our national life." An Administration bill went in, sponsored by Maryland's senators, and it looked as if the legislative process would as usual become the appropriate mill in which to grind out all the differences of opinion in the course of perfecting an acceptable authorizing law.

Chairman Jackson of the Senate and Interior and Insular Affairs Committee, had a chance to put in the measure for President Johnson again in the 91st Congress, reminding it that,

In the original capital city design by Pierre L'Enfant, he recognized the need for the preservation of scenic beauty, and other open spaces as a prerequisite rather than an afterthought of good environmental planning.

The recently completed Potomac Study and its recommended establishment of a national river have greatly broadened the concepts for Potomac planning, conservation, and development; and our vision of what a riverscape, protected and developed as a permanent scenic and recreational asset, can mean to the nation and do for the future of this region. . . . We see that we cannot address ourselves merely to the protection of one bank, but must regard the total riverscape as a unity if it is to retain its charm and beauty and serve the people adequately.

Then the Administration changed. The Office of Management and Budget, long vexed that the national river proposal had been a presidentially sanctioned maverick corrals and anxious to exercise a wise frugality in federal spending wherever possible, locked up all Potomac measures pending a good look at them.

There was still a head of steam behind Potomac matters, however. Senator Jackson pressed for action on the national river proposal, and Representative Gude of Maryland put in his own national river bill, aware that half-measures would never take care of recreation needs. "I like Potomac National River," said the new Interior Secretary, Walter Hickel. "It has meaning for the entire country." Reminded by aides that it was the darling of the previous Administration, his retort was, "So what? If it is a good project, let's go with it!" His advisory board on national parks backed him up enthusiastically.

But the C & O Canal people, conservationists, and politicians alike insisted on having their park at long last. The rest of the river could wait, though without a tie to the canal side and the support of canal lovers, protecting the Virginia–West Virginia side of the Potomac alone seemed a lamed proposal. After assessing the political climate, the Department of the Interior acquiesced to the phased approach to riverscape conservation, and recommended the park as a first step toward broader Potomac preservation. A C & O Canal National Historical Park of some 20,000 acres was authorized. Time will tell if it is the right approach. It will at least save half a river, and half a loaf is better than none, after all. With the C & O Canal park backers satisfied and gone, however, protecting the other riverside that has no historic cause for preservation may prove a friendless effort. Perhaps the other half of the conservation may come about when Virginia and West Virginia find they are left out of the environmental quality and economic benefit to be expected. Then again, that other half may be free enterprise's part of the Potomac pie, divvied up in the spirit of compromise and the political art of the possible. If so, when campfires burn low along the canal park; when the moon shines through the giant sycamores; when the whippoorwill calls and the voices of old canalers and rivermen seem to whisper in the river mists, Ticki-Tacki Towne across the narrow water may well jazz up the scene.

While the Federal Interdepartmental Task Force was mapping model conservation plans upon the Potomac landscape, another governmental group was equally hard at work. Its planning, however, utilized legal language rather than maps and resource inventories, for it was building the legal machinery by which the water and related resources of the whole Potomac Basin could be planned and managed down the years ahead. Called the Potomac River Basin Advisory Committee, the group was formed by the governors of the four basin states and the Commissioners of the District of Columbia to monitor, coordinate, and assist the federal effort and keep the states' concerns in view. Most important of the committee's assignments, however, was to work out the best possible kind of permanent interstate organization to plan, develop, and manage the resources of the basin.

Despite a strong sense of sovereignty on the part of all Potomac Basin governments, most realized, in the words of the compact eventually drafted, that "the wisest and most efficient uses of the available resources of the Potomac River and its tributaries may be determined only through the continuing process of fully coordinated and comprehensive planning which is responsive to all the interests and jurisdictions of the basin." Moreover, since none had overall jurisdiction, a single basin agency was necessary to carry out those plans.

The Advisory Committee worked for a year and a half on a preliminary draft of a Potomac Basin Compact, published it for study and comment, and then revised and improved it further before submitting a final draft to the governors in 1968.

Under the Compact, a six-man Potomac River Basin Commission (comprised of the governors or their appointees) would draw up a Comprehensive Water Resources Plan, adopt a water resources program annually, and review proposed projects relating to the river to prevent conflicts with the plan. The Commission could regulate the flow and supply of water; oversee water quality criteria and management; intercede for and indemnify those abused by pollution; delineate flood plains; review projects that might affect flooding; operate flood control facilities; promote soil conservation practices; and, with the consent of the state affected, sponsor water-related recreation projects.

There was, of course, strong local opposition to the cession of local authority. Moreover, a power struggle developed between the jurisdictions with the bulk of the basin land and those with the majority of the population. The proposed commission membership of states, the District of Columbia, and the United States actually struck a fairly good balance between rural and urban interests, West Virginia and Pennsylvania being largely rural so far as the Potomac is concerned, Maryland and Virginia, both rural and urban, and the District of Columbia urban. But still they pulled and hauled.

To guide the Advisory Committee were the Delaware River Basin Compact, already in force, and the completed but then unratified Susquehanna Compact. The Potomac group, however, attempted something no other drafting committee had yet dared to do: it recognized the indivisability of the river's water and the related land resources. Controversial Article 9, entitled "Other Public Values" (besides water) declared "that, in addition to water resources management, the purposes of this compact are to preserve and promote the aesthetic and other values inherent in the historic, scenic and environmental amenities of the Potomac River Basin for the enjoyment and enrichment of future generations and relate such values to the economic health of the basin and the promotion of the orderly development of the basin." The compact called for an Amenities Plan, for the whole Potomac Basin. It could establish river zones along the Potomac wherein scenic, historic, or recreational values of particular significance are given special protection, as well as create other parks, parkways, trails, wetlands, natural areas, and recreational open space. Bitterly attacked, of course, as a usurpation of environmental self-determination by local jurisdictions, Article 9 was deeply under-mined, so that those local jurisdictions would have veto powers over Compact Commission land conservation programs. It still survived in the Compact proposal, however, and although Com-mission control over land uses could not begin until 1980 and would be severely limited by local zoning as well as the local veto powers, it was a step toward coordinating the protection and uses of an entire valley for lasting public benefit.

Alas for the Compact and all those years of work, West Virginia seems to have done it in. Virginia ratified it, then Maryland; but a special committee of the West Virginia legislature recommended it be given "no further consideration." Potomac landowners with political clout apparently feared that despite the watered-down land regulation, the public might someday want to get to the river, and that prerogatives of local government might be reduced. "No way," they said in effect. The Advisory Committee which drafted the Compact still hopes that West Virginia and Pennsyl-vania, which has cooled toward the Compact, will keep an open mind and their citizens in opposition will come to realize that regional management of resources is not a communist scheme after all.

Is it wishful thinking now to hope that a model Potomac may yet come about, if not by virtue of any conservation Camelot along its shores or an intergovernmental mechanism, then through the democratic process of dialogue and give-and-take decisions? After all, that process has enabled the various watershed associa-tions and land trusts of the East to inch their way toward broadly supported conservation goals. In such a way, grassroot America can conceivably form a deep, firm conservation sod, though many exploitive, despoiling weeds of species flourishing succulently since frontier days must be painfully pulled in the process. Such sod building is slow, for weeds proliferate and can kill reluctant grass, and weeds are rampant along the Potomac as on almost every river. Along with the sod building, America also needs visions of ideal solutions, "impossible" dreams come true, grand designs and model programs to fertilize and stimulate our democratic evolution from an exploitive to a conservative civilization. We need a catalyst for riverscape protection. Thomas Jefferson once wrote George Washington that "nature has declared in favor of the Potomac." Jefferson had commerce in mind at the time, but national focus and a beautiful riverscape still relatively unscathed by our exploitations have lent new meaning to his words. Today the Potomac offers opportunity to establish a model river wherein a successful pattern of federal, state, and private cooperation in environmental stewardship can be built.

A Potomac National River, developed and integrated with a Potomac Compact with which it would be completely compatible: that would indeed be a "big plan" in Daniel Burnham's sense, with magic to stir the blood of all, at least, who do not simply regard river valleys as troughs. What a pittance it would cost compared to the treasuries of revenues we lavish upon imminent obsolescence. And what an inspiration it could be to communities and nations everywhere with rivers to care for and enjoy. Perhaps it is not a lost cause, for as Burnham said, "A noble, logical diagram once recorded will never die, and long after we are gone will be a living thing, asserting itself with ever-growing insistency." I hope so, but although rivers seem eternal, time in our age runs out on their beauty and their freedom. A model Potomac, wisely managed as a whole, its finest reaches and historic qualities preserved, can proclaim to the world that the rivers which water our land shall also forever delight the souls of men.

Credo

Rivers are choice national assets reserved for all
the people.

—William O. Douglas in "My
Wilderness—East to Katahdin"

I BELIEVE in these words of Justice Douglas; I wish they now applied to rivers as I believe we must define them—not waterways only but wholenesses of water course and bordering banks. The riversides, in addition to the quality of the flowing water, are what make the streams beautiful and recreative and meaningful. "Any river is really the summation of a whole valley," Hal Borland has written. "It shapes not only the land but the life and even the culture of that valley. The trees that grow on its banks and all the greenness there may be common elsewhere but they still are special to that river. So are the birds, the insects, the animals that live along that river's bank. And the river has its own swarming life.... To think of any river as nothing but water is to ignore the greater part of it." Yet we often advocate the spending of millions to cleanse water and ignore the soiled and preempted banks. Only a very few river reaches in America are wholly reserved for all the people—those in the Scenic Rivers System and others in park or forest reservations. Only one of large size, the Allagash, exists in the East.

I believe we should do for our waterways what we do for most of our other routes; even for the minor streets of our residential communities. Along our asphalted roads the rights-of-way are wider than the pavement. There are protective edgings of green and places to pull off and rest. Our biggest and finest arteries have rights of way wide enough that their scenic qualities are protected from intrusion, and they remain green and pleasant ways. In our towns there are sidewalks along the streets where people may freely stroll. Moreover, many neighborhoods require a setback of buildings without obstructing fences, so that a green sheath of trees and lawn, even though privately owned, is guaranteed to remain, keeping the route a more beautiful one to utilize.

No green sheaths, no bordering walkways exist along most of our finest water routes, although sometimes there is a setback required to keep building out of the way of possible floods. Often that also is lacking, however. If we could treat our rivers like our roads, we could have beautiful, permanent river parks through every part of our country.

But the time is late. After all, most of our riversides are privately owned. Is it worth all the effort and cost to try to do it now? Yes, I believe it is. For there is no element of our environment more handsome, more recreative than our waterways. They designed our land for living. How well they are loved and kept will influence all living that surrounds them, for few jewels are set in brass. They are the best, and in some places the only corridors along which we may pass from the contrived to the natural world in our search for self-renewal and understanding.

Waterways compose the earth's circulatory system. If their flow is uncontaminated and unblocked; if their pulse is strong and steady, we shall know we have a well earth, for like man's circulatory system, river water and river life tell us much of health and sickness. If waterways are healthy, they should be as free as healthy people from confinements and quarantines. They should be free to communicate in every way: through aesthetics, recreative pastimes, scientific inquiry.

But how shall we protect and restore our rivers? Pollution has at last touched our conscience, and water cleansing has captured our technological imagination. We are therefore hard at work on new methods, new discoveries to combat our filth. Costs stagger but do not scare us, though it may take anywhere from half a billion to two and a half billion dollars to clean up the Potomac River alone. We must put ingenuity and money unstintingly behind prevention and cleanup, until we may, if we wish, place our water supply intakes below our sewage discharges. More states need to follow New Hampshire's example in requiring specific state approval for any waste disposal system within a thousand feet of a waterfront. Our riversides could be spared from many a sleazy cottage development if the developer were required to put up a bond in advance guaranteeing adequate sewage disposal. Such controls would help not only to keep the water clean but also the riverscapes open.

I believe we must put together our humpty-dumpty planning authority and land use controls now fragmented in countless local government jurisdictions. Building the legal machinery necessary to effect adequate land conservation in America will, I fear, take far longer and be much more difficult than the technological accomplishments needed to stop and cure pollution, though, as has been noted, the two must proceed together. Few states in the East have made much headway in even inventorying their riverine resources and deciding what conservation is desirable. Vermont, for example, is just beginning, though no state is prouder of its scenic beauty or more dependent upon it. West Virginia, Virginia, and Maryland have charted a logical course of action, rudimentary or inadequate as are the measures they have adopted to date. As a first step in holding the line against riverscape deterioration, West Virginia's Natural Streams Preservation Act blows the whistle on damming and channeling its best waterways, though it pays no attention to what goes on along the banks. Virginia and Maryland have at least identified the most important of their streams deserving scenic protection, though the politicians shudder at the lumps they will get if they go after that protection.

To put into practice thriftily the principle of treating our rivers like roads, complete with adequate roadsides, would require two basic governmental-legal changes. One would be the consolidation of planning and land use control authority, either in state hands or by means of river authorities or compacts created to oversee and manage river resources. The other is the extension of the principle of zoning more fully to cover not only health and safety but also less obvious aspects of human welfare, such as preservation of aesthetic and recreational values. Extension of policing powers is risky business, of course, and if done at all, should be based on thoroughly researched and broadly based tenets. We must also research further the psychological benefits of outdoor recreation, the penalties of crowding, the social benefits of clustering dwellings as compared with the biological consequences of consuming green space with sprawl. Such may reveal sound reasons for zoning not now supportable on strictly interpreted health and safety grounds. Moreover, if zoning of riversides is part of a logical plan, generally respected in the community involved, rather than a special restriction, the control is more likely to stand up under legal scrutiny. Now few communities along rivers have such plans.

In the avaricious jungle of present-day real estate and industrial development; amid the shambles of long-fractured planning authority, conservationists private and public are groping for new ways to control the fate of our riverscapes. Some try education and persuasion; others, the policing powers. Both ways are important. The only sure way, however, is to buy, and buy now. That is true of any landscape, but especially so of rivers, focal lines of land development pressures that wind through many jurisdictions. If our willingness to do this equals our willingness to have fine highways and fast airplanes, we shall gladly bear the cost, knowing that what we buy will not, for once, be evanescent. Then the "not one cent for scenery" curse against our land will have been lifted.

Buying Eastern landscapes is an appallingly expensive proposition. But we are like King Tarquin of Rome to whom a priestess offered nine priceless books of prophecy and secrets of divine favor. When the king balked at the price, she burned three volumes; then three more, until he gladly paid the original price for the three remaining. We must pony up before all our river treasures are consumed. If we wait until our planning laws change, the riverscape will be long gone. If we cannot buy many, we should certainly buy the best. Then, perhaps, appreciation of them will encourage other means of preserving the beautiful dendritic pattern of green-edged waterways that grace our land.

Unlike some art collecting, we should by no means regard our preserved riverscapes simply as museum pieces to be peered at by the curious. They must become catalysts, demonstration areas of what respect and care can mean in enhancing the total matrix of our lives. And the chances are that they will pay their way well. The tax loss a community may sustain when land and development potential go off the tax rolls as the result of a conservation project is more than offset by economic benefits it generates. These include the money spent by recreationists and the taxable private businesses that spring up to serve them. Moreover, when the permanence of an amenity like an unspoiled river is secured, the monetary value of the surrounding lands increases. It makes the valley a more attractive, and therefore valuable, place to live.

What is needed, then—now—is an action program, and that requires money, lots of it, private and public. Until recently, the only financing at work to save environment was private philanthropy and some state purchasing now and then. It was not until 1961 that the Congress consented to appropriate money to buy a natural area for the National Park System—Cape Cod National Seashore. Other such areas had been either carved out of the public domain or accepted as gifts from private or state donors. Compared to other philanthropies, however, conservation has received minor attention from private purchasing power. The Rockefeller and Mellon families have, of course, given impressively both of money and land for parklands. Other individuals

have donated personal holdings out of a desire to see them preserved as they have loved them. Many also will contribute to a
special conservation project they hold dear, or respond to an
emergency plea to save an exceptional resource.

But, as Aldo Leopold has pointed out, our ethics are people-
rather than land-oriented. Our charity is therefore usually aimed
at direct human assistance in such fields as education, medicine,
and other care rather than preserving environment for human
welfare and happiness. Most of the eleemosynary organizations
with money to give away are more likely to provide scholarships
for Patagonians than to buy a mountain or a river or a seashore
for posterity. Even historical preservation seems to capture the
fancy of the generous more readily than does the preservation of
natural scenes. The human associations, I suppose, make the difference, plus the pleasure of watching restoration progress.

Every week, classified advertisements in the newspapers list
scores of extraordinary conservation opportunities in choice lands
offered for sale. Bureaucracy can seldom move in time or lacks
funds or authority to snap up such opportunities. But a charitable
foundation or an individual or corporation looking for a tax de-
duction and valuable good will could work conservation wonders
by picking up such properties with little or no risk of ever losing
if a conservation agency failed to assume their management. If a
property, once sold, stays in a single ownership, sometimes the
opportunity to buy it comes again, though at a vastly larger cost
to taxpayers. If the land is subdivided, however, the chances to
protect it for public benefit are usually nil. So if a piece of land
for sale represents an important scenic and recreational resource
to a community, it behooves some civic-minded body to buy it
for the public good.

Even the most generous and alert private action can only do a
small part of the environmental protection job we need, however.
Unless there is broad-based public concern and willingness to bear
whatever financial burden is necessary to protect the environment,

our conservation efforts will be marginal. Notes Dr. Lynton K. Caldwell, professor of government at Indiana University:

Private means cannot be mobilized to a degree sufficient to buy the lands and the easements and to fight the legal battles necessary to safeguard ecological values everywhere. The setting aside of specific natural areas and sanctuaries through private and public effort should be pushed with full vigor. But the prospects for their survival as ecological islands amid environments of biophysical ruin could hardly be optimistic.

Even though America's population growth were arrested today, the present industrial technology would continue its push to exploit every niche in the North American biosphere. Even to let the natural environment alone now requires positive protective action. Nothing will remain untouched that public administration does not protect. There is at present no end of talking and writing about the environmental crisis of our time, but action proportionate to the need has yet to appear.

Of course there has been some encouraging action. The recent state bond issues to buy open space are prime examples, as is Congress's willingness now to buy parkland. Yet there remains the double standard of dollars for dams and roads and other comparatively ephemeral public works and pennies for parks and other permanent environmental assets. That double standard has got to go. It is starting to, I think; I hope. "I guess if we can spend a billion and more for some destroyers, we can spend $20 million on a park," I heard a Senate aide muse aloud not long ago.

In buying land, government must salve a dreadful political prejudice against this kind of public action. It is the fear of the power of eminent domain. No private person likes to be disturbed in his ownership or activities. The power of the state forcibly to buy private property for public benefit is always resented. It is a gut resentment, of course, but much of it stems from the fact that the private property owner fears he will get gypped. Sometimes he does. Moreover, his resentment is heightened when he thinks that the purpose for which the land is being condemned is a frivolous one. As one landowner put it, "No legislative body should delegate the awesome power of condemnation for any purpose as trivial as recreation." Although resenting condemnation to build a school or a dam or a new road permitting salesmen to whiz faster to their customers, the property owner may at least understand it, for does not America progress through construction? But he may well feel that to condemn for parks is "unnecessary": just a scheme to let one man roast weenies on what was another man's private property. He suggests, therefore, that conservation programs be built only of land willingly sold, thus assuring that many of our parks will be patchwork or else composed of swamps, deserts, and rockpiles passed up by realty hawks.

Landowners' groups are opposing eminent domain bitterly. No doubt they were indirectly responsible for the impotent scenic rivers law passed in Virginia. Yet without eminent domain, as without the power of taxation, government cannot carry out the public will. Public conservation programs without eminent domain can be compared to sending a policeman out to keep the peace without the power of arrest. Moreover, as William H. Whyte has pointed out, eminent domain assures that one landowner does not make a mockery of the cooperation of others in conserving the scenery or open space of a vital area. It assures that the taxpayer, having voted a program, can see it through and gets a square deal.

Although the law requires it, the landowner sometimes doesn't get a square deal. Government land buyers, taking the taxpayer's interest to heart, often drive a hard bargain. "Fair market value" established by conservative appraisers is usually based on the lowest comparable sales in the neighborhood. Moreover, the couple condemned out of a $500 cottage can seldom find another place to live save a $10,000 house in town. Guess who goes into debt for the difference? Landowners who contest the appraised values and sue have obtained some handsome court awards, but legal action can be expensive and exhausting. The federal government recognized this inequity when it enacted the Uniform-Relocation Assistance and Real Property Acquisition Act of 1970, but this law helps only partially.

I believe that condemnation purchases should be generous to the point of giving a bonus. A land acquistion specialist threw up his hands in horror at this suggestion, pointing out that in so doing an agency would defeat its purpose by driving up the price of land. But I would rather see the public pay ten percent too much for a property than lose it altogether in a political debacle because of a penny-wise reluctance to make public acquisition as easy as possible on landowners having to sell.

Owners of private property have two other basic values inherent in their ownership besides that of fair cash value for their property: private enjoyment of it undisturbed (and, within legal limits, according to their own lights), and expectation of future value. The latter is the investment aspect of land ownership. To many landowners enjoyment of property is as important as cash value. A landowner cares much about knowing that "this is my domain; I have the right to manage it in ways that express and develop my own personality and character." Fortunately land condemned for park and other recreational use can usually avoid disturbing this second cherished right. The builders of dams, highways, and the like must have immediate possession of the land to carry out their project. They must turn the private owner out. Most land conservation projects can allow him to live his life out undisturbed on the land he loves, by means of life tenancies, or lease-back agreements. Generally, these have been discretionary on the part of the government buyer, who weighs the public interest in immediate possession against the private interest and lower cost in granting a delay. This creates uncertainty and fear, and public purchasing of land for conservation use might be a lot more popular and less frequently opposed if continued occupancy was made a matter of right. Public land managers may gasp in dismay at such a notion, for continuing tenancies can postpone and frustrate public use programs. But I do not think the temporary inconvenience to the public is worth the risk of losing the land as a result of determined political opposition.

Unfortunately, nothing can be done to compensate a landowner for what may be his future financial expectations from his property. The taxpayer cannot be asked to pay today what a property owner thinks his land may be worth ten years hence. It can only be assumed that, if he gets fair value for it, he can go elsewhere and make a comparable investment. Nor can another important expectation ever be satisfied if land is bought for public purposes: the hope to bequeath it to one's heirs.

Except in extremely wealthy families, however, dynastic landholding is passing in America, where many millions of families move each year. There is little assurance that heirs either can or will keep the ancestral property in the family. The family patriarch had better resign himself to the probability that the home farm will be sold out within a generation or two. His descendants are now so mobile, so subject to being blown across the country by winds of fortune, that they cannot be counted on to retain the old estates. And those are often becoming either too expensive or too valuable to keep. If an owner wants the land to stay as is, his most certain assurance is to see it in public trust, perhaps with suitable strings attached to keep the public stewards committed.

As public land purchasing to preserve environment becomes more and more imperative, fairness and consideration must be the order of the day. Government must bend over backwards to make the buying as painless as possible, otherwise battle lines between landowners and conservationists will be drawn. The only losers can be the environment and beyond that the American people as a whole. The speculators will always squawk, of course, but with a square deal and a lifetime occupancy most private residents can take satisfaction and pride in their private stewardship's becoming a public trust.

In seeking to protect our most beautiful Eastern rivers, two

general approaches are discernible. One involves the wild river
and river park idea. When the quality of a riverscape is so high
and so fragile that any adverse use may destroy it, then outright
purchase is needed. It is needed also when a river is so important
for public use that it, or at least a section of it, must be completely dedicated to that purpose. One example needing absolute
protection is the wild river whereon even a few developments
can destroy its secluded character. Another example is an urban
riverscape or one which millions of people can count upon
throughout the seasons for recreation. Small rivers especially
need complete protection if they are to serve either as natural
areas or as community parks. Intrusions have a greater impact
upon little streams; also, more length is required along them to
provide adequate and various recreation. Big rivers can withstand
more intrusion and can offer more recreation in proportion to the
length so used. They can serve both as recreation resources and as
scenic amenities with a lesser degree of outright ownership. Land
use controls more readily meet conservation objectives along
large rivers than they do on small ones, unless, of course, major
public recreation needs are to be served. Thus, there are more
options open in ways to protect large rivers than small ones. That
is fortunate, in a way, for the conservation problems along the
larger streams tend to be big and knotty.

Small wild rivers like the Cacapon, larger ones like the Upper
Hudson, the Penobscot's branches, the St. John; semi-wild ones
like the Rappahannock and Pine Creek; rural beauties like the
Ausable and the upper Connecticut, should be safeguarded as
unique and precious treasures. Some exceptionally productive
streams like the Battenkill and Ausable might well be managed
as fishing parks. Other beloved and beautiful streams such as the
Upper James, Shenandoah, Potomac's South Branch, Juniata,
Unadilla, Upper Delaware, Housatonic, Androscoggin, and Saco
could also appropriately be treated as river parks. Large rivers and
river reaches, where short sections can suffice for park use but
which are important as design elements in their regions, might

be protected by a combination of park zones and general development controls. This approach would be much like England's method of park protection. The Susquehanna, Lower Delaware, Connecticut, and James could be treated thus, though the James is peculiarly suited to being a large river park. So is the Potomac, where a variety of river characteristics plus much historical significance and scenery provide exceptional and diverse recreational opportunities to large numbers of people.

Whenever we think of "national assets reserved for all the people," we must grapple with the problem of how much use those assets can appropriately sustain. Most who like river outings look forward to enjoying them as journeys into serenity and seclusion. Even people who go in groups want to savor in their own company the pleasures of the river world. To visualize a river as jostlingly filled with recreationists as our streets are filled with drivers is to evoke a very bad dream. Yet that is exactly what may happen to our rivers in the name of recreation if we do not regulate their use.

Regulation of outdoor activities is about as antipathetic an idea as a frontier-reared nation can contemplate. In our own subconsciousness we are all voyageurs, anglers, hunters in an American wilderness. We have room to roam, or so it says in what we regard as an outdoor Bill of Rights. But there are now 200 million of us, and, in most of the East we live 450 to the square mile. Our population density shows up in the very water itself. For example, it soon may be necessary to treat everything that empties into the Charles River to preserve tolerable water quality. And if our rivers, particularly our Eastern waterways, are to give us the pleasure they can uniquely provide, we are going to have to regulate our recreational use of them as well as to purify them. The same holds true of any public area of quality where quietude, perception, and appreciation of environment are important objectives. The pleasure drive along a parkway turns into a nightmare in bumper-to-bumper traffic. The leisurely golf game is no fun when the fairways are jammed and there are lines waiting to

tee off. Being linear and travel routes, rivers are especially suscep-
tible to overcrowding. In fact, capacity standards for river use in
two states—Louisiana and Wisconsin—call for a half-mile of aver-
age-size river per pair of boatmen!

We accept regulated use in most of our recreational pursuits.
We acknowledge "full house" signs in our theaters and know
enough to plan ahead and get reservations for them and many
other places, from airplanes to restaurants. We respect the regulated use of fragile historic places, and few of us demand to lie
down on George Washington's bed or try on Abraham Lincoln's
hat. But we expect to trample and fondle our natural environment to our heart's content. William Vogt expressed this matter
well when he wrote:

If our great museums and art galleries were used as recklessly and
harmfully as are our wild lands, there would be a national
scandal and a national sense of shame. Yet the environment of
wild geese or the pasque flower, whose sighting Aldo Leopold
recognized as a necessity for many of us (certainly as much of a
necessity as a view of Picasso!), is as vulnerable as a Gobelin or
the walls of the Sistine Chapel. So little respect for these environments have those in charge that they constantly advocate "accessi-
bility" without provision for adequate protection.

A visit to a national park or a journey down a scenic river will
have to become a privilege rather than a right if by the year 2000
quality experiences are to remain for us to appreciate. There are,
certainly, many imaginative ways by which our resource managers
can put more people pleasurably in the landscape. I expect we
shall always be able to allow multitudes to view the great scenic
and natural wonders they own and want to admire, the Grand
Canyons and Old Faithfuls, even if we have to move the visitors
by mass transit. I foresee, however, that opportunities for private experience, for the refreshment of being alone in the
natural wild, or of that simple yet deep companionship of two or
a few quietly sharing an appreciation of nature's subtle beauties—

those we shall have to ration out in some fair equitable way. Of course they should never be regulated by pricing or favor but rather on the basis of caring enough, wanting them enough to plan ahead, qualify for using them, and gain the requested allotment of space and time for the experience. When we regard ourselves as sufficiently foresighted and thoughtful to have secured a weekend's outing on our favorite river; when we have perhaps passed a qualifying test, like that for driving, proving that we know how to conduct ourselves on the outing, we shall think it a privilege to be cherished rather than a right to be taken for granted. We shall then better take care of that river. We shall savor its charms and beauties, its thrills and its moods. We shall examine it more avidly and lovingly and gain more knowledge and understanding from it than ever before, and more jealously demand good care for it. The experience will be a rich feast rather than a common meal, and we shall remember it, the lessons it taught, the pleasure it gave us. Our friends and neighbors will envy our foresight, and status, just as now they might envy our good fortune in having secured tickets to the hit show or the championship game. They also will begin to plan and train, and having secured their opportunity, will likewise cherish it. So will appreciation of our outdoor heritage grow with its "privilege value," and with appreciation will come kind stewardship.

Thus, and only thus, amid a population explosion, will the quality of our environment survive. It has been estimated that ten percent of the United States' land area will be megalopolitized within the next thirty years. The Delaware Valley, for instance, will get more urban growth in the next quarter century than it experienced in the last two and a half centuries. Scenic little Vermont is already losing 10,000 acres to real estate developments, with three times that amount on the drawing boards. Under such pressure only the most stringent care and vigilant insistance on quality, will keep our environment sanative. As Dr. Caldwell has said, it cannot survive in museum-piece islands amid ecological ruin. We cannot, for example, maintain it by protecting one scenic river among ten sewers. We need massive land protection programs, diverting money if necessary from development programs, which can be carried out later, to land conservation programs, which cannot.

But even the most massive land protection programs will not succeed without public policy to back them up. Dr. Caldwell has pointed out that our American institutions of economics and government are better adapted to exploitation than either protection or self-renewing development. Conservation has been a defensive measure, aimed mainly at preserving our most spectacular landscapes, and often government has been the agent of those who would sacrifice environment to economic or political advantage. "Public ownership affords no guarantee of safety in the absence of public environmental policy that will lift the level of public decisions above bargaining among the various resource users," Dr. Caldwell has written, adding that until ecological concepts are somehow reflected in the law, administering environmental controls will not be fully successful.

Behind law and administrative policy stand the people who form them. Our environment, therefore, ultimately depends entirely on education, for people seldom will care for what they do not understand. Preserving resources in parks, forests, scenic rivers, seashores is of no avail if an unwitting, uncaring public tramples them down. Dr. Paul F. Brandwein of The Conservation Foundation has defined conservation as man's recognition of his interdependence with his environment and with life everywhere, and as a culture which maintains that relationship through whatever policies and practices are necessary to secure the future of a sanative environment. To secure it, he points out, we must first understand it, and to do that we must become part of it. This must happen early in our lives, he adds, for what we learn in school years presages what we do, or do not do, later on. Obviously, then, our environment and how we use it depends on education. Name it conservation education, environmental awareness, what you will: upon it rests the fate of this once and, we hope, future

Eden we call Earth. To date, conservation education is a token endeavor in America, often consisting largely of a field trip or two to what Dr. Brandwein calls "a concentration camp for organisms which otherwise cannot survive."

If we are to instill reverence for environment in our national ethos, that will have to be a principal goal in the educational process. Dr. Brandwein defines education as experience in search of meaning. If that is true, then American childhood, all of it, must grow up knowing the environment—what it does, how it works, how it affects us and we it, what necessities and what pleasures it affords. Amid all the recent furor of our new environmental awareness, much of our energy has been directed toward scolding and bringing to heel the environmental wrongdoers in our land. If those who politic and picket and inveigh against such sinning—particularly all who still have rapport with youth—could use some of that energy to take two children by the hand and lead them into the wonderland of nature, how kind and careful of it they as adults might become.

Neither billions spent nor lawsuits won, but education alone, can bring about a reverence for the earth. Only through education can the physical prison of urban living and the cultural prison of technologically contrived satisfactions be broken open, and American children *all* experience the natural environment. Only when everyone by experience understands the how and why and wherefore of environment will conservation action project itself into the mainstream of American life. Only then will ecology become a vital part of every decision that affects the earth.

To change the attitude and habits of thinking that have evolved over centuries of cultural development is a staggering proposition. Though we are beginning to admit that our superabundance is a myth, we still believe what Stewart Udall has similarly called the myth of scientific supremacy. We need not take care of things, we think, for we can always fix them. An ecologist, Raymond F. Dasmann, has described this trait by observing that

Americans are impatient with the slow processes of nature. They prefer the simplicity of a machine to the intricacies of a biota. The day by day problems of watershed management seem tiresome, whereas a large dam built to stop floods "for all time" has popular appeal. Even when we wish to preserve nature we like to get the job over with, and by some spectacular act of congress decreeing preservation forever. The continual small difficulties involved in the maintenance of any natural community tend to annoy the American temperament. Wildness is too unmanageable to suit the majority of the people.

A physician, Dr. Seymour Farber, has discussed the problem in the context of general human behavior down the ages. Citing Thomas Jefferson's concern with the encroachment of industrialism on the land he loved, Dr. Farber called it "the conflict between inwardness and outwardness." "Man has always tended to choose the latter," he noted. "Whether with stone ax, sword, or bulldozer, he has loved conquest and exploitation more than cultivation of the spirit. Mankind has reached a point where inwardness is being forced upon it by the sheer oppression of its own numbers. Man must look inward or perish."

A journalist, Colman McCarthy, put it more bluntly in the context of pollution: "Few dare say that pollution is in our national blood, a part of our mood and a basic to our economy, and until we get it out of all three—completely out—our country is doomed," he wrote. "Doomism is not popular among a people who have convinced themselves they can do anything; but eventually the unrevered earth will begin returning to us exactly what we have been giving to it: cruelty and poison."

The victims of this cruelty and poisoning that have suffered most are our Eastern rivers. At best we have neglected them; at worst, raped and mutilated, scorned and humiliated and enslaved them. In few places are rivers allowed to have dignity, to bring joy, to be clean arteries of life. Rivers have probably lost more productive capacity than most other environments, and in all

too many places they are fouled, scarred and tarnished wrecks of
what once were pure and attractive inlays of the land. Their flow
no longer brings beauty and pleasure but merely the wastes and
mistakes and sins of the people upstream. Yet, as Justice Douglas
has emphasized, the polluters and destroyers of our rivers do not
have monopoly rights, and people have broader interests than
exploitation. "Recreation, health, and enjoyment of aesthetic
values are part of man's liberty," the Justice wrote. "Rivers play
an important part in keeping this idea of liberty alive. They supply playgrounds and swimming holes. Their waters are for
artists as well as for merchants."

Yes, if we will remember that and do something about it. For
why must one mill ruin the water in miles of lovely waterway?
Why should our loveliest valleys be flooded out because of the
wrong development downstream, because other water sources are
more expensive or too little researched, or because it is the cheapest place for power? Why should a four-lane expressway bear down
like a juggernaut of doom on historic Harpers Ferry and its spectacular setting and nobody lift a finger to divert it? Why should
a beautiful river like the Shenandoah turn into a linear slurb
because governments have not guts enough to zone adequately or
are too timid or too lazy to preserve the riverscape? Why should
the gorgeous stream valleys that are gateways to the White Mountains go unprotected, with National Forests all around?

Why is Carderagus Creek, which could be the greatest orna-
ment and central charm of old York, Pennsylvania, locally known
only as "Inky-stinky," with its sole parkland a play area recently
bought to appease downtown social unrest? Why don't we allow
our best streams to be managed for fishing scientifically and not
judge their health by an inexpert angler's empty creel? Why are
our "choice national assets reserved for all the people" in the
hands of speculators, exploiters, or those who think that their
world will never change, their individual ownerships last forever?

To paraphrase a famous modern folksong of peace, "When will

we ever learn?" When will we decide what rivers shall remain wild and pristine, which valleys beautiful forever, and keep them so against all raids, sellouts, chiselings and betrayals, false emergencies, or cries of "laissez-faire"? When will we stop speaking of pollution *control* and espouse prevention and banishment? When will we start planning from what W. H. Whyte calls a "river's-eye point of view," letting our riverine beauty design and pervade the living areas we develop and the spaces we preserve? When will we plan not for the decades ahead but for the centuries, glorying more in a wholesome felicitous future than in a frontier past?

The answer to the whys is that we have yet no conscience in our concerns with nonhuman matters. We have not yet achieved the land ethic Aldo Leopold so eloquently pleaded for. The answer to the whens is when we develop that conscience, that ethic. The only way is through education, and what better classrooms are there than our rivers, the most vital and alluring of all inanimate things, wherein the whole story of life and earth, the health of it and the sickness, is found entwined with water's symbolic lifelike flow.

Take a child to a river; acquaint him with its wonder, its beauty, and its power; let him enter into the joy of running water, and it will not only be a playmate and playground but a teacher and classroom as well. If he fishes, it will teach quiet and patience and deftness. If he boats, it will teach self-reliance and the basic lessons of the consequences of right and wrong action— something city rearing often hides. As his mind matures, his knowledge will grow from wondering and fascination to study and research. He will become scientist as well as outdoorsman and will determine in his favorite stream the health of his region. Inevitably he will become artist as well, in appreciation if not in practice. Despite what trials life may bring, he will then have not only new worlds to explore but an old and beautiful world to care for and enjoy. And, as Thoreau once said, "Who hears the rippling of the rivers will not utterly despair of anything."

When children grow up caring, the only troubles that rivers will then need bear will be those of mind and body which beauty and recreation can wash away.

Bibliography of principal works quoted, and other germane reading

Agriculture, U.S. Department of—*Wild Rivers*, 1965 (with U.S. Dept. of the Interior)

Appalachian Mountain Club—*New England Canoeing Guide*, 1971

Bakeless, John—*The Eyes of Discovery*, Dover, New York, 1961

Bardach, John—*Downstream, A Natural History of the River*, Harper, New York, 1964

Borland, Hal—*Beyond Your Doorstep*, Knopf, New York, 1968

Boyle, Robert H.—*The Hudson River, A Natural and Unnatural History*, Norton, New York, 1969

Brandwein, Paul F., in *Future Environments of North America*, edited by F. Fraser Darling and John P. Milton, The Conservation Foundation, 1965

Brooks, Paul—*Roadless Area*, Knopf, New York, 1964

Bryan, Charles W., Jr.—*The Raquette, River of the Forest*, Adirondack Museum, 1964

Burmeister, Walter Frederick—*Appalachian Water*, Canoe Cruisers Association, Washington, D.C., 1962

Caldwell, Lynton K., in *Future Environments of North America*, The Conservation Foundation, 1965

Canby, Henry Seidel—*The Brandywine;* "The Rivers of America" series, Farrar, New York, 1941

Carmer, Carl—*The Susquehanna;* "The Rivers of America" series, Rinehart, New York, 1955

Carter, Randy—*Canoeing White Water—River Guide,* 1967, 1970

Cawley, James and Margaret—*Exploring the Little Rivers of New Jersey,* Rutgers University Press, New Jersey, 1961

Coffin, Robert P. Tristram—*Kennebec, Cradle of Americans;* "The Rivers of America" series, Farrar, New York, 1937

Dasmann, Raymond F., in *Future Environments of North America,* The Conservation Foundation, 1965

Dietz, Lew—*The Allagash;* "The Rivers of America" series, Holt, New York, 1968

Douglas, William O.—*My Wilderness—East to Katahdin,* Doubleday, New York, 1961

Eiseley, Loren—*The Immense Journey,* Random House, New York, 1957

Emerson, Ralph Waldo—*Nature,* 1836; *Essays,* 1844

Evans, Jay—*Fundamentals of Kayaking,* Ledyard Canoe Club, Dartmouth College

Farber, Seymour, in *Future Environments of North America,* The Conservation Foundation, 1965

Grady, Joseph F.—*The Adirondacks,* 1933

Graves, John—*The Creek and the City,* U.S. Department of the Interior

Gutheim, Frederick—*The Potomac;* "The Rivers of America" series, Rinehart, New York, 1949

Haig-Brown, Roderick L.—*A River Never Sleeps,* Morrow, New York, 1946

Hard, Walter—*The Connecticut;* "The Rivers of America" series, Rinehart, New York, 1947

Headley, J. T.—*The Adirondack, or Life in the Woods,* 1864

Interior, U.S. Department of the—*Wild Rivers,* 1965 (with U.S. Dept. of Agriculture), *The Nation's River,* 1968; *Land, People, & Recreation in the Potomac River Basin,* 1968

King, Thomas Starr—*The White Hills,* 1859

Leopold, Aldo—*A Sand County Almanac,* Oxford, New York, 1949

McPhee, John—*The Pine Barrens,* Farrar, Straus & Giroux, Inc., New York, 1968

Morgan, Ann Haven—*Field Book of Ponds and Streams,* 1930

Murray, William H. H.—*Adventures in the Wilderness, or Camp Life in the Adirondacks,* 1869

Netboy, Anthony—*The Atlantic Salmon, A Vanishing Species?* Houghton, New York, 1968

New York Commission on the Preservation of Agricultural Land—*Preserving Agricultural Land in New York State,* 1968

New York Temporary Study Commission on the Future of the Adirondacks—*The Future of the Adirondack Park,* 1970

Niles, Blair—*The James;* "The Rivers of America" series, Farrar, New York, 1939

Oldaker, Warren H.—*Report on Pollution of the Merrimack River and Certain Tributaries; Part III—Stream Studies—Biological,* U.S. Department of the Interior, 1966

Olson, Sigurd—*The Singing Wilderness,* Knopf, New York, 1956; *Open Horizons,* Knopf, New York, 1969

Pennsylvania Department of Forests and Waters—*Report on Water Resources Survey of Main Stem of Schuylkill River, Pennsylvania* (Water Resources Bulletin No. 4), prepared by E. H. Bourquard and Associates, 1968

Potomac Planning Task Force—*The Potomac,* U.S. Government Printing Office, 1967

Prime, W. C.—*I Go A-Fishing,* 1873

Riviere, Bill—*Pole, Paddle & Portage,* Van Nostrand-Reinhold, 1969

Saltonstall, Richard, Jr.—*Your Environment and What You Can Do About It,* Walker & Company, 1970

Scott, Genio C.—*Fishing in American Waters,* 1869

Sears, George Washington ("Nessmuk")—*The Adirondack Letters of George Washington Sears,* with explanatory notes and a brief biography by Dan Brenan, Adirondack Museum, Blue Mountain Lake, New York, 1962

Singmaster, Elsie—*Pennsylvania's Susquehanna,* 1950

Smith, Chard Powers—*The Housatonic, Puritan River;* "The Rivers of America" series, Rinehart, New York, 1946

Thoreau, Henry David—*A Week on the Concord and Merrimack Rivers,* 1849; *The Maine Woods,* 1864

Udall, Stewart L.—*The Quiet Crisis,* Holt, New York, 1963

Urban, John T.—*A White Water Handbook for Canoe and Kayak,* Appalachian Mountain Club, 1970

Van Dyke, Henry—*Little Rivers,* 1895; *Fisherman's Luck,* 1899

Vogt, William, in *Future Environments of North America,* The Conservation Foundation, 1965

White, William Chapman—*Adirondack Country,* Knopf, New York, 1967

Whyte, William H.—*Connecticut's Natural Resources, a Proposal for Action,* 1962; *The Last Landscape,* Doubleday, New York, 1968

Wildes, Harry Emerson—*The Delaware;* "The Rivers of America" series, Farrar, New York, 1940

Index

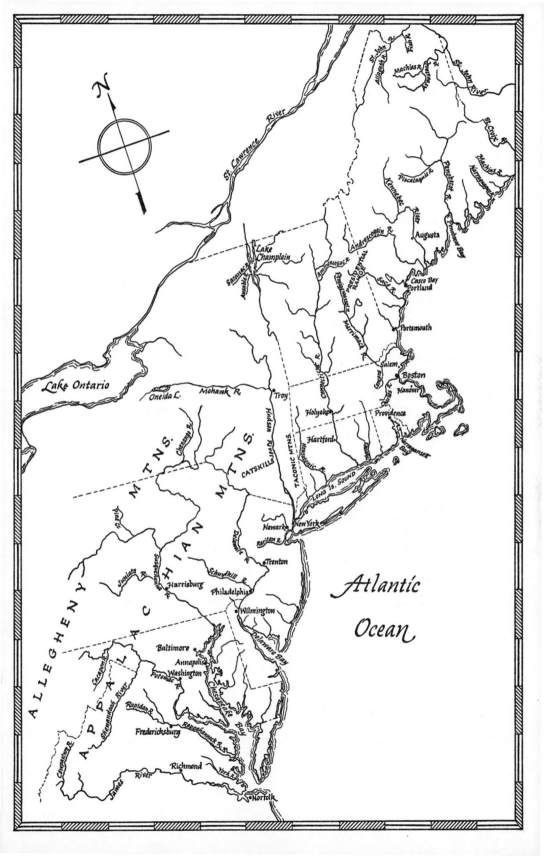